the God of Hope

A One-Volume Commentary on God's Promises

Joel F. Drinkard Jr.
& Dan R. Dick

Thomas Nelson
Since 1798

NASHVILLE DALLAS MEXICO CITY RIO DE JANEIRO

Published in Nashville, Tennessee, by Thomas Nelson. Thomas Nelson is a registered trademark of HarperCollins Christian Publishing, Inc.

Thomas Nelson titles may be purchased in bulk for educational, business, fund-raising, or sales promotional use. For information, please e-mail SpecialMarkets@ThomasNelson.com.

Typesetting: Barbara Dick

ISBN: 978-1-4185-4993-0

Printed in the United States of America

13 14 15 16 17 18 RRD 6 5 4 3 2 1

Contents

Old Testament

New Testament

Hope in the *Old Testament*

Hope in the *Old Testament*

According to conventional Christian theology, the Old Testament is a book of law, and the New Testament is a book of grace; the Old Testament is a book of judgment, and the New Testament is a book of mercy or salvation. While there are some generalized truths in those assertions, a fuller picture affirms that both Old and New Testaments include law and grace, judgment and mercy, and deliverance or salvation events. In the Old Testament, law is a part of covenant. *Covenant* is God's provision for relationship with humankind and all creation. One specific covenant, the Sinaitic covenant or Mosaic covenant made with the children of Israel, followed their deliverance by God from slavery in Egypt. That deliverance became the primary salvation event of the Old Testament, celebrated by the Israelites from that time forward. The Sinaitic covenant represented the formal agreement between God and the Israelites that marked their relationship. Much of the law or instruction of the Old Testament traces its origin to the Sinaitic covenant. Since the Sinaitic covenant is a direct outcome of the exodus, law (covenant) and grace (deliverance from slavery) are inseparable.

There are relatively few explicit occurrences of the term "hope" in the Old Testament. Indeed twenty-two of the thirty-nine books of the Old Testament do not include the word *hope* (compare with the New Testament, in which has the word *hope* occurs in twenty-four of the twenty-seven books). However, the theme of hope is pervasive throughout the Old Testament.

First, we will consider the type of literature of each book. In the Old Testament, we find law/instruction/regulations: the regulations to guide our relationships with God, fellow humans, and all creation. The regulations cover worship instructions, and what we would describe as civil, criminal, and moral regulations. We also find narrative, sections that primarily relate a story or recount history. We also have prophetic material—that warns of judgment on disobedience and promises blessing on obedience—that recounts past events, present situations, and future outlooks. And we also have wisdom and poetic material. The Pentateuch (or Law, Torah), especially Exodus through Deuteronomy, provides much of the legal and instructional material. Genesis and Joshua through Esther are primarily narrative. We find most prophetic material in Isaiah through Malachi. And Job through Song of Solomon contain most of the poetic and wisdom material. However, some narrative is found in all major sections, as are prophetic and wisdom and poetic material. Because of the narrative component, the metaphor of a journey seems most appropriate as a central theme for connecting our study of hope in the Old Testament. The first eleven chapters of Genesis describe a journey from creation to the fall, out of Eden, through the Flood to Shinar and Babel. The remainder of the narratives focus on journeys of people: to the promised land; to Egypt; out of Egypt to Sinai; back to the promised land; later into exile in Assyria, Babylon, and Egypt; and ultimately return.

The Biblical Basis of Hope

Throughout the Bible, our hope is centered in God and the acts/grace/mercy/purpose of God. Scripture—Old Testament and New Testament—makes abundantly clear that we find no real hope in ourselves or in other humans. People, friends, and family can be supportive and helpful to us. To view ourselves, our family, our government, or any other human agency as the ultimate source of hope, however, will bring only disillusionment and loss. (See Ps. 33:16–17: "No king is saved by his great army. / No warrior escapes by his great strength. / Horses can't bring victory; / they can't save by their strength" (NCV). Our ultimate hope rests in God alone. Hope and help go together.

> Do not put your trust in princes
> or other people, who cannot save you.
> When people die, they are buried.
> Then all of their plans come to an end.
> Happy are those who are helped by the God of Jacob.
> Their hope is in the LORD their God.
> He made heaven and earth,
> the sea and everything in it.
> He remains loyal forever. (Ps. 146:3–6 NCV)

There is a link that connects all of the Bible. This is the connection between Genesis (especially Gen. 1–2) and Revelation (especially Rev. 21–22). What we see in these "bookends" of the Bible are creation and new creation, paradise created and paradise restored, creation of heaven and earth, and creation of new heaven and new earth. All of the "no mores" of Revelation 21–22 (no more tears, no more mourning, no more pain, no more death) indicate the full and complete restoration of God's hope, plan, purpose for creation in the new creation. The end of Scripture fulfills the hope of the original creation. The rest of the Bible describes the journey from God's hope initiated in creation to God's hope consummated in the new heaven and new earth—a journey that began with the first human sin. All of Scripture describes the efforts—human and divine—to restore hope. All human efforts (and hope centered in humans or human agencies) ultimately fail. Only God's intervention "when the time was fully come" could ultimately restore God's vision.

We are still on the journey toward the restored hope of Revelation. We live in a fallen world, but one that has hope, genuine hope, that comes not from human efforts but from God's provision in Christ Jesus.

As we look through the Old Testament for markers of hope, we will look not just back into history of long ago and far away but at a journey we continue to travel today. We will not focus backward, dwelling on "what ifs." Instead, we will look for the elements of hope experienced in the Old Testament in the midst of sin and fallenness, and we will see reflections of our own journeys. The hope of the Old Testament focused on the future, as does all hope.

Having examined the connections between the testaments, we need to note that hope in the Old Testament differs significantly from New Testament hope and the hope we have as Christians. Old Testament hope did not have the fulfillment of the crucifixion and resurrection of Jesus Christ. The Old Testament could only "hope for" God's redemption of creation. The deliverance of the exodus and covenant grace did not restore creation to God's vision. The Old Testament picture of God is that of the eternal optimist. God's plan in creation is one of perfect union with God's will; so creation as God willed it and as God completed it, was good, very good. In a word, it was perfect. However, God gave to humans freedom and choice, without which we would be mere robots. God the Optimist freely gave humans choice, recognizing they could and would make bad choices. So God established laws to deal with the consequences of those bad choices. All are God's laws—physical, moral, or religious. Gravity is a physical law: if you jump off a cliff and try to fly, gravity will inevitably bring you down. In creation, Adam and Eve received only one law: "Of every tree of the garden you may freely eat; but of the tree of the knowledge of good and evil you shall not eat" (Gen. 2:16–17). Adam and Eve broke this law, bringing severe consequences for all humankind. God the Eternal Optimist is also God the Judge. God is also the Redeemer, however, the God of many second chances (the Eternal Optimist). God's plan is for perfect harmony and perfect relationship between God and all of creation. So God works to redeem all creation. Therein is our hope.

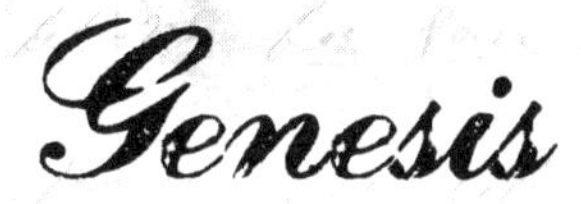

Genesis

God's Hope in Creation; Human Need of Redemption

The Pentateuch, or Torah, consists of the books of Genesis, Exodus, Leviticus, Numbers, and Deuteronomy. This corpus is traditionally ascribed to Moses. Indeed, many English Bibles, such as the New King James Version, refer to the books of the Pentateuch as "The First Book of Moses Called Genesis" and so on. Modern biblical scholars often date the Pentateuch in the form we find it in our Bibles to a much later period, even to the time of the Babylonian exile (587 BC) or later. For our purposes, the content of the text rather than its authorship or date is our primary concern.

Prehistory Hope

The book of Genesis may conveniently be divided into two parts: Genesis 1–11 and Genesis 12–50. Genesis 1–11, often called "prehistory," describes the creation of the universe and the marring of God's creation by sin. Genesis 12–50, usually called "patriarchal history," describes God's workings through the lives of successive generations of one family, the family of Abraham. We will follow this standard division in our study of hope in Genesis.

Hope at Creation: Genesis 1

Genesis 1 and 2 present two narratives of creation. The Genesis 1 account (1:1–2:4a) presents a macrocosmic view, that is, a big-picture view, of the creation of the universe: "In the beginning God created the heavens and the earth" (1:1). This first verse summarizes the whole narrative: God created heavens and earth—in a word, everything. In this first narrative we see God's vision, his plan, his purpose, and, as we will see shortly, God's hope for his creation. My assertion is simple: creation itself is an expression of God's hope. We see God's vision concerning creation expressed on the universal scale. This narrative depicts a universe filled with God's creation and ends with God's assessment of creation. After each creative act or set of acts, God sees the creative act as good (1:4, 10, 12, 18, 21, 25). Genesis 1:26–31 (NCV) describes the final and culminating act of creation on the sixth day:

> Then God said, "Let us make human beings in our image and likeness. And let them rule over the fish in the sea and the birds in the sky, over the tame animals, over all the earth, and over all the small crawling animals on the earth." So God created human beings in his image. In the image of God he created them. He created them male and female. God blessed them and said, "Have many children and grow in number. Fill the earth and be its master. Rule over the fish in the sea and over the birds in the sky and over every living thing that moves on the earth." God said, "Look, I have given you all the plants that have grain for seeds and all the trees whose fruits have seeds in them. They will be food for you. I have given all the green plants as food for every wild animal, every bird of the air, and every small crawling animal." And it happened. God looked at everything he had made, and it was very good. Evening passed, and morning came. This was the sixth day.

And after completing the task with the creation of humankind in God's image and likeness, God looks at all of creation and assesses it as very good. A simple outline of chapter 1 might read:

1. God did it.
2. God did it all.
3. God did it all good, very good!

So in effect, creation at the end of God's activity is a perfect expression of God's will, God's plan, God's purpose. Creation is the perfect expression of God's hope.

Hope at Creation: Genesis 2

Chapter 2 offers a different view of creation. It focuses on one small garden in the east, in Eden, and on one human couple, Adam and Eve. The Genesis 2 account of creation has, however, the same basic outline:

1. God did it.
2. God did it all.
3. God did it all good!

Hope and Sin Stories: Genesis 3–11

God's good creation and God's vision of creation, however, are quickly changed. The humans God created, good and with free will, soon fall to temptation. The result that we call the fall affects not only the humans but also all of creation. God's creation is no longer completely good. All creation shows the effects of the fall, not just humans. The rest of the Old Testament, indeed the rest of the Bible, is the narrative of God's vision of creation being restored. So in effect, Genesis 1 and 2 reflect God's original plan and vision of creation. Genesis 3 and following show God's plan to restore creation to its original goodness, God's original hope. If humans have any hope, it is grounded in God's plan. The hope we see in Scripture looks to the future, to God's way of restoring creation to its original purpose, God's original vision and plan.

Within Genesis 3–11, we see multiple sin stories. The first sin story is the fall, the original sin. The sin was the human attempt to be like God (3:5, 22). Indeed, every sin is, in one way or another, disobedience to God or to God's commands, and is, in reality, a human attempt to be like God, the created being trying to usurp the role and position of the Creator. (Interestingly, the Hebrew Bible uses the word *create* only with God as subject—never humans.) We have not experienced the vision, the plan of God before the fall, so we cannot know the hope of that original plan. We can and do experience the nature of God in a fallen world. Our hope lies in the fact that God is a God of love and mercy. The old gospel songs express something of that hope: "My hope is built on nothing less than Jesus' blood and righteousness" ("My Hope Is Built," Edward Mote, 1834) or "O God our help in ages past, our hope for years to come" (O God, Our Help in Ages Past," Isaac Watts, 1719). These songs express something of our hope in God.

The sin of chapter 3 disrupts the goodness of God's creation and vision. One might assume the situation is hopeless. All of creation suffers in the condition of sin. The earth feels the curse of humanity's fall. But even in the fall, hope is not lost. For the curse that seemed to offer only death is followed by God's grace and mercy, God's hope. God does not end sinners' lives at the moment of their sin. Instead God shows mercy. God provides garments for Adam and Eve to wear. They are expelled from the Edenic garden, and the ground no longer provides easy sustenance. Now they work by the sweat of their brows. The ground produces thorns, thistles, and nettles along with food. But humankind survives by God's grace, and that grace offers hope. Furthermore, God gives the gift of new life. A second generation is born, and in that new generation is new hope. Now there are farmers and herders, a diversification of occupations and increased hope.

But once again the hope is shattered in another sin story. The disobedience of the first generation becomes murder in the second generation: Cain kills his brother Abel. Surely if the disobedience of that first generation brought such severe judgment, the murder will end all hope. Cain is judged for his sin—the land no longer yields its fruits to him, and he becomes a wanderer, an outcast from society. Yet even in the midst of the horror of Cain's sin, God shows mercy. Cain still has his life, and he is given a wife and children. Even before we learn that Adam and Eve have additional children, we read of multiple generations of Cain's children (4:16–24). Furthermore, God gives Cain a protective mark so that no one will kill him despite his sin (v. 15). Even for Cain there is an element of hope. God not only continues to be merciful and offer Cain hope but also shows mercy and hope to Adam and Eve as they have numerous additional children (4:26–5:32).

By the end of Genesis 5, humankind has fulfilled at least part of God's original command in creation: they have been fruitful and multiplied. As humans have multiplied, so has human sin. This sin story includes God's displeasure and judgment:

> The LORD saw that the human beings on the earth were very wicked and that everything they thought about was evil. He was sorry he had made human beings on the earth, and his heart was filled with pain. So the LORD said, "I will destroy all human beings that I made on the earth. And I will destroy every animal and everything that crawls on the earth and the birds of the air, because I am sorry I have made them." (6:5–7 NCV)

God's judgment is a flood to destroy all living beings on earth—the loss of all hope for humankind. Yet once again, God shows mercy and provides hope: Noah finds favor in God's sight (v. 8). God spares Noah and his family and a remnant of all living creatures on the ark Noah constructs before the flood comes. At the end of the flood, God renews the promise, the blessing, the hope of creation; calling on all living things to be fruitful and multiply (8:17). God then specifically blesses humankind through Noah and his family with the renewed call to be fruitful and multiply and fill the earth (9:1). God also makes a covenant with Noah, Noah's family, and all living beings: God will never again destroy all the earth with a flood, and the rainbow in the sky is a sign and symbol of that covenant (vv. 8–17).

In Genesis 3–11, sin is pervasive as humans attempt to overstep the boundaries God established in creation. Sin is basically a human attempt to be like God. Yet even in the face of such sin, God offers hope. At every stage, in response to every sin, we find God not only judges and punishes sin but also shows grace and mercy alongside every judgment. The grace and mercy of God is the source of hope, offered fully in the terms of the covenant promises God makes with all humankind.

Hope in the Patriarchal History

Genesis 12–50, the patriarchal history, shifts the narrative and the hope. Now humankind is described as having multiplied and filled the earth. The narrative knows the great empires at the ends of the Fertile Crescent as well as large populations in the region known as Canaan. No longer will the narrative focus primarily on all of creation or all of humankind. Instead it focuses on God working to bring hope and blessing to all humankind (and ultimately to restore all creation) through covenant with one particular family across three generations. In each generation, the focus narrows on a smaller segment of the family. But this narrowing focus does not limit the availability of God's covenant promises and blessings. The strong covenant message is that the patriarchs are to be not only recipients of blessing but also vehicles of blessing for others.

Hope and Abraham

Abram becomes the first bearer of hope through his call in Genesis 12. God calls Abram to leave his homeland and his extended family and to go to a place God will show him. God promises to make Abram a great nation. He will be blessed and a vehicle of blessing: "in you all the families of the earth shall be blessed" (12:3). So the hope Abram receives is also hope for all people. But there is a problem: Abram has no children, and he is seventy-five years old. Abram's wife, Sarai, is barren. Nevertheless, he responds to God's call in faith and goes to Canaan. God reaffirms and expands the promise to Abram in Genesis 13. He promises Abram and his descendants land (specifically the land of Canaan) and descendants as numerous "as the dust of the earth" (13:16) and "count the stars. . . . So shall your descendants be" (15:5). Abram believes the Lord, and God reckons it to him as righteousness (v. 6). Abram places his hope in God. The narrative offers several attempts by Abram and Sarai to help God fulfill God's promises. Abram may have considered Lot as his heir. But when Lot and Abram separate (ch. 13), Abram apparently adopts Eliezer, his servant and steward, as his heir. When

God reaffirms his promise and states that Abram's own son will be his heir (ch. 15), Sarai (still barren) gives Abram her maidservant, Hagar, as wife. Hagar conceives and bears a son, Ishmael (ch. 16). Again, God reaffirms the covenant promise, stating that Ishmael is not to be the child of the covenant, and Sarai's child by Abraham will be. Ishmael will also be blessed and so experiences the hope of God's blessings, but he is not the promised one.

Time passes: Abraham is now ninety-nine and Sarah is eighty-nine. God again appears, reaffirms the covenant promises, renames the couple Abraham and Sarah, and announces that the next year they will have a son (chs. 17–18). Both Abraham and Sarah laugh at the announcement. They are well beyond child-bearing age. It is humanly impossible (18:11–12). From a human perspective, it is hopeless. And that is precisely the point. The covenant, the promise—the hope—lies neither in human hands nor in human actions but in God's will. And so, the next year, the (humanly) impossible happens, God visits Sarah, she conceives and bears a son, Isaac (ch. 21; see also Heb. 11:11–12).

Hope and Isaac

The covenant God made with Abraham is renewed with Isaac, extending hope to the next generation. At a time of famine, the Lord appears to Isaac, tells him not to go to Egypt despite the famine, and promises Isaac and his descendants that God will be with them, that they will become numerous, and that through them all the people of the earth will be blessed (26:1–5).

Hope and Jacob

The covenant is again reaffirmed with Jacob in similar words (28:13–14). Once again the hope promised to Jacob also brings hope to all the people of the earth. The explicit connection of the covenant with Abraham, Isaac, and Jacob is confirmed by numerous Old Testament and New Testament references to "the God of Abraham, Isaac, and Jacob."

Hope and Joseph

The Joseph narrative is of a different sort than the other patriarchal narratives. Although Joseph is the fourth generation of patriarchs, he never receives a theophanic covenant promise from God. The narratives of Abraham, Isaac, and Jacob are episodic—they are for the most part unconnected episodes. But with Joseph, the stories are all tightly interconnected. Jacob favors Joseph and gives him a special garment, making his brothers jealous. In addition Joseph has dreams that he interprets as his father, mother, and brothers all bowing down to him. When Joseph's brothers are caring for sheep away from home, Jacob sends Joseph to see how they are doing. Joseph's brothers first plot to kill Joseph, but finally sell him as a slave to a caravan going to Egypt.

In Egypt, Joseph is sold to Potiphar. Potiphar's wife tries to seduce Joseph, but he refuses her. She accuses him of assault, and he is thrown into prison. While in prison, Joseph interprets dreams for two of Pharaoh's attendants. The interpretations are accurate. When Pharaoh has dreams that none of his advisors or wise men can interpret, one of the attendants remembers Joseph and tells Pharaoh. Joseph interprets Pharaoh's dreams and is released from prison and made third in the kingdom. Egypt has seven years of plenty during which Joseph oversees the storage of an abundance of grain. Seven years of famine follow during which Pharaoh supplies food for the people, but most are forced to sell their possessions and land for the food.

The famine also affects Canaan, with the result that Jacob sends Joseph's brothers to Egypt for food—fulfilling the dreams Joseph had years before. When Joseph finally reveals himself to his brothers, he forgives them: "you meant evil against me; but God meant it for good, in order to bring it about as it is this day, to save many people alive" (50:20). God is the source of hope and deliverance for Joseph, for Jacob and his entire family, and for the Egyptians in this seven-year famine. Jacob and the entire family move to Egypt and are given choice land in Goshen, where they live long lives. Each piece of the Joseph narrative is tightly connected to an enduring message of hope in the goodness of God.

Hope in Jacob's Final Blessings

One additional passage expressing hope in Genesis is found in the midst of Jacob's deathbed blessing for his sons. Jacob says: "I have waited for your salvation, O LORD!" (49:18). The Hebrew word translated *wait for* carries the connotation of waiting expectantly or in hope. In many passages, especially in Psalms, the word is translated as *hope*. Just a few verses later, in the blessing of Joseph, Jacob describes God's actions: "By the God of your father who will help you / And by the Almighty who will bless you" (v. 25). The Hebrew word translated *help* is one that occurs in a number of passages alongside the word for *hope*. Our hope is in God, and God alone, because God is our only sure source of help. Genesis closes with the death of Jacob, Joseph, and his brothers, and with the Israelites outside the promised land. But far from being hopeless, the text reminds us of God's help as a source of hope. Because of the covenant promises to Abraham, Isaac, and Jacob, all people on earth share in the hope of God.

Exodus–Deuteronomy
Introduction

The books of Exodus, Leviticus, Numbers, and Deuteronomy are treated together in this study. These books all have the same historical time frame, essentially the time from Moses' birth to his death. These books represent the period of Moses' leadership of the Israelites. But more significantly, these books describe two primary deliverance acts of God on behalf of the Israelites: the exodus event, the deliverance of the Israelites from enslavement in Egypt, and the Sinaitic or Mosaic covenant in which God (re)establishes special relationship with the Israelites, the descendants of Abraham, Isaac, and Jacob. The primary time frame is a forty-year period from the call of Moses to be God's agent of deliverance from Egypt to Moses' death.

The locations move from Egypt to Mount Sinai and end in the plains of Moab overlooking the land of Canaan. In terms of hope, the books move from initial hopelessness as the Israelites are slaves in Egypt to hopefulness as the Israelites are encamped in the plains of Moab poised to enter Canaan, the promised land. But the journey in these books is anything but linear. There are numerous sidetracks, diversions, and setbacks due to the rebellion and disobedience of the Israelites.

Exodus

The book of Exodus picks up where the book of Genesis ended. The first few verses recapitulate the last chapters of Genesis. Exodus opens with the list of the sons of Jacob (1:1–5; compare Gen. 46:8–27), the death of Joseph (1:6; compare Gen. 50:26), and the multiplication of the descendants of Jacob (1:7; compare Gen. 47:27). At this point the Hebrews experience both despair and hope. Despair comes at the death of the generations of Jacob and Joseph. Yet there is hope in that God's promise to Abraham has been partially fulfilled—Abraham's offspring have indeed become numerous. Their situation has changed significantly since the end of Genesis, however.

The time reference for Exodus is approximately 350 years after the end of Genesis. The descendants of Jacob have gone from being honored resident aliens in Egypt to enslaved people. The biblical text describes the change tersely: "Now there arose a new king over Egypt, who did not know Joseph" (1:8).

Hope in a Hopeless Situation

From the human perspective the situation of the Israelites is hopeless; they are powerless to deliver themselves. The only thing they can do is pray—cry out to God. And that is the one thing that can (and does) give hope.

> Now it happened in the process of time that the king of Egypt died. Then the children of Israel groaned because of the bondage, and they cried out; and their cry came up to God because of the bondage. So God heard their groaning, and God remembered His covenant with Abraham, with Isaac, and with Jacob. And God looked upon the children of Israel, and God acknowledged them. (2:23–25)

They cry to God: God hears, remembers, sees, and knows (experiences) the suffering expressed in their prayers. Just as God in the incarnation became fully human to experience the human condition, so Exodus describes God as being present with God's people. God doesn't stop at hearing and seeing their suffering, but experiences it just like one of the Hebrew slaves.

In response to their cries, God prepares and preserves Moses to lead the Hebrews out of slavery to freedom. Moses is born to a Hebrew woman at a time when Pharaoh has ordered all male Hebrew babies to be killed. Moses' mother saves him and sets about to preserve him by placing him in a basket in the Nile. Providentially, Pharaoh's daughter comes to bathe in the river just below where Moses is in the river. She sees the infant, has compassion, takes the infant, and raises him in the palace. Years later, as an adult, Moses sees an Egyptian beating a Hebrew and kills the Egyptian. He flees Egypt and lives in Midian many years. He marries a Midianite woman, has children, and cares for his father-in-law's herds.

When the time is right, God calls Moses from a burning bush. God calls to Moses: "I am the God of your father—the God of Abraham, the God of Isaac, and the God of Jacob" (3:6). The call explicitly identifies God with the patriarchs and implicitly connects Moses' call with the covenant promises (and the hope) God established with the patriarchs almost four hundred years earlier. The call also assures Moses that God knows the situation of the Hebrews:

> And the LORD said: "I have surely seen the oppression of My people who are in Egypt, and have heard their cry because of their taskmasters, for I know their sorrows. So I have come down to deliver them out of the hand of the Egyptians, and to bring them up from that land to a good and large land, to a land flowing with milk and honey." (vv. 7–8)

Moses is to be the human agent God uses to deliver the Israelites from slavery. This message and call is not just for Moses. It is also a message to the Israelites—a message of hope embodied in the covenant relationship first promised to Abraham, Isaac, and Jacob:

> Therefore say to the children of Israel: "I am the LORD; I will bring you out from under the burdens of the Egyptians, I will rescue you from their bondage, and I will redeem you with an outstretched arm and with great judgments. I will take you as My people, and I will be your God. Then you shall know that I am the LORD your God who brings you out from under the burdens of the Egyptians. And I will bring you into the land which I swore to give to Abraham, Isaac, and Jacob." (6:6–8)

Note the promises, the hope of God's message. It is a message of great hope—the hope for the complete fulfillment of the promises made to Abraham, Isaac, and Jacob. Now instead of the covenant being with one individual (a patriarch, such as Abraham), it is with a people, the descendants of Jacob/Israel. Though Abraham's (and Jacob's) descendants are very numerous, they do not yet possess the land promised to them. In this one announcement, God gives a renewed hope to the people. This announcement answers the cry of the Hebrews. God acts on behalf of God's people to free them from bondage.

Hope is especially evident in God's continual presence with God's people, the visible presence in the pillar of smoke to lead them by day and the pillar of fire by night (13:21–22). God's continual presence with and provision for the people—the manna and quail (ch. 16) for food and the water in the wilderness (chs. 15–17)—is perhaps their greatest source of hope.

God provides even though the people continually rebel on the journey out of Egypt and toward the Mount Sinai. For example, at Baal-zaphon beside the Red Sea, God has brought the people out of Egypt and leads them with the pillar of cloud by day and pillar of fire by night (ch. 13). The people realize Pharaoh is pursuing them, and they cry out to God and complain that Moses brought them out to die in the wilderness (ch. 14). When they find no food, they murmur against Moses and Aaron—and God—that they will die of hunger (ch. 16). When they find no water (ch. 17) or only bitter water (ch. 15), they complain that they will die of thirst in the wilderness. And these complaints occur early in their journey, before they arrive at Mount Sinai (ch. 19).

Hope at Mount Sinai

Moses leads the Hebrews out of Egypt, to God's holy mountain, Sinai. There God initiates a covenant with the people.

> And Moses went up to God, and the LORD called to him from the mountain, saying, "Thus you shall say to the house of Jacob, and tell the children of Israel: 'You have seen what I did to the Egyptians, and how I bore you on eagles' wings and brought you to Myself. Now therefore, if you will indeed obey My voice and keep My covenant, then you shall be a special treasure to Me above all people; for all the earth is Mine. And you shall be to Me a kingdom of priests and a holy nation'. These are the words which you shall speak to the children of Israel." (19:3–6)

Hope is embodied in this Sinaitic, or Mosaic, covenant. Israel is to obey and keep the covenant. God will hold Israel in a special relationship—they will be a kingdom of priests and a holy nation. That relationship is Israel's hope, and this covenant lies at the heart of the Old Testament. The Israelites remember (and to this day the Jewish community remembers) and celebrate the exodus and the Sinaitic covenant as the primary deliverance and covenant acts of the Old Testament.

The covenant between God and the people of Israel at Mount Sinai has conditions. In the covenant God identifies himself as the one who delivers the Israelites and initiates the covenant, as Exodus 19 indicates. But the covenant requires obedience; Israel must keep the covenant. Only as Israel obeys the covenant will it experience its blessings and hope.

All of Exodus—really all of the Old Testament (and New Testament as well) shows there is no hope apart from God. Our only hope comes from God, God's character (grace, mercy, and steadfast love), and God's initiative. Genesis (and even more Exodus) shows the record of human sin—human failure—and God's grace in forgiveness and deliverance despite human sin, not because of anything deserving in humans. Moses, who led the people out of Egypt, was a murderer. The Israelites themselves were fickle and sinful.

The book of Exodus is a narrative of rebellion against God rather than faithfulness to God. While Moses is on the mountain receiving the covenant from God (chs. 20–31), the people along with Aaron, Moses' brother, make a golden calf image to worship (ch. 32)— breaking the commandments to have no other gods but Yahweh and to worship no graven or molten images. One would assume from all this sin that God would simply wipe out this rebellious people and start over with another group—but God does not. He judges and punishes the sin, but just as in Genesis, God shows grace and mercy. Hope is evident in God's continual presence with his people. In the instructions accompanying the covenant, God institutes worship practices and equipment. God's presence is symbolized by the tabernacle and the ark of testimony within the camp. God's presence is also symbolized by the tent of meeting, which may be a separate structure outside the camp where God meets with Moses and the elders. Despite their sins, Israel can take hope in God's covenant and in God's continual presence.

Leviticus

Proper and Obedient Worship and Hope

The book of Leviticus deals primarily with ritual and worship instructions and regulations. The book is set during the time the Israelites are at Mount Sinai. Leviticus picks up where Exodus ends, with the construction of the tabernacle. Leviticus opens with instructions for acceptable sacrifices and offerings (chs. 1–7). These sacrifices are to be brought to the priest in the tabernacle. (Once the Israelites were in the promised land and the temple was built, these instructions were also applied to the temple in Jerusalem.) A primary aspect of hope expressed in Leviticus is that which comes from proper and obedient worship. Leviticus describes and prescribes proper sacrifices and offerings one may bring to God as a sign of confession of sin, as a plea for forgiveness, and as a symbol of thanks for God's grace. It is not that the sacrifice assures forgiveness of sin; but a sacrifice, presented with a genuine repentant heart, expresses to God an awareness of the seriousness of sin and the honest search for forgiveness and reconciliation. The hope expressed in the sacrifices is that God will forgive and show mercy and steadfast love in response to a sacrifice rightly offered. Leviticus also defines what is clean and unclean, pure and impure, and how worshipers are to become and remain ritually clean and pure. It prescribes the ways to cleanse oneself from uncleanness or impurity.

Leviticus also includes instructions concerning the priests (chs. 8–10). It describes the regulations and instructions for the priests, the preparations for the ordination and consecration of Aaron and his sons to the priesthood, and the clothing they are to wear. The instructions delineate the sacrifices that are to accompany ordination. Within this section is the narrative concerning the death of two of Aaron's sons, Nabad and Abihu

(10:1–3). They do not obey the regulations concerning sacrifices, offerings, and incense to be brought before God and die as a result. The judgment shows all the people that disobedience to God's commands brings terrible judgment to those who disobey—even to those of the high priest's family. The judgment shows the serious nature of sin, God's absolute holiness, and the requirement of complete obedience when entering God's presence in the most holy places (Exod. 26:33). A greater level of obedience and holiness was required of the priests because they served in the tabernacle in the immediate presence of God in the most holy places.

Following the ordination and consecration of Aaron and his remaining sons, Leviticus gives instructions concerning ritual cleanness and uncleanness (chs. 11–16). These regulations include clean and unclean animals (what animals can and cannot be eaten—and what may or may not be offered to God), and conditions that make women and men ritually unclean. The implication of these regulations is that the body is a temple of God and is to be kept ritually clean and pure (1 Cor. 6:19). Within this section are the details of the Day of Atonement and the preparations and sacrifices made as part of that day. The Day of Atonement, the most sacred and holy celebration in Israelite worship, symbolizes the atonement, forgiveness offered to all the people of Israel for their sins. Sacrifices are brought before God on behalf of all the people, not just an individual. As such the Day of Atonement symbolizes the great hope of Israel in God. God is gracious and merciful, and forgiving of sin!

The Holiness Code and Hope

The last major section of Leviticus (chs. 17–26) is traditionally called the Holiness Code. It includes many moral and ritual regulations for the people. The basic premise of the regulations is that Israel is to live differently from the peoples around them because they have been set apart by God, because they have a special covenant relationship with God. As a result Israel is to live in a set-apart manner pleasing to God. Specifically, Israel is to avoid all idolatry and immorality as practiced by the Canaanites and other peoples. This difference is repeatedly emphasized in Leviticus:

> For I am the LORD your God: ye shall therefore sanctify yourselves, and ye shall be holy; for I am holy: . . . . For I am the LORD that bringeth you up out of the land of Egypt, to be your God: ye shall therefore be holy, for I am holy. (11:44–45 KJV)

> Consecrate yourselves therefore, and be holy: for I am the LORD your God. And you shall keep My statutes, and perform them: I am the LORD who sanctifies you. (20:7–8)

> And you shall be holy to Me; for I the LORD am holy, and have separated you from the peoples, that you should be Mine. (20:26)

These statements are both instructions and words of hope. They are words of hope because they speak of the special relationship Israel has with God, which the Canaanites and the other people around Israel do not have. Israel is to live differently and serve as an example for the nations; they are to be the means of bringing the other nations to know God and experience the same hope Israel has. Several conclusions from these verses are: God is holy and expects his people to be holy. God offers a special covenant relationship to the Hebrew people. That relationship is the source of hope, of life lived as God intends. That relationship requires a lifestyle that is pleasing to God—that is godlike. This is what God intended in creation from the beginning. Humans are created in God's image—godlike. Here God calls for holiness—apartness—as a way to be godlike! That holiness provides the hope humans have for a continuing relationship with God. By nature we humans are sinful; our lifestyles are not pleasing to God. But when we repent of our sins, seek God's forgiveness, and demonstrate our resolve by practicing the lifestyle pleasing to God—that holy lifestyle—we can have the hope of God's forgiveness and continuing relationship with us. Such is the hope of Leviticus!

Numbers

The book of Numbers picks up in the same location as the end of Exodus and the beginning of Leviticus, Mount Sinai. It also provides a specific time context: the first day of the second month in the second year after the exodus. The book of Numbers takes its name from the census, the numbering, God commands to be taken in preparation for the departure from Mount Sinai and the journey to the promised land. The book describes the departure from Sinai and the initial journey toward the promised land. Thus the book starts on a note of hope.

Complaints and Hope

The journey, however, becomes a nearly forty-year experience of wandering in the wilderness. After leaving Mount Sinai (10:11, 33), the people immediately start complaining and God sends judgment because of their complaints. The people then cry out to Moses, who prays to God, and the judgment ceases (11:1–4). But the rebelling and complaining continue. Even Aaron and Miriam, Moses' brother and sister, complain about Moses' authority because Moses had married a foreign woman. They contend that God spoke through them as much as through Moses. God is angry with Aaron and Miriam because of their presumption and judges them (ch. 12).

When the Israelites get near Canaan at Kadesh, God commands them to send spies into the promised land. The twelve spies spend forty days in the land and bring back a mixed report. They all report that Canaan is a land that "truly flows with milk and honey" (13:27), but ten of the spies say the Canaanites are too strong for the Israelites. Only Caleb and Joshua urge the people to enter and take the land. The people rebel against God's command and even suggest choosing another leader to take them back to Egypt. As a result, God judges the Israelites to wander in the wilderness until the whole generation over twenty years of age dies; only Caleb and Joshua of that generation will live to enter the promised land (chs. 13–14). The next thirty-eight years are spent wandering through the wilderness. Throughout that time the rebellions and complaints continue: the rebellion of Korah, Dathan, and Abiram (ch. 16); complaints about lack of meat and water (chs. 20, 21), and worshiping other gods (ch. 25). By the end of the book, the Israelites have reached the plains of Moab just across the Jordan River from the land of Canaan. Most of the older generation has died, including Aaron and Miriam. But the rebellions and sinfulness continue.

From this brief summary it would seem that the situation is completely hopeless. The Israelites commit sin after sin, and God's judgment is both swift and severe. It seems that Numbers depicts a people without any chance of hope. But that is only one side of the story—the human side. Yes, the Israelites are a sinful people. The people do rebel against God and God's commandments. God does judge the sin. However, alongside the depiction of human sinfulness and failure is a picture of God's grace. When God wants to destroy the entire people, Moses (and often Aaron with him) intercedes on behalf of the people. God responds to the pleas of Moses and Aaron and does not fully destroy the people. Instead he continually shows grace and mercy.

A New Generation and Hope

Although the end of the book indicates the death of the generation that left Egypt, it does not depict a hopeless situation. Instead at the end there is a new generation, and a second census shows they are as numerous as the previous generation. Also a new generation of leaders is in place to lead the people into the promised land. Aaron's son Eleazer is the new high priest, and Joshua is commissioned as Moses' successor. This new generation of Israelites has every reason to hope. God is present in their midst; they have achieved military success on the east side of the Jordan

River; they have newly commissioned leaders; and they are poised in the plains of Moab to enter the promised land. God continues to show grace and mercy to them.

One passage in Numbers particularly shows God's grace and the hope it brings—the Aaronic benediction:

> And the LORD spoke to Moses, saying: "Speak to Aaron and his sons, saying, 'This is the way you shall bless the children of Israel. Say to them,
>
> "The LORD bless you, and keep you:
> The LORD make his face shine upon you,
> And be gracious to you:
> The LORD lift up his countenance upon you,
> And give you peace."'
>
> So they shall put my name upon the children of Israel, and I will bless them." (6:22–27)

This passage has served as a benediction for Christians and Jews for over two millennia, a sign of the continual hope of God's blessing. Two of the earliest Hebrew inscriptions yet discovered are tiny silver amulets excavated from a tomb at Ketef Hinnom just outside Jerusalem. The two amulets date to the eighth century BC and were found to have a form of the Aaronic benediction incised on them. The hope this passage gives meant enough during the first temple period, to the one buried in the tomb or his family, that it was included with other grave goods. It reminds us, as it reminded Israel even before they left Mount Sinai, that God alone was the source of blessing for Israel in the Old Testament and for us today. God guards his people, makes his presence shine on them (that means God is present with his people), is gracious, shows grace or mercy to his people, and grants them peace. The final verse indicates that, with this blessing, God's name and God's presence are placed on the people of Israel. Therein lies Israel's hope—and ours. "If God is for us, who can be against us?" (Rom. 8:31).

Deuteronomy

Deuteronomy is the last book of the Law or Torah and the last of the books ascribed to Moses. The book is set in the plains of Moab just before the Israelites cross over the Jordan River to take possession of the promised land. The entire book of Deuteronomy is a series of messages delivered by Moses immediately prior to his death, followed by an epilogue containing Moses' farewell blessing and a report of his death.

The messages restate the mighty acts of God in delivering the people over the previous forty years: the exodus, the covenant at Sinai, and the wilderness wandering. Much of the book is a retelling and renewing of the covenant with a new generation born or reaching adulthood after the events of exodus–Sinai. The purpose is to bring this new generation into covenant relationship with God so they recognize that they are heirs of the covenant and bound by it:

> And Moses called all Israel, and said to them, "Hear, O Israel, the statutes and judgments which I speak in your hearing today, that you may learn them and be careful to observe them. The LORD our God made a covenant with us in Horeb. The LORD did not make this covenant with our fathers, but with us, those who are here today, all of us who are alive." (5:1–3)

The book reiterates the need to obey God's laws in order to receive God's blessing. Disobedience will result in God's judgment. The review of the wilderness wandering recounts the continual sinfulness of the people and God's judgment to show why the generation who left Egypt did not receive the gift of the land. So the message is intended both to warn and to promise the new generation—the ones who will enter the land—that they must remain obedient to receive and enjoy God's blessing. The hope is evident in God's faithfulness and gracious forgiveness when the people repent and obey him. The hope is evident because God continues to lead them, provide for their needs, and bring them to the very border of the promised land. God raises up a new leader to bring the people into the land. So there is hope—hope despite the sinfulness of the people, hope if they will be obedient, and most important, hope because God is a God of grace, mercy, love, and forgiveness. "Then He brought us out from there, that He might bring us in, to give us the land of which He swore to our fathers" (6:23).

The many words of promise in Deuteronomy rest on the premise of obedience. Great hope rests on Israel's obedience to the covenant. The conditions are clearly set forth: If you obey, blessings will come. But if you disobey, judgments, curses, will come:

> Behold, I set before you today a blessing and a curse: the blessing, if you obey the commandments of the LORD your God which I command you today; and the curse, if you do not obey the commandments of the LORD your God, but turn aside from the way which I command you today, to go after other gods, which you have not known. (11:26–28)

The blessings that follow from obedience include long life, well-being, and possession of the promised land:

> Therefore you shall be careful to do as the LORD your God has commanded you; you shall not turn aside to the right hand or to the left. You shall walk in all the ways which the LORD your God has commanded you, that you may live and that it may be well with you, and that you may prolong your days in the land which you shall possess. (5:32–33)

The call to obedience is stated eloquently in Deuteronomy 6:4–5, one of the most quoted passages in all of Scripture. Jesus referred to it as the greatest commandment (Matt. 22:35–40; Mark 12:28-31):

> Hear, O Israel: The LORD our God, the LORD is one! You shall love the LORD your God with all your heart, with all your soul, and with all your strength. And these words which I command you this day shall be in your heart; You shall teach them diligently to your children, and shall talk of them when you sit in your house, when you walk by the way, when you lie down, and when you rise up. (6:4–7)

The Hebrew word translated *hear* has the fuller meanings of heeding and obeying. One could just as accurately translate as "Listen, obey, O Israel. . . ." Hope is found at the beginning of the passage. The affirmation that the LORD is *our* God is the epitome of hope. We are commanded to love God with all our heart, soul, and strength. Israel also is commanded to teach the children, the next generation, all the aspects of covenant so they may experience the blessings God has promised. The responsibility is ours to teach our children and grandchildren—the next generation—about God, God's commandments, and the hope they can have in God and God's promises. Only in that manner can hope exist. Moses expresses that hope definitively to the new generation:

> For you are a holy people to the LORD your God; the LORD your God has chosen you to be a people for Himself, a special treasure above all the peoples on the face of the earth. The LORD did not set His love on you nor choose you because you were more in number than any other people, for you were the least of all peoples; but because the LORD loves you, and because He would keep the oath which He swore to your fathers, the LORD has brought you out with a mighty hand, and redeemed you from the house of bondage, from the hand of Pharaoh king of Egypt. Therefore know that the LORD your God, He is God, the faithful God who keeps covenant and mercy for a thousand generations with those who love Him and keep His commandments. (7:6–9)

The Israelites who hear Moses speak God's words take hope from these promises. This is also our hope.

At the close of Deuteronomy, the new generation is poised on the plains overlooking the promised land. They have new leadership, Joshua and Eleazer, ordained by God to lead them into the land. They have every reason to be filled with hope.

Joshua

The book of Deuteronomy set before the people of Israel the covenant conditions and promises. If Israel keeps the covenant, all the blessings of God would be theirs; if they do not, they face the judgment of God. The history books—Joshua, Judges, Samuel, and Kings—recount the narrative of Israel's life in the promised land from the entry under Joshua until their defeat, destruction of the temple, exile, and loss of freedom at the hands of the Babylonians in 587–586 BC. The narrative depicts the blessings Israel enjoys when obedient to the covenant. It also recounts Israel's sin and disobedience that lead to God's judgment. What we see in these narratives is that God alone is the source of hope for Israel. Israel can experience the fullness of hope if the people will faithfully keep the covenant relationship with God.

Hope for the Hopeless—A New Beginning

The book of Joshua heralds a new beginning for the Israelites. Exodus through Deuteronomy mark God's deliverance of the Israelites from slavery in Egypt, the covenant at Sinai, and their wilderness wanderings. Now they are at the very edge of the promised land. The book of Joshua is the story of their entrance and new beginning in the promised land. It marks a new beginning in several ways. The former generation has died. Only Joshua and Caleb of that generation remain as Israel enters the promised land. Israel crosses the Jordan River and enters Canaan, the promised land (ch. 2). The book of Joshua describes the fulfillment of both parts of God's promise to Abraham, Isaac, and Jacob—Israel now has many descendants of the ancestors and the land God promised to them.

The first chapters of Joshua describe the commissioning of Joshua, the crossing of the Jordan River, and initial encampment at Gilgal (chs. 1–5). Chapters 6–12 describe the conquest of the land. In the midst of the conquest account, Joshua and the people go to Mount Ebal as Moses had directed, build an altar, and offer sacrifices to God. Joshua writes on the stones there all the words of the law that God had given Moses. Then he reads to all the people all the words of the law and all the blessings and curses of the law (ch. 8). The land is then divided among the tribes as directed by God, first through Moses and now through Joshua (chs. 13–22). The book closes with Israel in the land, having rest and peace; Joshua gives his farewell address to Israel and concludes another covenant renewal at Shechem, which is followed by the report of his death (chs. 23–24).

From this overview we see God has, indeed, kept his covenant promises—the promises to Abraham, Isaac, and Jacob—and the promises reiterated in the Sinaitic covenant with the people of Israel. They now are numerous, a great people, and occupy the promised land. Israel has been obedient; God has kept his promises. There is every reason for Israel to have great hope.

However, the book of Joshua also describes a darker side of the narrative. Israel is not entirely obedient. The sins of Israel lead to some judgments from God. In the first battle against the Canaanites at Jericho, the people break faith. God commands that all the city be burned; the people were not to keep anything from Jericho. But Achan keeps some of the spoils. As a result when Israel next goes out to battle, they are defeated. The sin of Achan is discovered; Achan and all his family die for his sins (ch. 7). When Israel deals with the sin, the people are successful in battle against the inhabitants. In another example of failing to keep covenant, Joshua and the leaders of Israel are tricked into entering a covenant with the inhabitants of Gibeon. The Gibeonites deceive Joshua by pretending to be from a distant area; however, Joshua and the leaders do not inquire of God before agreeing to a covenant. That failure allows Canaanites to remain in the land and to be a snare to Israel (ch. 9). Furthermore, several passages indicate the Israelites are lax in completing the conquest and occupying the land:

- Ephraim does not drive out all Canaanites (16:10).
- Israel does not utterly drive out Canaanites (17:13).
- Israel is slack in taking possession of the land (18:3).

Among the portions of land that are not taken are Philistia (13:2–3), Phoenicia (13:5–6), Jerusalem (15:63), and the Jezreel Valley (17:14–18). All these territories and their inhabitants will be a snare to the Israelites in future generations. Because Israel does not take all the land, God allows the Canaanites to remain as a test of Israel's faithfulness (Judg. 3:1–5).

Joshua's farewell address (chs. 23–24) emphasizes the fact that while Joshua led Israel into the land, Yahweh gave the land to the Israelites. Continued blessing and hope is dependent upon the obedience of the people:

> Therefore be very courageous to keep and to do all that is written in the Book of the Law of Moses, lest you turn aside from it to the right hand or to the left, and lest you go among these nations, these who remain among you. You shall not make mention of the name of their gods, nor cause anyone to swear by them; you shall not serve them nor bow down to them, but you shall hold fast to the LORD your God, as you have done to this day. (23:6–8)

The covenant renewal ceremony at Shechem climaxes with Joshua's charge:

> Choose for yourselves this day whom you will serve, whether the gods which your fathers served that were on the other side of the River, or the gods of the Amorites, in whose land you dwell. But as for me and my house, we will serve the LORD. (24:15)

The people of Israel reaffirm their commitment to serve only God.

The book of Joshua closes with the account of the deaths of Joshua and Eleazer the priest, Aaron's son, and with the affirmation: "Israel served the LORD all the days of Joshua, and all the days of the elders who outlived Joshua, who had known all the works of the LORD which He had done for Israel" (v. 31). Israel has success and hope when they are obedient to God. However, Israel has hope only because God is merciful, gracious, and forgiving even when Israel is not fully obedient! Our hope also rests on the grace, mercy, and forgiveness God offers us.

Judges

The book of Judges depicts the moral decline of the Israelites following the death of Joshua and the first generation of leaders in the promised land. It begins with a recounting of the tribes' attempts to take their allotments—and the parts they could not take (ch. 1). The text then records:

> When all that generation had been gathered to their fathers, another generation arose after them who did not know the LORD nor the work which He had done for Israel. Then the children of Israel did evil in the sight of the LORD, and served the Baals; and they forsook the LORD God of their fathers, who had brought them out of the land of Egypt; and they followed other gods from among the gods of the people who were all around them, and they bowed down to them; and they provoked the LORD to anger. (2:10–12)

There is still hope if the people remain faithful to God. God raises up judges to lead them against the remaining Canaanites as long as the Israelites remain faithful to him (vv. 6–19). Much of the book of Judges follows a pattern: the people of Israel sin, primarily by worshiping other gods; God raises up a force to oppress the people of Israel; the people of Israel cry out to God due to the oppression; God raises up a deliverer, a judge, who leads Israel to victory over the oppressor; and the people of Israel have rest and peace during the life of the judge/deliverer. The pattern then is repeated as the people of Israel again forsake God after the death of the judge. The oppressors came from all regions around the Israelites: Mesopotamia, Moab, Canaan, Midian, Ammon, and Philistia.

The judges range from people of exemplary character to those who epitomize the sins of the people of Israel. One exemplary judge is Deborah, the one woman named as a major judge and a prophetess (4:4). All Israel comes to her for justice (4:5). Deborah is a wife (4:4) and a mother (5:7). As judge and prophetess, Deborah calls out Barak the commander of the army of Naphtali and Zebulun (4:6). The people of Israel respond to God's call through Deborah and defeat the much stronger Canaanite army. The people are obedient, and God blesses them with victory and freedom from oppression. The people's hope again rests on God's faithfulness to his covenant and Israel's obedience.

Samson is an example of a judge who epitomizes the sins of Israel. When an angel announces Samson's coming birth to his parents, they are instructed that he is to be a Nazirite his whole life. Nazirites traditionally refrained from cutting their hair, from wine or strong drink, and from touching anything dead. Samson seems to revel in being disobedient to God's covenant and to the Nazirite vow. He marries a Philistine woman (14:15–20), breaking God's commands not to marry any of the inhabitants of the land. He has an affair with a Philistine woman, Delilah (16:4). He reveals to her the secret to his strength, his unshaven hair. She betrays him and has him shaved. Samson loses his strength and is captured and blinded by the Philistines. Once his hair grows again, and he cries out to God asking for renewed strength, God answers him. Samson pulls down the roof of the Philistine temple to Dagon, killing more Philistines at his death than he had the rest of his life (v. 30). As a judge, Samson defeats the Philistines numerous times. But how much more successful might he have been if he had been more obedient to God and to his vows!

The closing chapters of the book show how far Israel has fallen into sin. The chapters are framed with the statement that "In those days there was no king in Israel; everyone did what was right in his own eyes" (17:6; 21:25). This implies that a king would lead them to do what is right. But a greater implication is that Israel is no longer doing what is right in God's eyes. They forget or abandon their covenant with God.

At the end of Judges the situation seems hopeless. There is no great leader on the horizon like Moses and Joshua. The Israelites relapse into sin, becoming indistinguishable from the Canaanites in their immoral behavior.

They break covenant with God and engage in inter-tribal warfare. They set up illicit shrines and forbidden images.

The book of Judges shows us that hope is based on God and God's grace, not Israel's character or actions. Hope resides not in humans—not even in humans called and used by God as judge or deliverer. The people of Israel repeatedly sin against God. God judges their sin by raising up oppressors. But God does not desire to punish his people, his creation. God desires grace and redemption. God is the God of second chances. God shows grace to all people, not because they deserve it, but despite their failure and sin. Hope derives not from any human action, but from the character of God—from God's grace. That hope is all Israel has at the close of Judges, and that is also our hope.

Ruth

Two books in the Bible, both in the Old Testament, bear the names of women: Ruth and Esther. In each book, the woman is the main character and heroine. The book of Ruth is set historically in the time of the judges (1:1) and is so placed in our Bibles. However, the book clearly must have been written later because it ends with a genealogy down to David, three generations after the setting of the book (4:17–22).

Full to Empty

Famine has hit the land of Judah, so the family of Elimelech from Bethlehem moves to Moab where there is food. After they live in Moab for some time, Elimelech dies. The situation is now critical; Naomi, Elimelech's wife, is left alone to raise her two sons, Mahlon and Chilion. The family remains in Moab because the famine is still affecting Judah (1:6). In time, the two sons marry Moabite women. Remember, the law forbade Israelites to marry foreigners (Deut. 7:3–4) and specifically forbade any descendant of an Ammonite or a Moabite from entering the assembly or congregation to the tenth generation (Deut. 23:3). Yet these Judeans marry Moabites. After some time, Mahlon and Chilion also die. Now the situation is completely hopeless for the three widows, one of whom is a foreigner in Moab.

A glimmer of hope comes with the news that the famine is over in Judah, and Naomi can return to Bethlehem where she has family. Both daughters-in-law offer to go with her, a statement that says much about Naomi and the concern and love her daughters-in-law have for her. The young women have nothing to gain by following her—they will be foreigners with no support group in Judah. Naomi tells both to return to their homes and families.

> Go back, my daughters, to your own homes. I am too old to have another husband. Even if I told myself, "I still have hope" and had another husband tonight, and even if I had more sons, should you wait until they were grown into men? Should you live for so many years without husbands? Don't do that, my daughters. My life is much too sad for you to share, because the LORD has been against me! (1:12–13 NCV)

This is the only explicit mention of *hope* in the book. Orpah does return to her family, but Ruth stays with Naomi and returns to Bethlehem with her:

> But Ruth said: "Entreat me not to leave you,
> Or to turn back from following after you;
> For wherever you go, I will go;
> And wherever you lodge, I will lodge;
> Your people shall be my people,
> And your God, my God.
> Where you die, I will die,
> And there will I be buried.
> The LORD do so to me, and more also,
> If anything but death parts you and me." (vv. 6–17)

Ruth, a Moabitess, puts her faith and hope in the God of Naomi. She leaves her family, her land, her family religion, to follow and help Naomi. There are a number of significant parallels between Ruth and Abraham—Abraham leaves his extended family, his homeland, to follow God's call.

To support both herself and Naomi, Ruth gleans the fields surrounding Bethlehem for food. The poor are permitted to take the grain left in the fields after it has been cut and gathered. She happens to come to the fields of Boaz, a kinsman of Elimelech. Boaz comes out to the fields and asks about Ruth; his men tell him she is Naomi's daughter-in-law. Boaz becomes her protector; he tells her to glean only in his fields and orders his men not to molest her. Boaz also tells her when she is thirsty to drink from the water his men have drawn. He tells his men to leave additional grain for her.

From Empty to Full

When Naomi learns where Ruth has been gleaning, she tells Ruth that Boaz is a relative of Elimelech, her deceased husband. Elimelech had property, which Naomi offers for sale. Jewish law gave the nearest kinsman first option to purchase (or redeem) the deceased's property, to keep it within the family (Lev. 25:23–25). With the property also comes the obligation to marry the widow, Ruth in this case, to provide offspring to perpetuate the family line (see levirate marriage, Deut. 25:5–6). Boaz, not the nearest kin, arranges for a public meeting with the nearest kin to offer the property and the marriage to him. The man is not willing to become the redeemer because it will mean splitting his own children's inheritance (4:5–6). So Boaz purchases the property and marries Ruth. She conceives and has a son, Obed. Naomi, who had been empty, widowed, and hopeless, is now blessed again through a new generation. Ruth, who was widowed and hopeless, is now a wife and mother. Boaz has offspring. Naomi, Ruth, and Boaz are blessed and full of hope. The hope reaches fruition as Ruth and Boaz are identified as direct ancestors of David (Obed became the father of Jesse who became the father of David, 4:17).

The book of Ruth is filled with hope. Naomi with her husband and sons moves from Judah to Moab because there is hope for food in Moab and only famine in Judah. After Elimelech's death, Naomi succeeds in raising two sons to adulthood, and they both marry, a renewed hope for new life. When both sons die, the situation is desperate and seemingly hopeless, but Naomi hears that the famine has ended in Judah—a glimmer of hope.

Ruth clearly puts her hope in the Lord, the God of Israel, the God of Abraham, Isaac, and Jacob. She abandons her whole heritage to follow Naomi, placing all her hope in a foreign land, the family of her mother-in-law and deceased husband, and in their God. Her hope is fulfilled in marriage, in security, in family. The book of Ruth teaches us that even strangers can and do find hope in God. The book of Ruth shows us there are no limits to God's mercy and grace. Gender, ethnicity, race, marital status, and national origin place no limit on God's grace or human hope. God's mercy and grace extend to all of God's creation.

In Ruth's hope, we also find hope. For Ruth's son becomes the grandfather of David and the ancestor of Jesus. Truly, through faith in the God of Abraham, Isaac, and Jacob all people of the earth can be blessed and have real hope.

First and Second *Samuel*

First Samuel

The books of 1 and 2 Samuel continue the narrative of Israel in the promised land after the time period covered in Judges. First Samuel opens with the birth narrative of Samuel, the last judge and the priest-prophet who anoints Israel's first two kings, Saul and David. These three—Samuel, Saul, and David—are the main characters in 1 Samuel.

Hope through Hannah and Samuel

The book of Judges ends with Israel seemingly in a hopeless state of sin. One tribe has acted as sinfully as the Canaanites and has been decimated. Illicit shrines and sanctuaries have been set up in defiance of God's commandments. There is no leader on the scene. The situation clearly appears desperate. First Samuel opens with Hannah, a distraught, barren woman, on a pilgrimage to the sanctuary at Shiloh where the ark is and where Eli and his sons are priests. She cries out in prayer, vowing that if God will give her a son, then she will dedicate the child to his service. God hears Hannah's prayer and grants her request. She has a son, Samuel. When he is weaned, Hannah takes him to the sanctuary at Shiloh where he lives and serves God. Hannah, who had been hopeless, is filled with hope as her prayer is answered. Her hope is further heightened when God blesses her with three more sons and two daughters.

Eli is an old man and righteous. His two sons, however, are very wicked (ch. 2). Eli confronts them about their sinfulness, but they will not listen to him. They die in battle when the Philistines defeat the Israelites and capture the ark of the covenant from the Israelites' camp, illustrating Israel's hopeless situation. The death of Eli's two sons, followed by Eli's death when he learns the outcome of the battle, only increases the Israelites' hopeless condition. God's hope and plan (ch. 4), however, does not waiver. In every place the Philistines bring the captured ark, God demonstrates his power over the Philistines and their gods: images of Philistine gods are broken, and people die from plagues. God does punish sinful Israel at the hands of the Philistines. At the same time, God punishes the Philistines and provides hope for Israel with the return of the ark. The Philistines even send gifts with the ark—probably a recognition of the power of Israel's God over their gods.

There is further hope in the person of Samuel. The young boy brought to the sanctuary to minister to God under Eli's tutelage receives a prophetic message from God that promises hope beyond the tragedies of Eli's family (ch. 3). Samuel grows up to be the last judge-deliverer. He is also a prophet, bringing God's word to the people. He takes on the priestly role of offering sacrifices to God and anoints Israel's first two kings, Saul and David. Samuel is the evidence of God's continuing to bless Israel and continuing to be a source of hope.

Evidence of that hope can be seen as Samuel challenges the people to put away all false gods and serve only God; the people pledge to do so. Samuel then calls for an assembly of the people at Mizpah, apparently for covenant renewal. When the people gather at Mizpah, the Philistines learn of the gathering and attack them. Samuel offers sacrifices and prays to God, and God routs the Philistines (7:10–11). Samuel sets up a stone and names it "Ebenezer" (literally, stone of help) because God helped them (v. 2). God is indeed Israel's hope when Israel repents and is faithful to him.

The People Hope for a King

When Samuel is old, he appoints his two sons to be judges. But Samuel's sons are not righteous like Samuel; they take bribes and pervert justice. The elders of Israel come to Samuel, confront him about his sons, and ask for "a king to rule over us like all the other nations" (8:5). Samuel is upset over the demand for a king and prays to God. God tells Samuel to grant their request and explains that the people are rejecting, not Samuel, but God, as they have since the exodus. Samuel warns the people of the dangers and costs of human kingship (8:6–18).

God reveals to Samuel that Saul is to be the first king (9:17). Samuel anoints Saul and relates God's commission: "And you shall reign over the people of the LORD and you will save them from the hand of their enemies round about" (10:1 RSV). Saul certainly seems kingly. He is described as being more handsome and taller than anyone else in Israel (9:2). Saul is also quite successful on the battlefield:

> When Saul became king over Israel, he fought against Israel's enemies all around. He fought Moab, the Ammonites, Edom, the king of Zobah, and the Philistines. Everywhere Saul went he defeated Israel's enemies. (14:47, NCV)

The depiction seems quite hopeful despite God's warnings. However, a couple of facts indicate all may not be that hopeful. Saul is of the tribe of Benjamin, and his home is in Gibeah (10:26; 14:16). At the end of Judges, the people of Gibeah and the tribe of Benjamin were behaving as the sinful inhabitants of Sodom and Gomorrah had acted. That behavior led to the decimation of much of the tribe of Benjamin (Gen. 19; Judg. 19–21). Furthermore, despite Saul's success on the battlefield, he disobeys God's commands, and God rejects him (15:26). Ultimately Saul and three of his sons die in battle at the hands of the Philistines (31:6).

Shortly after God rejects Saul and well before Saul's death, he sends Samuel to anoint Saul's successor, David of the tribe of Judah. More important (and with hope), God describes David as a man after his own heart (13:13–14). He is not an obvious choice for king, young and inexperienced, but this indicates clearly that David brings God's hope for Israel, not Israel's hope to be like other nations.

David has great success. He defeats and kills Goliath, the Philistine. Even while Saul is still alive and seeking to kill David, the younger man is a successful warrior and leader. He does not fight against Israel or Saul's forces, but only against the enemies of Israel. He becomes so widely known that the people sing: "Saul has slain his thousands, and David his ten thousands" (29:5). Although I Samuel closes with the death of Saul, it also ends with hope in David, a man after God's own heart.

2 Samuel

The book of 2 Samuel opens with David learning of the death of Saul and his sons. David moves to Hebron where the leaders of Judah anoint him king of Judah. But Abner, Saul's army commander and cousin, takes one of Saul's remaining sons, Ishbosheth, and makes him king over Israel (2:8–10). After two years, Abner and Ishbosheth are assassinated (chs. 3–4). After that, the elders of Israel all come to David at Hebron, make a covenant with him, and anoint him king over Israel (5:1). David is now king over all twelve tribes of Israel in a way Saul never was, living out God's hope for a united and obedient people.

A Kingdom United in Hope

David captures Jerusalem, a city that until then had never been in Israelite hands (5:6–8). Jerusalem is on the border between Judah and Benjamin but had remained in Jebusite hands. David takes up residence in Jerusalem, a stronghold that he names the city of David (vv. 7–9). In joyous hope and celebration, he brings the ark of the covenant from Baale-Judah to Jerusalem (ch. 6), making it a major Israelite shrine as well as the political capital of his kingdom. He subjugates neighboring people as his vassals, creating an empire from the Euphrates River to the border of Egypt. He then proposes to build a temple for God to house the ark of the covenant. However, God sends a message through the prophet Nathan that David is not to build the temple, but that his son and successor will build it (ch. 7).

The message does contain a promise from God: he will build a "house" for David—a dynasty—and David will never cease to have a descendant on the throne as long as he and his descendants remain faithful to God (7:2–13). David has been extraordinarily successful to this point. God has blessed him at every point. Israel has every reason to be hopeful.

Hope Endangered by Human Pride

For all his success and blessing, David is flawed, and his flaws lead to new hopelessness in the royal family and, ultimately, for all of Israel. One expectation of kings is that they are to lead their troops in battle. One spring, following many victories (ch. 8), David sends his army against the Ammonites, but he stays at home in Jerusalem (11:1). One evening from his rooftop, he sees a young woman bathing. He inquires who she is. Even when he learns she is Bathsheba, wife of Uriah the Hittite, David invites her to the palace and commits adultery with her. When Bathsheba later reports that she is pregnant, David tries to cover up his sin. He first invites Bathsheba's husband back from the battlefield and sends him home to spend time with Bathsheba. But Uriah is too dedicated a warrior and does not go home. David then has Uriah killed in battle so he can marry Bathsheba (vv. 2–27). God's judgment on David is swift. Nathan the prophet confronts David with a parable. David, when confronted, acknowledges his sin and seeks God's forgiveness. God forgives David, but brings severe judgment on David and Bathsheba (ch. 12).

The remainder of 2 Samuel details much of the turmoil, sin, and tragedy within the family of David. The child born to David and Bathsheba dies. One of David's sons, Amnon, rapes his half sister, Tamar. Tamar's brother, Absalom, has Amnon killed. Absalom flees from David and spends three years in exile. He is allowed to return to Jerusalem but not allowed to come into David's presence for another two years. Even after David reconciles with Absalom, Absalom conspires against his father. Four years later, Absalom goes to Hebron and is proclaimed king. The rebellion is so widespread that David flees from Jerusalem. The army loyal to David fights Absalom's army; David's army prevails and Absalom is killed. As David is returning to Jerusalem after Absalom's death, Sheba, a Benjaminite leads another rebellion against David. This rebellion also is crushed. These events show the extreme dysfunction in the royal family and disunity in the kingdom. The narrative certainly indicates that sin has severe consequences.

Despite the family dysfunction and downfall, the Davidic kingdom seems to prosper. Near the end of 2 Samuel, however, we read of other problems. David deals with a three-year famine due to bloodguilt Saul had brought on Israel by breaking covenant with the Gibeonites. David resolves this by handing over seven of Saul's grandsons to be executed by the Gibeonites.

The last chapter of 2 Samuel closes with David, incited by the Lord's anger at Israel's sins, taking a census of Israel and Judah. Joab, David's army commander, objects because he thinks the census is something David desires for personal gain rather than for God's glory. After taking the census, David realizes he has sinned and confesses his sin to God. As judgment, God offers David three options: a three-year famine, three months of David fleeing his enemies, or a three-day pestilence. Rather than accepting judgment that would apply only to himself, David chooses the three-day pestilence, and seventy thousand people across the nation die. When the pestilence reaches Jerusalem, God stops it at the threshing floor of Araunah. David prays to God that any further punishment fall on him and his family. Through the prophet Gad, God tells David to build an altar to him on the threshing floor. David purchases the threshing floor from Araunah, builds an altar, and sacrifices to God on the site where the pestilence stopped, bringing an end to the punishment.

Second Samuel ends there, with another message of hope following judgment. David's sins and the sins of his family result in terrible judgment from God. But there is hope. David is still on the throne of the united monarchy of Israel. The books of Kings will carry the narrative forward.

Hope will find fruition through another generation. The site of David's sacrifice will become the location of the temple in Jerusalem. At the end of 2 Samuel, we don't have the whole story. But God's mercy, David's penitence, his building an altar and offering sacrifices to God point to hope. The hope, as always, lies with God forgiving sin and showing mercy on David and the kingdom.

First and Second *Kings*

First Kings

The book of 2 Samuel closes with David having reigned as king over Israel for many years. His census of Israel is sinful and results in a three-day pestilence that kills seventy thousand. David confesses his sin to God; he purchases the threshing floor of Araunah (where the pestilence stopped), builds an altar, and offers sacrifices to God. The plague stops. There is hope in God's forgiving mercy.

Solomon's Rise and Fall

First Kings opens after that episode. David is now very old. The matter of succession to the throne is critical in the first chapter. Adonijah, apparently the oldest of David's surviving sons, gathers leaders of Judah, offers sacrifices, and is proclaimed king. But Nathan the prophet, Zadok the priest, and others go to Bathsheba and David. David selects Solomon, Bathsheba's son, to succeed him. At the end of the chapter, David dies, and Solomon is firmly established as king of a still-unified Israel.

Solomon's reign begins in great hope. Solomon is known as a wise ruler. He offers sacrifices to God at Gibeon. In a dream, God asks what Solomon would request from him. Solomon asks for a discerning mind, wisdom. God grants Solomon wisdom and also riches, honor, and long life if Solomon remains obedient to God's commandments. The following chapters of 1 Kings depict Solomon's great achievements, God's blessings for Solomon's obedience.

> There were as many people in Judah and Israel as grains of sand on the seashore. The people ate, drank, and were happy. Solomon ruled over

> all the kingdoms from the Euphrates River to the land of the Philistines, as far as the border of Egypt. These countries brought Solomon the payments he demanded, and they were under his control all his life. . . .
>
> Solomon controlled all the countries west of the Euphrates River—the land from Tiphsah to Gaza. And he had peace on all sides of his kingdom. During Solomon's life Judah and Israel, from Dan to Beersheba, also lived in peace; all of his people were able to sit under their own fig trees and grapevines. . . .
>
> His wisdom was greater than any wisdom of the East, or any wisdom in Egypt. He was wiser than anyone on earth. (4:20–21, 24–25, 30–31a NCV)

Solomon begins to build the temple for God (chs. 5–6). The temple is the central sanctuary, the place representing God's dwelling place, the focal place for worship of God for all the land. With the completion of the temple, the position of Jerusalem is fully established as the political and religious center—the central sanctuary—of the kingdom-empire. God's covenant promises to Abraham are fulfilled. Abraham's descendants are numerous and possess the promised land. Israel's hope is fulfilled. Everything seems great, a sign of God's blessing. In his dedication of the temple, Solomon repeats the promises of blessing for obedience to God's commandments and the warning of judgment for disobedience (ch. 8). God appears again to Solomon and repeats the promise that if Solomon remains obedient he will always have an heir on the throne of David. If, however, Solomon and his descendants turn aside from following God and turn to other gods, Israel will be cut off from the land, and the temple will be destroyed (9:1–9). The kingdom-empire is at its height; the king is greatly blessed; hope is running high.

Solomon, however, like his father before him, and like all of us, is flawed. He marries many foreign women (seven hundred wives and three hundred concubines) contrary to God's commands that Israelites are not to marry foreign women because they turn away Israel's heart from God to the worship of other gods. In his old age, Solomon turns away from God and also worships Ashteroth, Milcom, Chemosh, Molech, and other foreign gods. He builds shrines and sanctuaries for these foreign gods in and around Jerusalem (11:1–8). God's judgment on Solomon is that the kingdom will be divided after his death, that his son will have only one tribe remaining (vv. 9–13), a remnant of the original hope of Israel. In Solomon's last years, God raises up adversaries against him: Rezon, an Aramean leader, and Jeroboam, who leads the Northern Kingdom of Israel after the kingdom splits (vv. 14–39).

The Kingdom Divided

After Solomon's death, his son Rehoboam succeeds him. Rehoboam goes to Shechem to be made king of the united kingdom. Jeroboam and other leaders of Israel ask him to lighten the heavy burdens Solomon had placed on Israel. Rehoboam refuses. Ten of the twelve tribes reject Rehoboam and make Jeroboam king of the Northern Kingdom of Israel. The united monarchy is no more. The judgment God pronounced against Solomon is fulfilled under Rehoboam, in part as a result of his own willfulness. Rehoboam remains king of the Southern Kingdom of Judah, which includes the tribes of Judah and Benjamin (12:1–25).

Jeroboam makes Shechem his capital. He sets up calf images representing God in sanctuaries at Dan and Bethel to keep the people from going to Jerusalem to worship (vv. 26–33). He also sets up high places to other gods and creates new festivals. These acts are the basis of the sins that Jeroboam caused Israel to commit (14:14–16).

Much of the latter part of 1 Kings focuses on Israel and the disobedience of Israel's kings against God and God's laws. Jeroboam's sins are repeated by later Israelite kings, contributing to the destruction of the kingdom of Israel two hundred years later (2 Kings 17:20–23). The great hope of a united monarchy is destroyed as the disobedience of the rulers leads the people into sin and hopelessness.

Ahab and Elijah

The story of one king of Israel, Ahab, is told in great detail, and it introduces a new source of hope in the words and actions of the prophet Elijah. Ahab marries Jezebel, the daughter of the king of the Sidonians. Ahab worships Baal, the Phoenician god, builds a temple and altar for Baal in his capital city Samaria, and also makes an image of the goddess Asherah (16:30–33). God sends the prophet Elijah to pronounce judgment against Ahab and Israel. The first judgment is a three-year drought. At the end of that time Elijah proposes a contest between himself and the prophets of Baal on Mount Carmel (ch. 17). Elijah alone faces 450 prophets of Baal. After Baal fails to respond to the cries of his prophets, God responds to Elijah's prayer. The prophets of Baal are killed and the drought ends—new hope emerges (ch. 18).

In a direct and powerful encounter with God, Elijah receives hope for his personal future and for the future of Israel as God names Elisha as Elijah's successor (ch. 19).

God gives Ahab numerous victories over the Arameans (ch. 20), but Ahab and Jezebel continue their sinful ways. Jezebel has Naboth, a faithful Israelite, killed to give Ahab Naboth's vineyard. When Elijah speaks God's judgment against Ahab and his family—everyone in his family will be killed—Ahab tears his clothes, puts on sackcloth, and fasts in repentance. God responds to Ahab's repentance by delaying the judgment until after Ahab's death (ch. 21). Again we see an element of hope. Repentance, even by an extremely sinful person, can bring blessing. Note that God's judgment is not averted, but it is delayed. The same was true of God's judgment on Solomon.

Second Kings

While much of 2 Kings continues the narrative of the kings of Israel and Judah, with little evidence of hope, the prophets Elijah and Elisha lift up the promise of hope in their obedience to and reliance on God (chs. 2; 4–8). As to the kings, every king of Israel is described in terms of sin. Of the kings of Judah, eight are good, but only two are depicted in a fully positive light: Hezekiah and Josiah. Both of these kings institute significant, if short-lived, reforms.

Hezekiah

Hezekiah is quite unlike his predecessors on the throne:

> Hezekiah did what the Lord said was right, just as his ancestor David had done. He removed the places where gods were worshiped. He smashed the stone pillars and cut down the Asherah idols. Also the Israelites had been burning incense to Nehushtan, the bronze snake Moses had made. But Hezekiah broke it into pieces. Hezekiah trusted in the Lord, the God of Israel. There was no one like him among all the kings of Judah, either before him or after him. (18:3–5, NCV)

God blesses Hezekiah with great success, bringing hope for Judah because of Hezekiah's faithfulness and God's graciousness. Hezekiah is able to expand Judah's control again into former Philistine territory. He reigns at the height of Assyrian expansion in the region. The Assyrians have already conquered the Arameans when Hezekiah comes to the throne and will soon capture Samaria and all Israel (vv. 9–12). Hezekiah even stops paying tribute to the Assyrian king (v. 7). As a result the Assyrians invade Judah, take all the fortified cities, and besiege Jerusalem. Hezekiah submits to Sennacherib, the king of Assyria, and sends a tribute of three hundred talents of silver and thirty talents of gold. Sennacherib then sends his top officials to convince the leaders of Jerusalem that it is folly to trust in God because no other god has saved his people from Sennacherib (vv. 13–37).

Hezekiah tears his clothes, puts on sackcloth, goes to the temple, and sends servants to the prophet Isaiah. Isaiah sends a word of assurance to Hezekiah from God. Hezekiah receives a letter from Sennacherib that says

God will not be able to save Jerusalem from him. Hezekiah takes the letter to the temple, spreads it before God, and prays for him to deliver Jerusalem from Sennacherib. Isaiah delivers an oracle of deliverance from God, saying the king of Assyria will not enter the city or take it. That night an angel of God destroys much of the Assyrian army; Sennacherib returns to Assyria without taking Jerusalem (19:5–37). Even in the face of grave odds, the faithful and obedient can take hope—not from human hands, but from faith in God.

Later, Hezekiah becomes very sick, and Isaiah delivers a message from God telling Hezekiah to put his house in order for he is about to die. Hezekiah prays to God and God heeds Hezekiah's prayer, heals him, and grants him another fifteen years of life. Faithfulness to God and praying to him brings hope. Hope is dependent on God.

Hezekiah is succeeded by his son Manasseh, who undoes all the reforms of Hezekiah and introduces even more idolatries than earlier kings. He even burns one of his sons as an offering.

> Because Manasseh king of Judah has done these abominations (he has acted more wickedly than all the Amorites who were before him, and has also made Judah sin with his idols), therefore thus says the LORD God of Israel . . . "I will stretch over Jerusalem the measuring line of Samaria and the plummet of the house of Ahab; I will wipe Jerusalem as one wipes a dish, wiping it and turning it upside down. So I will forsake the remnant of My inheritance and deliver them into the hand of their enemies; and they shall become victims of plunder to all their enemies, because they have done evil in My sight, and have provoked Me to anger since the day their fathers came out of Egypt, even to this day." (21:11–12a, 13–15)

JOSIAH

The other good king is Josiah, great-grandson of Hezekiah. In the eighteenth year of his reign, Josiah orders repairs and renovations to the temple. In the course of the work, the high priest Hilkiah discovers a book of the Law (22:8). This book of the Law, considered by many scholars to be the book of Deuteronomy or portions of it, provides the basis of Josiah's reforms. The prophetess Huldah warns Josiah of imminent judgment because the people have not been obedient to the Law, God's instructions (vv. 14–20). In response Josiah gathers a convocation of leaders of Judah and Jerusalem:

> The king went up to the house of the LORD with all the men of Judah, and with him all the inhabitants of Jerusalem—the priests and the prophets and all the people, both small and great. And he read in their hearing all the words of the Book of the Covenant which had been found in the house of the LORD. Then the king stood by a pillar and made a covenant before the LORD, to follow the LORD and to keep His commandments and His testimonies and His statutes, with all his heart and all his soul, to perform the words of this covenant that were written in this book. And all the people took a stand for the covenant. (23:2–3)

The reforms Josiah institutes are the most sweeping recorded. He removes all the syncretistic cult objects that had been brought into the temple since the time of Solomon; he also destroys high places in Judah and Jerusalem. He even destroys and defiles the altar and high place at Bethel and all the high places of Samaria and kills their priests. He sweeps away all the mediums, wizards, abominable practices, and idols throughout the land. He commands the people to keep Passover, something not done since the days of the Judges. His acts are summarized:

> Now before him there was no king like him, who turned to the LORD with all his heart, with all his soul, and with all his might, according to all the Law of Moses; nor after him did any arise like him. (v. 25)

Josiah's reforms bring God's blessing on Judah and a measure of hope. Nevertheless, God's judgment against Judah and Jerusalem because of the sins of Manasseh is not averted, though it is delayed (vv. 26–27; see 22:18–20).

Summary

The books of Samuel and Kings recount life in the land for about five hundred years. They describe Israel's life under the last judges and then under the monarchy. Unfortunately, most of the narrative is one of Israel's repeated sinfulness, which brings repeated judgment by God.

Finally, the two monarchies of Israel and Judah pay the ultimate price. The Northern Kingdom, Israel, is defeated by the Assyrians in 722–721 BC. Much of the population is killed or taken captive by the Assyrians, and foreign people are resettled in Israel among the remaining population. The Southern Kingdom, Judah, is defeated by the Babylonians in 587–586 BC. Again, much of the population is killed or taken captive. Judah is placed under Babylonian government. Second Kings ends with much of the population, especially the leaders, exiled from the promised land due to their sinfulness.

But even in that situation there is hope. The last words of 2 Kings record that in the thirty-seventh year of exile King Jehoiachin is released from prison by the king of Babylon and is given a place at the table of the king of Babylon for as long as he lives (25:27–30). The words of release and provision by the king of Babylon offer some hope. The people are in a foreign land, exiled from the promised land. But they were out of the land before—first in Egypt (at the end of Genesis) and then in the plains of Moab (at the end of Deuteronomy). In each case, God brought them to the promised land, so there is hope that he will do it again, if the people repent and obey God and his commandments. There is hope that God will be merciful and forgiving and restore his people.

The focus of these books is on the human leaders God provides for Israel—the judges and kings. Much of the narrative details the successes and failures—the sins—of these human leaders. Certainly God uses these people, but hope is not found in such leaders—all humanity is sinful and fallible. Hope is found in God, who is merciful and forgiving when sinful humans repent and seek him.

Another element of hope within the books of Samuel and Kings are those spokespersons God sends to both warn and instruct the people about God's judgment and his will for the people. These prophets were men and women sent by God to kings and leaders to announce God's word. Many of their names are familiar to us—Samuel, Nathan, Elijah, Elisha, Gad, and Isaiah—but other prophets are unnamed:

> At the same time a prophet came to Ahab king of Israel. The prophet said, "Ahab, the LORD says to you, 'Do you see that big army? I will hand it over to you today so you will know I am the LORD'." (1 Kings 20:13 NCV)

The prophets may be designated as servants of God:

> The LORD used every prophet and seer to warn Israel and Judah. He said, "Stop your evil ways and obey my commands and laws. Follow all the teachings that I commanded your ancestors, the teachings that I gave you through my servants the prophets." (2 Kings 17:13 NCV)

Prophets' words warn of imminent judgment because of the sin of the king or leader (consider Nathan confronting David) and bring instruction, or words of promise and assurance (Isaiah's message to Hezekiah during Sennacherib's invasion).

The prophets are great figures of hope. Even if their messages are warnings of judgment, they also offer the hope that judgment is not the final word. Hope resides in the possible blessing or restoration beyond judgment. These servants of God and their messages become the focus of the section of the Old Testament we call the Prophets. Their message provides much of the hope later realized in the coming of the Messiah, the Christ, in the New Testament. A part of that hope looks back to the covenants between God and Abraham, Isaac, and Jacob in Genesis; between God and the children of Israel at Sinai; and between God and David. But all prophetic hope looks to future fulfillment beyond the desolation at the end of 2 Kings: the people exiled from the land and under domination of a foreign power. The hope is that, if the people repent and are obedient to God, he will remember the covenants and show mercy to his people, restoring the blessings promised in the covenants.

HOPE BEYOND *Torah and History*

The book of Chronicles in the English Bible is in the section often called the Historical Books that contains Joshua–Esther. In this arrangement the English Bible is following the Greek Old Testament, the Septuagint. The Hebrew Bible is divided into three major sections: Torah or Law (Genesis–Deuteronomy); *Neviim* or Prophets, divided into two parts—Former Prophets (Joshua, Judges, Samuel, Kings) and Latter Prophets (Isaiah, Jeremiah, Ezekiel, and the Book of the Twelve Minor Prophets); and Writings (the remainder of the Old Testament, including Chronicles). As previously noted, the word *hope* does not occur often in the Old Testament. What is even more interesting is the lack of words for *hope* in the Torah and Former Prophets, in Genesis through 2 Kings. The one occurrence of "hope" in English Bibles is Ruth 1:12. But in the Hebrew Bible, Ruth is in the Writings section. Even when we consider Hebrew words expressing hope or waiting expectantly, such words occur only twice in the Torah and Former Prophets: Genesis 49:18 and 2 Kings 6:33. What is clear from this evidence is that words for *hope* in both Hebrew and English translations are found almost entirely in the Latter Prophets and the Writings. These materials are also the ones considered to be the latest material in the Old Testament.

One reason for this expression of hope in the Latter Prophets and Writings is the nature of the material. The book of Psalms has almost twice as many occurrences of the word *hope* than any other Old Testament book (see the chapter on Psalms). The size of the book of Psalms partially accounts for this, but the material in Psalms is also part of the answer. Psalms contains prayers, praises, laments, and petitions addressed to God by worshipers. Expressions of hope as they address God are expected.

Likewise, the Latter Prophets contain warnings of judgment on Israel and Judah unless they repent and turn to God. But the Prophets also include strong messages of hope, even beyond judgment. In addition to this consideration, the later date of the Latter Prophets and Writings may be a major factor in the expression of hope. Historically, during the time period of the Latter Prophets and Ezra, Nehemiah, and Chronicles—from the eighth to the fifth century BC—the chosen people moved from the *possibility* of domination by foreign powers and loss of nationhood to the *reality* of exile. Both the threat and the reality of destruction at the hands of foreign powers led to increased expressions of hope in God and God's deliverance. Historically, even after the return from exile and rebuilding of the temple, Judah remained under foreign domination (Persian and Greek-Hellenistic), to the end of the Old Testament period. But the end of exile and the rebuilding of the temple provided a basis for hope—or as Jeremiah says, "a future and a hope" (Jer. 29:11).

First and Second *Chronicles*

The books of 1 and 2 Chronicles cover much of the same time period as 1–2 Samuel and 1–2 Kings, basically the period of the monarchy. However, 1 Chronicles begins with eight chapters of genealogies that go all the way back to Adam. The last verses of 2 Chronicles speak of Cyrus's edict of restoration, dated to 538 BC, that permits the exiled peoples to return to their homeland. However, the genealogy of King Jehoiachin (called Jeconiah, 1 Chron.) who is taken as a captive to Babylon in 597 BC, lists eight generations of descendants (1 Chron. 3:17–24), ending with seven brothers: Hodaviah, Eliashib, Pelaiah, Akkub, Johanan, Delaiah, and Anani. This genealogy pushes the date for Chronicles to about 400 BC. This extensive genealogy provides an element of hope linking the returning generation with earlier generations of God's people. God has not forgotten or abandoned them; he is still at work restoring the people.

The theological perspective of Chronicles differs from that of Samuel and Kings, which have a preexilic monarchical perspective until nearly the end of 2 Kings when the fall of both the Northern Kingdom of Israel and the Southern Kingdom of Judah are reported. The closing words of 2 Kings record the release of King Jehoiachin from prison in Babylon, offering a bit of hope. However, the people are still in exile. Chronicles closes with the announcement of Cyrus's edict allowing the exiles to return home. The perspective then is exilic and looks toward a postexilic future.

Hope through Idealized Monarchy

Chronicles also differs significantly from Samuel and Kings in relating the history of the period of the monarchy. Chronicles focuses on the Davidic monarchy only, depicting it as the only legitimate monarchy and

Jerusalem as the only legitimate place of worship. Saul's kingship is almost completely disregarded except for his final battle with the Philistines and his death. The division of the monarchy under Rehoboam is described as rebellion, and none of the kings of the Northern Kingdom of Israel are considered legitimate. Both David and Solomon are described as ideal kings. No mention is made of the human flaws of either man. David's adulterous affair with Bathsheba and its consequences are not mentioned. The only sin of David's that is mentioned is his census near the end of his reign (1 Chron. 21). David is credited with great military success and faithfulness to God for bringing the ark of the covenant to Jerusalem. He is also credited with collecting much of the material for the temple, enlisting craftsmen (1 Chron. 22:1–5), and drawing up the plans of the temple (1 Chron. 28). David is not permitted to build the temple because he has been a warrior and has shed much blood (1 Chron. 22:8). Solomon, as a man of peace, will be the one actually to build the temple. Solomon also is described as an ideal king, surpassing his father, David, in wisdom, riches, and greatness. He has unparalleled success in establishing the kingdom. No mention is made of his many wives and sin later in life (1 Kings 11).

Chronicles makes clear that blessing comes from obedience to God and God's laws. The books of Chronicles repeatedly demonstrate that sin brings immediate judgment in the life of the individual, and that obedience brings immediate blessing from God. Three main theological underpinnings for Chronicles relate to hope. The first is the Sinaitic or Mosaic covenant that establishes Israel as God's people and sets forth the principles for maintaining a right relationship between God and his people. As the people of Israel-Judah obediently follow the Sinaitic covenant, they have continuing assurance and hope of God's blessings. The second underpinning is the Davidic covenant that establishes right government by God for his people. David and his successors are God's chosen leaders for the people of Israel. As David and his successors are obedient to God and God's covenant, they and the people they govern have the assurance and hope of God's blessings. The third underpinning is right worship centered in the temple, with the right priesthood and religious leaders. If the priests and religious leaders remain faithful to God, instruct the people in God's covenant-law, and maintain right worship and actions, Israel-Judah can rest in the hope of God's blessings. All these underpinnings rest ultimately on God, not on the people or leaders. The people and the leaders are not the source of their hope; only God is.

The only explicit reference to hope in the books of Chronicles is in the midst of a prayer by David, giving thanks for all the gifts and offerings for the temple: "We are like foreigners and strangers, as our ancestors were. Our time on earth is like a shadow. There is no hope [*miqveh*]" (1 Chron. 29:15 NCV). The verse means there is no hope ("none abiding," KJV) in human beings. Humans amount to nothing compared to God. Human lifespan is short; God is eternal. Even the best and most faithful of humans—including those surrounding David as he prays, and David himself—provide no real hope. Real hope is found only in God.

This understanding of hope can be seen in a slight, but significant, difference in the report of Nathan's prophecy to David when David proposes to build the temple for God. In 2 Samuel 7, God affirms through Nathan that David will have a successor, God will establish the successor's kingdom (2 Sam. 7:13–14), and in so doing will also establish David's kingdom ("your kingdom," 2 Sam. 7:16). In 1 Chronicles 17, the wording is similar: God will establish the successor's kingdom (v. 11). However, verse 14 says: "I will establish him in My house and in My kingdom forever; and his throne shall be established forever." The slight, but very significant, difference is that God says he will establish his ("My") kingdom rather than David's ("your") kingdom. Chronicles emphasizes whose kingdom the monarchy really is. David is the king, but the kingdom is God's. For an audience in exile in Babylon or just returning to Judah, that is a very hopeful message. God judged the kings and the people for their sinfulness. Now God is restoring the people to Jerusalem and Judah. They can have hope because the kingdom is God's; it is not David's, or Babylon's, or Persia's—even if Persia is the world power controlling Judah.

Hope through Royal Repentance

Shortly after the division of the monarchy, during Rehoboam's reign, he and the people forsake God's law. As a result of their sin, Pharaoh Shishak of Egypt invades Judah and Jerusalem (2 Chron. 12:1–2). The prophet Shemaiah comes to Rehoboam and other leaders of Judah pronouncing judgment: "Thus says the LORD: 'You have forsaken Me, and therefore I also have left you in the hand of Shishak'" (v. 5). Rehoboam and the leaders then humble themselves and declare, "The LORD is righteous" (v. 6). God sees that Rehoboam and the leaders humbled themselves and sends a second message by Shemaiah:

> Now when the LORD saw that they humbled themselves, the word of the LORD came to Shemaiah, saying, "They have humbled themselves; therefore I will not destroy them, but I will grant them some deliverance. My wrath shall not be poured out on Jerusalem by the hand of Shishak. Nevertheless they will be his servants, that they may distinguish My service from the service of the kingdoms of the nations." (vv. 7–8)

The passage shows how God judges sin and disobedience; it also shows that repentance and humbling oneself to God can bring deliverance after judgment. This message of hope, recurring frequently in Chronicles, is a fitting word to an audience that has faced exile in Babylon and has just heard that a return to Judah and Jerusalem is possible. If those returning to Judah learn from the sins of the previous generations and remain faithful to God and God's law, then their restored community in the land will be blessed and hope-filled.

Chronicles has additional information concerning Asa, king of Judah. First Kings affirms Asa as one whose heart was wholly true to God his whole life (1 Kings 15:14). Chronicles records two prophets who take messages of God to Asa. The first, Oded, tells Asa that if he seeks God he will find him. Asa and all Judah with him institute religious reform (2 Chron. 15). However, Asa later breaks his alliance with Baasha of Israel, using silver and gold from the temple to bribe Ben-Hadad, king of Aram-Syria, to ally with him instead. Hanani, another prophet, chastises Asa for depending on Ben-Hadad rather than on God. Hanani also tells Asa he will have wars from that time on. Asa becomes angry and imprisons Hanani (2 Chron. 16). Asa develops a severe foot disease; but rather than seeking God for help, he relies on physicians and dies from the disease (vv. 12–13). Chronicles again indicates that even kings blessed for their righteousness come under judgment when they trust in themselves or other human help rather than seeking God. The message is a warning but also a message of hope. Faithfulness and seeking God always brings blessing and hope.

Chronicles emphasizes the hope that repentance and trust in God can bring. As in 2 Kings 21:10, 2 Chronicles 33:9 describes Manasseh as being more wicked than his predecessors. However, Chronicles includes an account not found in Kings: Manasseh is captured by the Assyrian king and taken captive to Babylon. There Manasseh humbles himself, repents, and prays to God (vv. 10–12). God hears Manasseh's prayer and repentance and forgives him. Manasseh is restored to Jerusalem and to the throne. There he undertakes major reforms (vv. 13–17). The hope here is that even the most wicked who are judged and exiled can be restored if they repent and trust in God.

The Promise of Hope Fulfilled

Second Chronicles closes with many of the Jews still in exile in Babylon, then under Persian rule. The last verses of the book report the rise of Cyrus to power and his edict allowing the Jews to return to their homeland and rebuild the temple in Jerusalem. This is the promise of hope fulfilled for both the exiles and those remaining in Jerusalem. Second Chronicles is the last book in the Hebrew Bible. It closes the third division, the Kethubim or Writings, so the Hebrew Bible ends with a strong message of hope. In one sense the hope of 2 Chronicles is fulfilled with the return of the Jews to Judea after 539 BC and the rebuilding of the temple in 520–515 BC. Even after the destruction of the temple by the Romans in AD 70, 2 Chronicles provides hope to Jews dispersed throughout all nations. They might also be able to return to Jerusalem, a hope still present today in the closing words of the Passover Seder: "Next Year in Jerusalem!"

Ezra–Nehemiah

The books of Ezra and Nehemiah are the latest of the historical books in the Old Testament. They cover a period of postexilic history in the fifth century BC, following the first return from exile in Babylon. Both these individuals' names indicate a measure of hope to the restored community. The name *Ezra* in Hebrew means "help" and is one of the words associated with hope in the Old Testament. The name *Nehemiah* in Hebrew means "Yahweh has compassion."

Ezra

The book of Ezra opens with the report of the decree of Cyrus authorizing the return of the exiles to Judah and Jerusalem along with much of the treasure Nebuchadnezzar had taken to Babylon. This is followed by a list of the heads of families and the number of their descendants who return (chs. 1–2). Shortly after their return to Jerusalem, the people rebuild the altar on the temple grounds and reestablish offerings, regular worship, and festivals. They also lay the foundation for a rebuilt temple (ch. 3). There is great hope among the Jews, and they undertake the restoration with great enthusiasm. (This text follows the standard usage of referring to the religious and ethnic community after the exile as Jews; the Hebrew term is actually *yehudi*, "Judean" or "Judahite.") God seems to be blessing in extraordinary ways, and the people are faithfully serving him. God is faithful to his covenant promises to the people of Israel. They had rebelled against him, worshiping other gods; they were judged for their sins and exiled from their land. But now, they have repented, and God graciously and mercifully restores them. Hope for full restoration abounds.

However, troubles soon emerge. After the Assyrians destroyed the Northern Kingdom and exiled most of the population, they brought in foreigners who settled in the land and inter-married with those who remained. Their descendants now live in the province of Samaria. They also worship God and ask to join in the effort to rebuild the temple. But the Jews who have returned from Babylon reject their offer, saying only the returnees from Babylon have been authorized by Cyrus to rebuild the temple. Many biblical scholars argue that this refusal has more to do with the fact of the intermarriage of Israelites in the former Northern Kingdom with foreigners than with Cyrus's authorization. The leaders of this rebuffed group then discourage the Jews from rebuilding the temple, and they send letters to the Persian king Artaxerxes, saying the Jews are plotting rebellion against Persia. Artaxerxes orders the work in Jerusalem to cease, and the cessation remains in effect until the second year of the reign of Darius (ch. 4). Thus the great hope and enthusiasm of the rebuilding is dashed.

Beginning Again

The prophets Haggai and Zechariah prophesy to the people of Jerusalem, and the work on the temple begins again. Judah at this time is under the governance of the province Aram-Syria, called "Beyond the River" in Ezra and Nehemiah. Tattenai, the Persian governor of Aram-Syria, comes to Jerusalem and asks Zerubbabel the governor of Judah for proof of authorization to rebuild the temple. The leaders of Judah reply that Cyrus ordered the rebuilding. Tattenai reports this in a letter to King Darius of Persia, and asks for a decision concerning the rebuilding. In searching the records, Cyrus's decree is found. Darius orders Tattenai to allow the work to continue and, furthermore, to cover all the costs from the resources of Aram-Syria. The rebuilding of the temple is completed in the sixth year of Darius's reign. Sacrifices and offerings accompany the rededication. The Jews and those who joined them celebrate the Passover and the Feast of Unleavened Bread with joy (chs. 5–6). Again, Ezra expresses great hope—the people have returned from exile and the temple stands once again. They are faithful in their worship of God. Everything points to an even more hope-filled future.

The Priest-Scribe Ezra

The remainder of Ezra (chs. 9–10) deals with the priest-scribe Ezra and the focus of his mission to Judah and Jerusalem—addressing the issue of intermarriages with "the peoples of the lands" (9:1). This is the same concern behind the refusal to allow others living in the land to join in rebuilding the temple. Ezra gathers an assembly of the people, he prays to God confessing the sin of the people in having mixed marriages, and they make a covenant with God to "put away all these wives and those who have been born to them" (10:3). Ezra prays, in part:

> But now, for a short time, the LORD our God has been kind to us. He has let some of us come back from captivity and has let us live in safety in his holy place. And so our God gives us hope and a little relief from our slavery. (9:8 NCV)

The phrase including "hope" says literally in the Hebrew "our God makes our eyes bright/light."

After hearing Ezra's prayer and confession, one of the leaders responds:

> Shechaniah the son of Jehiel, one of the sons of Elam, spoke up and said to Ezra, "We have trespassed against our God, and have taken pagan wives from the peoples of the land; yet now there is hope in Israel in spite of this." (10:2)

Shechaniah speaks of the hope that God will forgive the sin of intermarriage and continue to bless the returnees when they divorce their foreign wives and disavow their children. Purity in marriage is crucial to avoid the sin of worshiping other gods (Ex. 34:11–16; Deut. 7:1–4; 20:16–18). The book closes with a list of the Jewish leaders who divorce their foreign wives. The Jews are obedient; they have hope of continued blessing as they remain faithful to God and God's commandments.

The concern here is clearly religious—the holiness of the people before God—and not ethnic or racial. This is obvious from the numerous Old Testament examples of Jews who marry foreigners and are blessed by God and not condemned. Both Ruth and Esther are examples of mixed marriages. Mahlon is an Israelite, a Judean, who marries a Moabite woman, Ruth. Esther is an Israelite exile who marries a Persian king. Both women are heroines who bring great hope and blessing to the Israelites because of their faithfulness to God. The issue is not mixed marriages or ethnic origin but faith in God and faithfulness in following God's word.

Nehemiah

The book of Nehemiah opens in the twentieth year of King Artaxerxes, after the temple has been rebuilt in Jerusalem. Nehemiah is one of the Jewish leaders still in exile. He rises to a position of importance in Persia as a cupbearer to the king. He also has contact with people who have returned to Judah and Jerusalem. When Nehemiah asks about conditions in Jerusalem, they report that the situation is very bad. The city walls and gates of Jerusalem remain in ruins. Nehemiah is distressed over the report; he prays to God, confesses the sins of the people, and asks God for mercy (ch. 1). Nehemiah then asks the king for permission to go to Jerusalem and rebuild the walls and gates. The king sends him with letters to the governor of Aram-Syria, giving him safe passage and instructing the officials to provide the materials needed to rebuild the walls and gates. Later Nehemiah is called governor (8:9; 10:1; 12:26) and apparently is appointed as governor from the beginning. Nehemiah undertakes the journey accompanied by a contingent of soldiers. After making a secret, nighttime inspection of the walls and gates, he enlists the elders and leaders and begins the task of rebuilding and repairing (chs. 2–3). The very act of rebuilding and repairing is a source of great hope for both the returning Jews and those who had remained in the land. It is a sign of God's blessing, and has the support of the Persian king.

However, there is opposition to the rebuilding led by Sanballat, governor of Samaria, Tobiah the Ammonite, Geshem the Arab, and other non-Jews in the land. They scorn and ridicule the work; when that does not dissuade the workers, Sanballat and his cohorts begin to threaten the workers. Nehemiah and the Jews continue their rebuilding; half the work force builds while the other half guards the work and workers with weapons. The Jews work with one hand and keep a weapon ready in the other hand (chs. 3–5). Sanballat and Tobiah then plot to discredit Nehemiah. They hire a prophet to tell Nehemiah there is a plot to kill him, and that he should go into the temple for safety. But Nehemiah tells them he is not permitted to enter the temple. The Septuagint, the Greek translation of the Old Testament, states that this is because Nehemiah is a eunuch and to enter the temple would break God's law (Deut. 23:1). Nehemiah recognizes the evil intent of the plot and refuses to break the law. The work is completed in fifty-two days (6:15). Nehemiah then oversees a massive dedication of the rebuilt walls and gates:

> Now at the dedication of the wall of Jerusalem they sought out the Levites in all their places, to bring them to Jerusalem to celebrate the dedication with gladness, both with thanksgivings and singing, with cymbals and stringed instruments and harps. And the sons of the singers gathered together from the countryside around Jerusalem, from the villages of the Netophathites, from the house of Gilgal, and from the fields of Geba and Azmaveth; for the singers had built themselves villages all around Jerusalem. Then the priests and Levites purified themselves, and purified the people, the gates, and the wall. So I brought the leaders of Judah up on the wall, and appointed two large thanksgiving choirs. One went to the right hand on the wall toward the Refuse Gate. (12:27–31)

> Also that day they offered great sacrifices, and rejoiced, for God had made them rejoice with great joy; the women and the children also rejoiced, so that the joy of Jerusalem was heard afar off. (v. 43)

The accomplishment of the rebuilding of the walls and gates of Jerusalem are symbols of great hope to Nehemiah and the people. It indicates that God has, indeed, heard Nehemiah's prayers and has answered them. For the people, it is evidence that God is blessing and further restoring them.

Nehemiah also reports an assembly of all the people at the Water Gate in Jerusalem where Ezra reads the Law to them:

> Now all the people gathered together as one man in the open square that was in front of the Water Gate; and they told Ezra the scribe to bring the Book of the Law of Moses, which the LORD had commanded Israel. So Ezra the priest brought the Law before the assembly of men and women and all who could hear with understanding on the first day of the seventh month. Then he read from it in the open square that was in front of the Water Gate from morning until midday, before the men and women and those who could understand; and the ears of all the people were attentive to the Book of the Law. So Ezra the scribe stood on a platform of wood which they had made for the purpose; and beside him, at his right hand, stood Mattithiah, Shema, Anaiah, Urijah, Hilkiah, and Maaseiah; and at his left hand Pedaiah, Mishael, Malchijah, Hashum, Hashbadana, Zechariah, and Meshullam. And Ezra opened the book in the sight of all the people, for he was standing above all the people; and when he opened it, all the people stood up. And Ezra blessed the LORD, the great God. Then all the people answered, "Amen, Amen!" while lifting up their hands. And they bowed their heads and worshiped the LORD with their faces to the ground. Also Jeshua, Bani, Sherebiah, Jamin, Akkub, Shabbethai, Hodijah, Maaseiah, Kelita, Azariah, Jozabad, Hanan, Pelaiah, and the Levites, helped the people to understand the Law; and the people stood in their place. So they read distinctly from the book, in the Law of God; and they gave the sense, and helped them to understand the reading. (8:1–8)

It may well be that many of the people need help to understand the reading because they do not understand Hebrew. Aramaic has become the common language throughout the Babylonian and Persian empires. Many of the people, including returnees from exile and those who remained in the land, speak only Aramaic and do not understand the Scriptures being read in Hebrew. With individuals and Levites helping the people understand the reading, many, both returnees and those who had remained in the land, hear and understand the law for the first time.

Following the reading of the Law, the people celebrate the Feast of Booths for seven days and live in temporary shelters, a celebration not kept in that manner since the days of Joshua (ch. 8).

> Now on the twenty-fourth day of this month the children of Israel were assembled with fasting, in sackcloth, and with dust on their heads. Then those of Israelite lineage separated themselves from all foreigners; and they stood and confessed their sins and the iniquities of their fathers. (9:1–2)

Their confession is followed by a lengthy prayer recalling the mighty acts of God in creation, in choosing Abraham, in delivering the people from Egypt, making covenant with them at Sinai, and bringing them into their land. The prayer confesses the sins of the people and God's judgment that led to their exile. But God has been merciful and has brought them back into the land. The people enter into a covenant with God, reaffirming their commitment to obey God and God's law. This is another strong reason for hope. The people hear and understand the law for the first time; they confess their sins and covenant to be obedient to God. They have the hope of continued blessing and further restoration.

Nehemiah serves as governor for twelve years (5:14) and returns to Susa in Persia. At a later time, he returns to Jerusalem for another term as governor (13:6). Upon his return Nehemiah discovers the high priest Eliashib has allowed Tobiah the Ammonite to have a room in the temple courts, the people of Judah are doing work on Sabbath, and Jews and foreigners are selling goods on Sabbath. Nehemiah immediately institutes religious reforms, removes Tobiah from the temple, restores the priests' portions of offerings, and orders proper Sabbath observance. He also discovers one of Eliashib's grandsons has married Sanballat's daughter. Nehemiah removes him from serving as priest. He vigorously opposes marriages between Jews and foreigners. Nehemiah's purpose is to restore full observance of the Law, the Torah, to the restored community in Judah and Jerusalem (ch. 13). The reforms give cause for hope. God has blessed the people, and the reforms Nehemiah institutes offer every reason to anticipate even more blessing from God. A community completely committed to right relationship with God can take hope from the promises God has fulfilled in the past and continues to fulfill in the present.

Esther

The book of Esther describes the deliverance of Jews, exiled in Persia, from a plot of genocide. The Persian king Ahasuerus is usually identified as Xerxes I, who ruled over Persia from 486 BC to 465 BC. The book has several interesting features. It is one of the last books accepted into the Jewish Canon, delayed in part because the name of God never occurs in the book. Although God is not explicitly mentioned in the book, God's presence and protection clearly underlie the entire story.

The opening of the book of Esther offers a hopeful description of the condition of the Jews living in Persia. Although they were originally brought into the region as exiles from their defeated homeland, there is no evidence that they are persecuted or restricted in any manner. They own homes and property in Persia; they rise to positions of importance and power in the Persian bureaucracy. For example, Ezra, priest and scribe, is sent back to Jerusalem by the king of Persia to teach God's law to those in Jerusalem; Nehemiah is cupbearer to the Persian king; and Esther becomes queen. God definitely blesses God's people, even those who live in a foreign land. God's blessing and hope are not limited to the promised land.

Esther's Selection

The setting of the book is Susa, one of the capitals of the Persian Empire and the location of the winter palace of the Persian kings. Ahasuerus (Xerxes I) is described as ruling an empire of 127 *satraps*, or provinces, from Egypt to India. In the third year of his reign, Ahasuerus hosts a huge banquet, with leaders from across the empire in attendance, that lasts 180 days (1:1–4). After that he hosts a seven-day banquet in his winter palace for all those in Susa. Vashti, the queen, holds a banquet for the women at the same time. On the seventh day of his banquet, Ahasuerus orders Queen Vashti to come wearing her crown to show off her beauty to all the guests; Vashti refuses. For refusing to obey the king and, thus, insulting all the Persian leaders, Vashti is banished as chief wife and queen. When Ahasuerus's anger abates, a search is undertaken to find a new queen.

Now Esther, the daughter of Abihail, enters the picture. Esther is an orphan. She has been raised by her cousin Mordecai and adopted by him as his daughter. They are Jews and faithful worshipers of God. They are descendants of the Jews brought to Babylon and Persia at the time Jerusalem was conquered in 597 BC and 587 BC. Esther is young and very beautiful. She is among the young women selected to be considered as the new queen. She follows the instructions of her uncle Mordecai and does not reveal that she is a Jew. Esther finds favor with Hegai, the eunuch in charge of the search. Hegai provides her with the choicest ointments and foods and seven chosen maids from the king's palace. Hegai also gives her the best place in the harem (2:5–10). After a year of preparation, the young women are brought to the king one by one. Esther finds favor with the king; he loves her more than any of the other young women, and he selects her to be his new queen. The king then hosts a great feast in honor of Esther (vv. 11–18).

During the entire process of preparation and selection, Mordecai comes daily to the palace gate to see how Esther is doing. Just after Esther is selected as queen, Mordecai discovers a plot—two of the king's attendants are planning his assassination. Mordecai reports this plot to Esther who reports it to the king in Mordecai's name. The plot is investigated and found to be true, and the two attendants are executed (vv. 19–23).

Esther's Opportunity

The hopeful condition of the Jewish people is soon threatened. Sometime after the foiled assassination plot, the king promotes a man named Haman to a very important position, above all of the other nobles around him. As a result of this promotion, all the king's servants must pay homage to Haman and bow down before him. Even those in the king's gate do so. However Mordecai, who also is among those who sit in the gate of the palace, refuses to bow down and pay homage to Haman. So Haman becomes incensed with Mordecai and seeks to destroy him. Haman learns that Mordecai is of Jewish background and develops a plot to destroy all the Jews in the land. He goes to the king and tells him about this foreign people who live in the empire and do not obey the laws of the king or the laws of the empire. He offers a huge bribe to the king, ten thousand talents of silver, to allow Haman to destroy these people throughout the empire. The king agrees and gives Haman the royal signet ring to sign and seal an edict. Haman prepares the edict, seals it with the king's signet ring, publishes it in all the languages of the kingdom, and sends it all over the kingdom. The edict states that on a particular day all the Jews will be killed. When Mordecai and the Jews in Susa learn of this edict, they all weep, fast, and put on sackcloth. The situation seems hopeless. The edict of the king cannot be changed (ch. 3). Haman does not name the people to be destroyed in the king's presence, but does name the Jews in the edict.

Esther's attendants learn that Mordecai is sitting in sackcloth and fasting, and they tell Esther. She sends one of her attendants to ask Mordecai the reason for his mourning. Mordecai sends back word to Esther of the plot by Haman to destroy all of the Jewish population throughout Persia. Esther reports back to Mordecai that it has been a month since she has been called to appear before the king; to enter the king's presence without being called brings a death sentence, unless the king extends his scepter. Mordecai warns Esther that she will not escape Haman's edict, though no one currently knows she is Jewish. If she does not go to the king about the edict, there will come some other way to rescue the Jewish people, but she and her family will certainly perish. Mordecai challenges Esther: "Who knows whether you have come to the kingdom for such a time as this?"

(4:14). Esther asks Mordecai to instruct all the Jews in Susa to fast for three days and three nights and says she will do the same. After fasting and praying, she will go to the king, and if she perishes she perishes (v. 16). God is never mentioned explicitly, but the hope of all the people is certainly placed in God. They will all fast and pray, making supplication to God, and leaving the outcome in God's hands.

Esther's Request

After three days of fasting and prayer, Esther dresses in her royal attire and enters the king's presence. The king immediately holds out his scepter to her and asks for her request. She asks that he and Haman attend a banquet she has prepared that day. At the banquet the king again asks her petition, offering up to half his kingdom. Esther's request is that the king and Haman come to another banquet the next day; at that time she will make known her request. As Haman heads home, he sees Mordecai in the gate, and Mordecai refuses to bow down to him; Haman is furious. He tells his family and friends about his success and how Mordecai refuses to pay him homage. His wife and friends suggest he build a gallows and suggest to the king that Mordecai be hanged on it. Haman does so (ch. 5).

That night the king cannot sleep, so he has one of his attendants read to him from the chronicles of the king. The attendant happens to read about Mordecai reporting the plot against the king. The king asks what honor was bestowed on Mordecai and discovers there was none. The next morning Haman goes to the king to ask permission to hang Mordecai. When he arrives, the king asks him what should be done to honor one the king wishes to honor. Haman assumes the honor is for him and tells the king the one to be honored should be dressed in royal robes, placed on a royal horse, and ridden through the city with a herald proclaiming this is what is done for the one the king honors. The king then orders Haman to do so for Mordecai the Jew, and to be the herald proclaiming it. The king clearly knows Mordecai is a Jew, but does not know the Jews are the people Haman wishes to destroy. Haman does as ordered, then returns home mourning and reports the events to his family and friends. They tell him he will not prevail over Mordecai. The king's attendants then arrive and take Haman to the banquet (ch. 6).

When the king and Haman arrive at the banquet, the king again asks Esther for her request. Esther responds with the request for her life and the life of her people. She explains: "we have been sold, my people and I, to be destroyed, to be killed, and to be annihilated (7:4). Just as Haman had not named the people he planned to destroy, so also Esther does not indicate who her people are. The king is enraged and asks who dares do such a thing. Esther answers that the wicked Haman had done so. The king is exceedingly angry and storms out to the garden. Haman stays in the room, pleading with Esther for his life. The king comes back into the room and sees Haman has fallen on the couch where Esther is; the king accuses Haman of assaulting Esther. Haman is then taken out and hanged on the gallows he built for Mordecai (vv. 5–10).

God's Deliverance

The book of Esther clearly demonstrates the providential hand of God in directing human affairs even without direct mention of God. The book also clearly demonstrates the principle of divine retribution—that God blesses the righteous and judges the wicked. Haman is judged for his wicked plan. Although the edicts are still in force, God is in control, and this gives the people hope.

When the king's anger subsides, he gives Haman's house to Esther, and gives Mordecai the signet ring he had taken back from Haman. Esther begs the king to revoke the edicts Haman had written. The king tells Esther and Mordecai to write a new edict in the name of the king and seal it with the royal signet ring because no one can revoke a decree made in the name of the king. The new decree states that all Jews are to gather and defend themselves, to destroy, kill, and annihilate anyone who tries to harm them or their property. It is published in all the languages of the kingdom and sent all over the kingdom. The Jews all across the land celebrate, and many people convert to Judaism because of what happened (ch. 8).

The one explicit reference to hope in the book is found in Esther 9:1:

> Now in the twelfth month, that is, the month of Adar, on the thirteenth day, the time came for the king's command and his decree to be executed. On the day that the enemies of the Jews had hoped [*siber*, waited, hoped for] to overpower them, the opposite occurred, in that the Jews themselves overpowered those who hated them.

Here the hope of those who hate the Jews is dashed; but the hope of the Jews is fulfilled—they are delivered. God honors and responds to their prayers and fasting and blesses Esther's courageous actions.

The situation of the Jews after Haman's edict was sent out seemed hopeless. But God had not forgotten or abandoned the people. Even in a foreign land, even under the domination of a pagan world empire, God is still in control. The Jews hope in God and continue to serve God faithfully; they prevail and prosper.

Job

The book of Job is classified as one of the Wisdom books in the Old Testament. Apart from the book itself, Job is mentioned only in Ezekiel 14:14, 20 along with Noah and Daniel as notable righteous individuals. The book has few indicators of time or place. Job is characterized as a righteous person who faithfully worships God, but he does not appear to be an Israelite. He lives in the land of Uz, a place whose location is also quite ambiguous. In Genesis 10:23 in the table of nations, the descendants of Noah, Uz is a son of Aram who is a son of Shem. Lamentations 4:21 offers a possible connection of Uz with Edom ("daughter of Edom, you who dwell in the land of Uz"). The book of Job itself calls Job "the greatest of all the people of the East" (1:3), implying Uz is east of where the author is from, presumably Israel. The other ambiguous aspect of Job is its time period. There are few indicators of when Job lived. While many conservative scholars argue for the patriarchal period as the setting for Job, most critical scholars date the composition of the book to the sixth to fourth centuries BC.

The book of Job has a prose prologue (chs. 1–2) and epilogue (42:7–17). The remainder of the book (3:1–42:6) is a series of speech cycles by Job, his three friends, a fifth person, Elihu, who appears suddenly in Job 32, and God. The prologue sets the stage for the speech cycles and establishes the context of Job's situation—information neither Job nor his friends know. There are more words for hope in Job than any other Old Testament book except Psalms. All the occurrences are in the speeches by Job, his three friends, and God.

A look at the structure of Job aids understanding the explicit messages of hope in the book. Described simply, the prose introduction (chs. 1–2) is followed by an opening speech by Job (ch. 3), then each of the three friends speaks to Job (Eliphaz, ch. 4–5; Bildad, ch. 8; Zophar, ch. 11). At the end of each friend's speech, Job responds (chs. 6–7, 9–10, 12–14). This cycle is repeated twice more (chs. 15–21; 22–27). Job has a closing speech to the friends (chs. 28–31). At this point Elihu appears and speaks (chs. 32–37). God then engages Job in dialogue (38:1–42:6). The book closes with an epilogue describing Job's restoration and blessings. In Job's opening speech and the first cycle of speeches, Job and each of his friends use words of hope. But in the second and third cycles of speeches and closing speech, only Job uses words of hope. Job speaks sixteen of the occurrences of words of hope in the book.

The book opens with a description of Job: "that man was blameless and upright, and one who feared God and shunned evil" (1:1). Job is not only completely righteous but also blessed with a large family—seven sons and three daughters (v. 2). Job is very wealthy, with large flocks and herds and many servants tending them. He is described as: "the greatest of all the people of the East" (v. 3). Job's children are grown and have their own homes where they regularly gather and feast (v. 4). Job is so scrupulously righteous that he offers sacrifices to God on behalf of his children after they have feasts, just in case they might have sinned against God (v. 5).

The scene changes to God's throne room in heaven. Present are God, the sons of God, and Satan. Two sets of dialogue ensue between God and Satan. God opens the dialogue by asking Satan: "Have you considered My servant Job, that there is none like him on the earth, a blameless and upright man, one who fears God and shuns evil?" (v. 8).

God describes Job using exactly the same words the writer of the book used in verse 1. Satan responds by saying Job is righteous and worships God only because God has blessed Job and protects him. If God were to stop blessing and protecting Job, Job would cease worshiping and would curse him (vv. 9–11). God allows Satan to bring disasters on Job: all of Job's herds and flocks are destroyed or stolen, many of his servants are killed, and all of his children are killed (vv. 12–19). Job's response is not as Satan expects, however. Job grieves, but he does not blame God (vv. 20–22): "Naked I came from my mother's womb, / And naked shall I return there. / The LORD gave, and the LORD has taken away; / Blessed be the name of the LORD" (v. 21).

In a second scene in heaven, God again asks Satan if he has seen Job's response to disaster:

> Have you considered My servant Job, that there is none like him on the earth, a blameless and upright man, one who fears God and shuns evil? And still he holds fast to his integrity, although you incited Me against him, to destroy him without cause. (2:3)

Satan's second response is that God still protects Job, that he has not allowed Satan to touch Job's person. So God allows Satan to afflict Job but not take his life. Satan afflicts Job with painful boils (vv. 4–7). Job's response is again mourning and sitting on an ash heap, but he maintains his integrity and does no wrong (vv. 8–10).

Job's three friends hear of all that has befallen Job, so they come to mourn with him and to comfort him. When they see his great grief, they sit with him seven days and seven nights without speaking (vv. 11–13), comforting with their silent presence.

The speeches open with Job cursing the day of his birth, asking why he could not have died at birth so that he might have rest. Speaking of that day Job says: "May the stars of its morning be dark; / May it look for [*qavah*, hope for, wait for] light, but have none, / And not see the dawning of the day" (3:9). Job bemoans his current situation; he says death would be better, for in death he would have rest. In death the wicked cease troubling, the weary find rest, prisoners find rest, slaves are free—he prefers death (ch. 3).

Throughout the speeches between Job and his friends, Job maintains his innocence and righteousness and cannot understand why disaster has befallen him. The three friends begin by consoling Job. But their theological position is clearly defined by their understanding of divine retribution—God blesses righteousness and judges sinfulness. Their position is very rigid and also posits that all blessings (good things) mean God's approval of one's righteousness and all bad things (disaster, evil) indicate God's judgment of one's sinfulness. The friends' theological position appears to offer no exceptions: Job must be an unrepentant sinner for all these disasters to have befallen him. We know from the prologue that Job is righteous and innocent. The friends' presumption is wrong and, therefore, their theological position is flawed.

Bildad's First Speech

Nevertheless, the friends and Job both make some accurate observations concerning hope. In Bildad's first speech, he affirms Job: "Is not your reverence your confidence [*kesel*]? / And the integrity of your ways your hope [*tiqvah*]?" (4:6). Then, Bildad shifts and makes his point—Job must not be in a right relationship with God and has committed some sin to bring all these disasters on himself: "But as for me, I would seek God, / And to God I would commit my cause" (5:8).

> But He saves the needy from the sword,
> From the mouth of the mighty,
> And from their hand.
> So the poor have hope [*tiqvah*],
> And injustice shuts her mouth.
>
> Behold, happy is the man whom God corrects;
> Therefore do not despise the chastening of the Almighty.
> (vv. 15–17)

Bildad suggests that Job should seek God and commit his cause to God—implying that Job has not done so.

Job responds to Bildad, making it clear that he has, indeed, committed his cause to God. His grief is great, and God has loosed terrors on Job (6:1–8). "Oh, that I might have my request, / That God would grant me the thing that I long for [*tiqvah*]!" (v. 8). Job's request, his hope, is that God will crush him and cut him off (v. 9). He sees no advantage in prolonging his life because that merely prolongs his pain and misery. "What strength do I have, that I should hope [*yachel*]? / And what is my end, that I should prolong my life?" (v. 11). But Job has not necessarily given up all hope. Taking both halves of verse 13 as questions, Job states a strong hope: "Is not my help [`*ezer*] with me? / And is abiding success banished from me?" (v. 13, author's translation).

Job is affirming his help as being with him—and in so many other Old Testament texts, God is one's help, one's only certain help. Job contrasts God as help with human help. He describes human help as being like wadis that flow with water in the rainy season but dry up in summer. When people come searching for water, they are disappointed:

> The caravans of Tema look,
> The travelers of Sheba hope for [*qavah*] them.
> They are disappointed because they were confident
> [*batach*, trust, hope];
> They come there and are confused. (6:19–20)

Job declares his innocence and asks Bildad to show him where he has erred (v. 24). He describes the human condition as one of hard service:

> Is there not a time of hard service for man on earth?
> Are not his days also like the days of a hired man?
> Like a servant who earnestly desires the shade,
> And like a hired man who eagerly looks for [*qavah*] his wages,
> So I have been allotted months of futility,
> And wearisome nights have been appointed to me.
> When I lie down, I say, "When shall I arise,
> And the night be ended"?
> For I have had my fill of tossing till dawn.
> My flesh is caked with worms and dust,
> My skin is cracked and breaks out afresh.
>
> My days are swifter than a weaver's shuttle,
> And are spent without hope [*tiqvah*]. (7:1–6)

Even hired laborers can hope for wages, but Job laments that he has faced months of futility and sleepless nights. His sores fester, refusing to heal. The days pass quickly but are spent without hope of healing. Job sees his condition as hopeless, though he cannot understand why. He turns his questions to God:

> Have I sinned?
> What have I done to You, O watcher of men?
> Why have You set me as Your target,
> So that I am a burden to myself?
> Why then do You not pardon my transgression,
> And take away my iniquity?
> For now I will lie down in the dust,
> And You will seek me diligently,
> But I will no longer be. (vv. 20–21)

Job questions God, but he does not lose faith in him. He continues to address God and honestly ask the nature of his sin.

Bildad argues for the justice of God. He tells Job that *if* Job will sincerely seek God and *if* he is righteous, *then* God will bless him (8:5–6). The implication is that Job is not seeking God and is not righteous. Bildad then uses an example of a papyrus plant. It has to have marshy conditions to survive, but even with water, it is the first plant to wither (vv. 11–12). Bildad's point is:

> So are the paths of all who forget God;
> And the hope [*tiqvah*] of the hypocrite shall perish,
> Whose confidence [*kesel*] shall be cut off,
> And whose trust [*batach*] is a spider's web. (vv. 13–14)

There is no hope for those who forget God. Bildad closes his speech with the affirmation, "Behold, God will not cast away the blameless, / Nor will He uphold the evildoers" (v. 20).

In his response, Job appears to agree with Bildad: "Truly I know it is so, / But how can a man be righteous before God?" (9:2). However, the book's introduction (1:1) and God's speech (1:8) establish that Job is blameless and upright, fearing God and shunning evil. In responding, Job acknowledges that God made him and gave him life (10:8–12), and if he sins God will not acquit him (vv. 14–15).

Zophar's First Speech

Zophar opens his speech with a direct accusation against Job:

> But oh, that God would speak,
> And open His lips against you,
> That He would show you the secrets of wisdom!
> For they would double your prudence.
> Know therefore that God exacts from you
> Less than your iniquity deserves. (11:5–6)

Zophar's position is clear: Job is guilty of sin, and that sin is the cause of all the disasters that have befallen him. If Job will just acknowledge any iniquity, then God will restore him:

> And you would be secure, because there is hope [*tiqvah*];
> Yes, you would dig around you, and take your rest in safety.
> You would also lie down, and no one would make you afraid;
> Yes, many would court your favor.
> But the eyes of the wicked will fail,
> And they shall not escape,
> And their hope [*tiqvah*]—loss of life!" (vv. 18–20)

Zophar understands that those in right relationship with God have hope, but the only hope the wicked have is death. Zophar's faulty logic is that all disaster is a judgment for sin. Job has suffered many disasters, therefore, he must have sinned much.

Job's response to Zophar is harsh, rejecting his friend's accusations. Job affirms his righteousness and his own assessment of his situation. He affirms that God holds every life in his hands and that he blesses the righteous and judges the wicked (ch. 12). Job then asks to speak directly with God, who will not speak in platitudes like his friends have (13:1–13). Job expresses his faith, his hope, in God. Job is willing to present his case directly to him:

> Though He slay me, yet will I trust [*yachel*, wait for, hope in] Him.
> Even so, I will defend my own ways before Him.
> He also shall be my salvation [*yeshu`ah*],
> For a hypocrite could not come before Him. (vv. 15–16)

Job is confident God will deliver him. His faith and his hope remain strong despite his friends' charges. He continues his response by addressing God. He speaks of hope using an example from nature: "For there is hope [*qaveh*] for a tree, / If it is cut down, that it will sprout again, / And that its tender shoots will not cease" (14:7). However, Job's hope does not necessarily include a resurrection hope. In the same speech he adds: "If a man dies, shall he live again? / All the days of my hard service I will wait [*yachel*], / Till my change comes" (v. 14).

The change Job hopes for is most likely a change in his circumstance, healing or recovery from his disease. But as Job continues to address God, he grows more despondent. He says to God: "As water wears away stones, / And as torrents wash away the soil of the earth; / So You destroy the hope [*tiqvah*] of man" (v. 19). Notice two things. Job is still addressing God; he has not lost his faith. Nor does he say God is destroying him. He says that because God does not answer him, he is destroying his hope. Job wants answers. He wants God to tell him why all these disasters have befallen him.

Second Speech Cycle

In the second cycle of speeches, Job speaks more of death and the grave:

> If I wait for [*qavah*, hope for] the grave as my house,
> If I make my bed in the darkness,
> If I say to corruption, "You are my father,"
> And to the worm, "You are my mother and my sister,"
> Where then is my hope [*tiqvah*]?
> As for my hope [*tiqvah*], who can see it? (17:13–15)

But Job is not hopeless. He says, "*If* I wait for the grave as my house, *If* I make my bed in darkness . . . . Where then is my hope?" But Job does not say the grave *is* his hope. Later in the same cycle of speeches, Job appears to speak more harshly in his statements about God: "He breaks me down on every side, / And I am gone; / My hope [*tiqvah*] He has uprooted [*nasa`*, removed] like a tree" (19:10). Nevertheless, Job has stated previously that there is hope in a tree; even if it is cut down it will sprout again (14:7). So while Job says God has removed his hope, it too can sprout again!

Third Speech Cycle

In the third cycle of speeches, Job speaks of hope only once. He speaks of God as creator and of God's control over all creation. Job still maintains his innocence and righteousness (chs. 26–27) and says the hypocrite has no hope: "For what is the hope [*tiqvah*] of the hypocrite, / Though he may gain much, / If God takes away his life?" (27:8). Although Job says God has made his life bitter, he acknowledges God gives him breath. Job will not give up his integrity (vv. 2–6).

Job cries out to God in his closing speech: "I have become like dust and ashes. I cry out to You, but You do not answer me" (30:19–20). God does not answer him. Job describes his condition as being like dust and ashes—like death itself, and he continues: "But when I hoped for [*qavah*] good, only evil came to me; / when I looked [*yachel*, waited for] for light, darkness came (v. 26 NCV).

Finally God appears to Job and his friends. Unlike the expectation of the friends, God does not condemn Job. Instead God challenges Job to dialogue. He asks if Job has to put God in the wrong in order to justify himself. The question is: Can God be just and Job be righteous? Does it have to be either-or? Can it be both-and? God never answers Job's questions about why all the disasters have befallen him. He does cause Job to realize he cannot comprehend the greatness of God (chs. 38–41). Job acknowledges:

> I know that You can do everything, ...
> Therefore I have uttered what I did not understand,
> Things too wonderful for me, which I did not know. . . .
>
> I have heard of You by the hearing of the ear,
> But now my eye sees You. (42:2–5)

Job gains a new understanding of God and of himself. He understands that he can affirm both the goodness and justice of God and his own righteousness—as God does.

Job's last words demonstrate his new understanding: "Therefore, I reject, despise, and I am sorry, I repent, concerning dust and ashes" (v. 6, author's translation). Unlike traditional translations, in this modern translation, Job does not grovel in repentance before God. Remember, he is and remains blameless and righteous. What Job repents of is dust and ashes. In Job 30:19, Job says he is like dust and ashes—like one dead. He feels God-forsaken. Now God has responded to Job and challenged him to see things from God's perspective. Job has done so, and that satisfies him—Job no longer wants to die. He is ready to live. Job more fully understands his creaturehood, his humanity, and God's divinity. Furthermore, Job has his hope fully restored. Whether he remains covered by festering sores or is fully healed, he has hope. He has hope because God has answered and affirmed him.

In the epilogue God chastens Job's friends because they were wrong about Job and about God; Job prays for them and God accepts Job's prayer. God restores Job; he restores double what Job previously had in possessions and gives him seven more sons and three more daughters, and Job lives to the age of 140 years, to see his great-grandchildren.

The book of Job teaches us that we have hope in God. As the traditional marriage vows say, "for better or worse, in sickness and in health," we recognize that not even death can separate us from the love of God (Rom. 8:38–39). That is Job's newfound hope and ours! Job's hope is not his healing and double restoration. His hope is God's response, face-to-face dialogue, and presence. Job has hope and assurance that God is with him. As Christians we have that hope with a much deeper hope of God-with-us in the Christ event.

Psalms

Psalms is unlike most books of the Old Testament in that it is not a single book. Instead Psalms is a diverse collection of hymns, prayers, laments, and related genre that were used in temple worship (those used in the period of the monarchy) and in private devotional worship. We tend to think of the psalms as pieces of private devotion, yet clearly many were used in corporate worship in the temple in Jerusalem during the monarchy as well as in the rebuilt temple after the exile. The individual psalms are not necessarily related to one another—though some are grouped by content or theme or by other devices (for example, Psalms 9–10 together comprise one alphabetic acrostic—a psalm in which each verse or line has as its first letter succeeding letters of the Hebrew alphabet, *aleph*, *beth*, *gimel*, etc.).

For over a century, scholars have used a form-critical approach to discuss the psalms—dividing them into a limited number of primary genres or forms, typically: hymns of praise, community laments, individual laments, thanksgiving psalms, and royal psalms. They also identify a number of lesser genres (fewer examples) including: wisdom psalms, enthronement psalms, and liturgies. Such an approach is definitely helpful to understand the book of Psalms, and the psalms' genre will be mentioned in this study. However, this study will focus on a limited number of psalms and on a number of key themes that recur in the book of Psalms—often across the genres. My first premise is that the book of Psalms has two primary foci: God and the worshiper (the individual or the community who is calling on God). The focus on God is the proper focus for worship. Worship, right worship, must always have God as its central focus. We see this focus clearly in the hymns of praise. God is praised especially based on his character and attributes—righteousness, justice, mercy, steadfast love, faithfulness—and on what he has done, is doing, or will do (the mighty acts of God in creation, in history, and in continuing acts). It is these aspects of God's character and actions that most closely tie the psalms to our theme of hope. Worshipers are a second focus of the psalms; they know God is concerned about them and cares for them. So the needs and cares of the worshipers, the petitions expressed by the worshipers, are also expressed in the assurance that God hears and knows their needs. The worshipers cannot resolve these needs by themselves. Their only hope is that God who hears and knows will respond to their needs. The good news of the psalms is that God does hear and does help; that is the basis of the worshipers' hope and the assurance of their hope.

Praise Psalms

Psalm 33

Psalm 33 offers a great example of a hymn of praise to God. It shows many typical elements of such hymns as well as our theme, hope. The psalm begins with exhortations to praise God. The worshipers are called upon to rejoice, praise, make melody, sing, play skillfully (vv. 1–3). They are to use their voices and musical instruments in their praise. The setting is clearly a community worship occasion. The exhortations are all plural, indicating that the psalm is not intended for individual or private devotion but for a community or congregational worship with multiple worshipers and musicians. The worshipers are described as righteous and upright, indicating that they properly prepare themselves for worship—they confess their sins and seek forgiveness; they have a right relationship with God. (See Psalms 15 and 24 as two examples of entrance liturgies that express the confessions worshipers make to affirm they are properly prepared for worship and have a right relationship with God.) Psalm 33 continues by describing why people should praise God (vv. 4–5):

> For the word of the Lord is right,
> And all His work is done in truth.
> He loves righteousness and justice;

The earth is full of the goodness of the LORD.

The words used to describe God's attributes and works are (Hebrew—English): *yashar*—right, upright, *'munah*—truth, faithfulness, *tsedeqah*—righteousness, *mishpat*—justice), *chesed*—goodness, steadfast love. These same attributes are repeated frequently in the Bible as characteristics of God and characteristics he expects of his people.

The psalmist considers God's works in creation and in nature (vv. 6–9) before comparing his work with humankind, contrasting his counsel and plans with human counsel and plans (vv. 10–11). God's counsel and plans stand forever; human plans and counsel fail and come to nothing. The psalm closes with God considering all human works (vv. 13–15) and reminds the worshipers and us that no humans can save themselves, not kings or mighty warriors or horses:

No king is saved by the multitude of an army;
A mighty man is not delivered by great strength.
A horse is a vain hope for safety;
Neither shall it deliver any by its great strength.
Behold, the eye of the LORD is on those who fear Him,
On those who hope in His mercy,
To deliver their soul from death,
And to keep them alive in famine.

Our soul waits for the LORD;
He is our help and our shield.
For our heart shall rejoice in Him,
Because we have trusted in His holy name.
Let Your mercy, O LORD, be upon us,
Just as we hope in You. (vv. 16–22)

Those who place their ultimate hope in kings, armies, or horses find their situation hopeless (vain hope, *sheqer*, literally, deception, falsehood, lie). All hope placed in humans and human institutions and human power will ultimately fail. The only genuine hope for humans is God—those who hope (*yachal*—to wait expectantly, to hope) in God's mercy (*chesed*—steadfast love, lovingkindness, mercy) find deliverance and life (vv. 18–19). In these verses hope is paired with help (Hebrew *'ezer*). The psalmist recognizes that we find genuine help only from God, and that help becomes the source of our hope. The old Isaac Watts hymn says it well and correctly: "O God our help in ages past, our hope for years to come." The psalmist could well have spoken those words. God has proved again and again to be the psalmist's help. That help is the basis of his assurance that God is his hope in the present and will be in the future. Likewise, hope is paired with waiting (here *chakah*—to wait, to await) for God and trusting (Hebrew *batach*) in him, in his holy name. The Hebrew concept of waiting is not our idea of watching a clock or watching for a pot to boil. Instead it is waiting expectantly or with anticipation. That expectation and trust undergird the psalmist's hope and ours.

Lament Psalms

Within the lament psalms we find a similar pairing of hope and help. As in the praise psalms, so also in lament, the psalmist recognizes that God and God alone is the source of genuine help and hope. Help and hope are paired frequently in the book of Psalms.

Psalms 42–43

In Psalm 42, an individual lament, the psalmist remembers pilgrimages to Jerusalem at previous festival times (v. 4). But now he is suffering such distress that even his friends ask, "Where is your God?" (v. 3). The psalmist is genuinely seeking God (vv. 1–4). The repeated refrain in Psalms 42–43 (42:5, 11; 43:5) expresses the psalmist's faith that God is his hope and his help:

> Why are you cast down, O my soul?
> And why are you disquieted within me?
> Hope in God, for I shall yet praise Him
> For the help of His countenance. . . .
>
> Why are you cast down, O my soul?

> And why are you disquieted within me?
> Hope in God; For I shall yet praise Him,
> The help of my countenance and my God. (42:5, 11)

Quite interestingly, the Hebrew word translated "help" in each of these refrains is the Hebrew noun *yeshua`*, which more often is translated as "salvation, deliverance." The verb form *yasha`* is translated "to save" or "to deliver." This is the Hebrew basis for the name Jesus. The point is that God is the psalmist's help, deliverance, and salvation. As such, God is our hope also. There is a variation in the refrain between verses 5 and 11. In verse 5, the psalmist praises God for the help of God's "countenance," literally God's face (*panim*). This refrain emphasizes God as the source of help, as in frequent phrases that speak of God causing his face to shine on one (Num. 6:24–26). The image understands God as looking directly at one—as we might say face-to-face—and as a result helping, saving, delivering. In verse 11, and also in Psalm 43:5, the psalmist praises God for help ("the help of my countenance") and for being his God. In the same face-to-face depiction, the psalmist's face represents the psalmist's entire being, just as God's face represents God's entire being.

Psalm 16

In another lament, the writer of Psalm 16 calls out to God to "preserve" (*shamar*—watch, guard, keep) him for he has trusted (*chasah*, literally, to seek refuge) in God (v. 1). He clearly expresses the joy that true hope—hope in God—brings: "Therefore my heart is glad, and my glory rejoices; / My flesh also will rest in hope" (v. 9). The word translated as "hope" in this verse (Hebrew *batach*) is the same word translated as "trust" in Psalm 33:21. So again we find trust and hope connected. Trust in God leads to the hope one has.

Psalm 22

The psalmists appear at times to reach the depths of despair in their cries to God. Psalm 22, an individual lament, records such a cry. The words describe one who feels forsaken, abandoned by God: "My God, My God, why have You forsaken Me? / Why are You so far from helping Me, / And from the words of My groaning?" (v. 1). The help (*yeshua`*) that seems so far removed from the psalmist is the same word as in Psalm 42. It is the salvation or deliverance that God alone can bring. Despite the seeming despair of the words, the psalmist does not lose faith or hope. He continues with assurance based on the experience of his ancestors:

> Our fathers trusted [*batach*] in You;
> They trusted [*batach*], and You delivered them.
> They cried to You, and were delivered;
> They trusted [*batach*] in You, and were not ashamed. (vv. 4–5)

The trust or faith of past generations reflected their relationship with God. Because of that relationship, God delivered his people. In addition the psalmist expresses his lifelong trust as he renews his call to God: "From My mother's womb You have been My God. / Be not far from Me, / For trouble is near; / For there is none to help [*`ezer*]" (vv. 10b–11). The call to God is still desperate, but it is not despair. His statement that there is no one to help takes meaning from the context. The psalmist has no help apart from God. He calls on God and asks God to be near him. God, and only God, is his help. A few verses later the psalmist repeats his faith in God alone as his help:

> But You, O Lord, do not be far from Me;
> O My Strength, hasten to help [*`ezer*] Me!
> Deliver Me from the sword,
> My precious life from the power of the dog.
> Save [*yasha`*] Me from the lion's mouth
> And from the horns of the wild oxen!
> You have answered Me. (vv. 19–21)

God as his only help is the one who can deliver him and save him from all adversity. In the last phrase the psalmist affirms that God indeed hears and answers his prayer. And the psalmist then affirms that he will relate to the congregation what God has done:

> I will declare Your name to My brethren;
> In the midst of the assembly I will praise You. . . .

> For He has not despised nor abhorred
> the affliction of the afflicted;
> Nor has He hidden His face from Him;
> But when He cried to Him, He heard. (vv. 22, 24)

This experience of answered prayer gives a new message of faith and hope to the psalmist. From the depths of his despair he cries out to God. He never loses his hope. And his faith and hope are proved valid by God's deliverance. The details are not specified. We are not told if the despair is caused by physical illness and injury or by oppression from others. Nor are we told how God answers. But the psalmist experiences the reality of deliverance. It should be noted that Christ quotes the opening words of this psalm on the cross.

Psalm 139

Psalm 139 is classified as an individual lament. Yet the psalm expresses great hope without even mentioning the word. Hope is clear from the affirmations the psalmist makes:

> Where can I go from Your Spirit?
> Or where can I flee from Your presence?
> If I ascend into heaven, You are there;
> If I make my bed in hell, behold, You are there.
> If I take the wings of the morning,
> And dwell in the uttermost parts of the sea,
> Even there Your hand shall lead me,
> And Your right hand shall hold me.
> If I say, "Surely the darkness shall fall on me,"
> Even the night shall be light about me;
> Indeed, the darkness shall not hide from You,
> But the night shines as the day;
> The darkness and the light are both alike to You. (vv. 7–12)

There is no place the psalmist can go that separates him from God and God's presence (*panim*, literally, God's face). The verses express God's omnipresence. God is always present with the psalmist, which fills the psalmist with hope and praise even within lamentation. This is the hope often expressed in Scripture as the promise of God's presence, God-with-us, *Immanu-el*, of Isaiah 7, and "Lo, I am with you always" of Matthew 28:18–20.

Psalm 31

Psalm 31 is another example of an individual lament. As in so many of the other lament psalms, great trust and hope in God is expressed by the psalmist. The opening verses give voice to that hope:

> In You, O Lord, I put my trust [*chasah*];
> Let me never be ashamed;
> Deliver me in Your righteousness.
> Bow down Your ear to me,
> Deliver me speedily;
> Be my rock of refuge,
> A fortress of defense to save [*yasha`*] me.
>
> For You are my rock and my fortress;
> Therefore, for Your name's sake,
> Lead me and guide me. (vv. 1–3)

The psalmist puts his trust in God. The Hebrew verb *chasah*, "to trust," is often translated as "taking refuge" and the related noun as a place of refuge or safety. So the hope of the psalmist is in God, who offers refuge and safety. He is also the one who delivers and saves the psalmist. The Hebrew word for "save me" is the verb *yasha`* mentioned previously in Psalm 42. This is another example of a cluster of words used by psalmists to express hope in God and to voice petitions for help to God. The climax of the psalm is a word to the worshiping community: "Be of good courage, / And He shall strengthen your heart, / All you who hope in the Lord" (v. 24). This word for hope is the Hebrew *yachal*, hopeful waiting or waiting expectantly. The psalmist expresses assurance that hope placed in God will be fulfilled.

Psalm 71

Psalm 71 has many parallels to Psalm 31. It begins with almost identical words:

> In You, O Lord, I put my trust [*chasah*];
> Let me never be put to shame.
> Deliver me in Your righteousness, and cause me to escape;
> Incline Your ear to me, and save [*yasha`*] me.
> Be my strong refuge,
> To which I may resort continually;
> You have given the commandment to save me,
> For You are my rock and my fortress. (vv. 1–3)

The basis for the psalmist's faith is God, who is the rock, fortress, and refuge. God is the one who is able to deliver and save.

> For You are my hope [*tiqveh*], O Lord God;
> You are my trust [*batach*] from my youth. (v. 5)

> But I will hope [*yachal*] continually,
> And will praise You yet more and more. (v. 14)

God is the psalmist's hope (*tiqveh*). The Hebrew noun *tiqveh* is one of the primary words for hope along with the related verbal form (*qavah*). The Hebrew clause has no verb; in English the verb "to be" is understood in such constructions. The statement becomes a timeless affirmation: God has been my hope; God is my hope; God will be my hope. All these affirmations are included in the verbless clause, "God my hope." The psalmist continually waits expectantly for that hope to be realized again. Because God does repeatedly answer the psalmist's petitions, he will praise God more and more. His hope in God and his praise to God both continually increase.

Psalm 46

Psalm 46, a song of Zion, expresses the hope of the community in God. The worshiping community lifts praise to God: "God is our refuge [*chasah*] and strength, / A very present help [*`ezrah*] in trouble" (v. 1). There is reference to Zion, the city of God, in the psalm (v. 4), but the city is not the refuge and help for the community: God is. God is indeed in the midst of the city, and God will help. The repeated refrain of praise well states the hope: "The LORD of hosts is with us; . . . / The God of Jacob is our refuge [*misgav*]" (vv. 7, 11). The Hebrew word *misgav* depicts a fortress high up in a mountain. The hope of the community is not the holy city with its walls and towers for a fortress; the hope is in God, God's presence is the hope, and God alone is the refuge or fortress. Notice also the promise of God's presence in another verbless clause: God of hosts with us (*'emmanu*, with us)—past, present, future.

PSALM 62

Psalm 62 is a trust song, a sub-type of the lament with a focus on trusting God:

> Truly my soul silently waits for God;
> From Him comes my salvation.
> He only is my rock and my salvation;
> He is my defense;
> I shall not be greatly moved. (vv. 1–2)

The psalmist affirms that God is his only salvation. His wait is one of expectation. God is his hope. The psalmist uses three terms to describe the reason for his hope in God. Twice he says God is his "salvation" or deliverance (*yeshua'*); he further describes God as his "rock" and "defense" or "refuge" (*misgav*), the same word used in Psalm 46 as "refuge." The psalmist continues to affirm hope in God:

> My soul, wait silently for God alone,
> For my expectation is from Him.
> He only is my rock and my salvation;
> He is my defense;
> I shall not be moved.
> In God is my salvation and my glory;
> The rock of my strength,
> And my refuge, is in God.
> Trust in Him at all times, you people;

> Pour out your heart before Him;
> God is a refuge for us. (vv. 5–8)

The psalmist again uses the images of God as "rock," "salvation" (*yeshua`*), and "defense" or "refuge" (*misgav*). The word "expectation" in verse 5 is the primary Hebrew noun for hope (*tiqveh*) and is translated as hope in many versions. In addition the psalmist adds another word for "refuge" (*macheseh*, from the same word family as *chaseh*) twice in verses 7 and 8. This piling on of words describing the attributes of God demonstrates the psalmist's hope.

Psalm 121

Psalm 121 is another trust psalm. Although the word *hope* does not appear in the psalm, the word *help* does occur twice:

> I will lift up my eyes to the hills—
> From whence comes my help?
> My help comes from the Lord,
> Who made heaven and earth. (vv. 1–2)

The psalmist begins by affirming God as his help (*`ezer*), using first-person pronouns. Then immediately the psalmist begins to address another worshiper:

> He will not allow your foot to be moved;
> He who keeps you will not slumber.
> Behold, He who keeps Israel
> Shall neither slumber nor sleep.
>
> The Lord is your keeper;
> The Lord is your shade at your right hand. (vv. 3–5)

God, who is the psalmist's help, is also the one who keeps (*shamar*—keep, watch, guard) the worshiper. The psalmist affirms God as the one who watches over, guards, and keeps the worshiper. The psalmist may be a priest addressing a worshiper with words of blessing. Such an interpretation fits well with the last verses of the psalm that also use the word *keep* ("preserve" in the NKJV) three more times:

> The LORD shall preserve you from all evil;
> He shall preserve your soul.
> The LORD shall preserve your going out and your coming in
> From this time forth, and even forevermore. (vv. 7–8)

Not only has God proven to be guardian-keeper for the psalmist in the past and in the present (vv. 1–2), but the psalmist assures the worshiper that God will be the worshiper's guardian-keeper in the present and future.

Petition Psalms

PSALM 130

Psalm 130 is one of the penitential psalms—psalms that confess sin and seek forgiveness and restoration. The psalmist begins with confession and petition for forgiveness, followed by hope in God's mercy:

> Out of the depths I have cried to You, O LORD;
> Lord, hear my voice!
> Let Your ears be attentive
> To the voice of my supplications.
> If You, LORD, should mark iniquities,
> O Lord, who could stand?
> But there is forgiveness with You,
> That You may be feared.
>
> I wait [*qavah*] for the LORD, my soul waits [*qavah*],
> And in His word I do hope [*yachal*].
> My soul waits for the Lord
> More than those who watch for the morning—
> Yes, more than those who watch for the morning.
>
> O Israel, hope [*yachal*] in the LORD;
> For with the LORD there is mercy,
> And with Him is abundant redemption.
> And He shall redeem Israel
> From all his iniquities.

The psalmist places hope in God's forgiveness and mercy. He says he waits expectantly (*qavah*, the verb form related to *tiqveh*—hope, wait expectantly) for God. In addition to this anticipation, he hopes (*yachal*) in

God's word. The psalmist knows that God's word is the scripture of the Law and Prophets; he hopes in the promises and instructions in God's word. The psalmist closes by addressing the nation Israel, calling Israel to hope (*yachal*) in God even as he does. He also affirms God as the source of "mercy" (*chesed*—steadfast love) and ransom or "redemption" (*padah*). He affirms that if Israel hopes in God and follows his word—covenant commandments—God will ransom/redeem Israel from Israel's sins.

Psalm 119

Psalm 119 is a wisdom psalm. It is an alphabetic acrostic with 22 stanzas of 8 lines each. It is the longest chapter in the Bible with 176 verses, located just two psalms after the shortest chapter—Psalm 117 with 2 verses. The wisdom focus of Psalm 119 is the Law, the commandments of God, and instruction in the Law. The hope expressed in Psalm 119 is hope in God's word—scriptures, instructions, and commandments—described in many different words: "And take not the word of truth utterly out of my mouth, / For I have hoped in Your ordinances" (v. 43). Here the hope (*yachal*) of the psalmist is in God's word as found in his ordinances or judgments (*mishpat*). God's word itself is also the basis of the psalmist's hope in these verses:

> Remember the word to Your servant,
> Upon which You have caused me to hope [*yachal*]. (v. 49)
>
> Those who fear You will be glad when they see me,
> Because I have hoped [*yachal*] in Your word. (v. 74)

In all of the above examples, the psalmist expresses past hope—in previous situations when the psalmist hoped in God's word. Because that hope was realized in the past, the psalmist has the same hope for the present and future:

> My soul faints for Your salvation
> [*teshua*`, a form closely related to *yeshua*`],
> But I hope [*yachal*] in Your word.
> My eyes fail from searching Your word,
> Saying, "When will You comfort me?" (vv. 81–82)

At the point of his petition, his hope has not been realized. Nevertheless, the psalmist still has the hope that God will respond and will bring the comfort (*nacham*—comfort, mercy) he seeks.

> You are my hiding place and my shield;
> I hope [*yachal*] in Your word. (v. 114)
>
> Uphold me according to Your word, that I may live;
> And do not let me be ashamed of my hope [*sever*]. (v. 116)
>
> I rise before the dawning of the morning,
> And cry for help;
> I hope [*yachal*] in Your word. (v. 147)

In each of these examples the hope expressed is past, fulfilled hope. But the expressed need is present. The psalmist can have hope in the present because of past experience of help from God. So the present cry for help is filled with hope. If the psalmist's hope is in God's word, it is also in the salvation he offers: "LORD, I hope [*sever*] for Your salvation, / And I do Your commandments" (v. 166). The hope the psalmist has is in God's salvation or deliverance (*yeshua`*).

PSALM 146

One last psalm to consider for the hope it expresses is Psalm 146. This hymn of praise again pairs hope and help, and it contrasts misplaced hope or trust—trust placed in humans—with genuine hope found in God.

> Praise the LORD!
> Praise the LORD, O my soul!
> While I live I will praise the LORD;
> I will sing praises to my God while I have my being.
>
> Do not put your trust [*batach*] in princes,
> Nor in a son of man, in whom there is no help [*teshua`*].
> His spirit departs, he returns to his earth;
> In that very day his plans perish.
> Happy is he who has the God of Jacob for his help [*`ezer*],
> Whose hope [*sever*] is in the LORD his God,
> Who made heaven and earth,

> The sea, and all that is in them;
> Who keeps [*shamar*, keeps, watches, guards] truth [*'emet*, closely related word to *'emunah*, truthfulness] forever,
> Who executes justice [*mishpat*] for the oppressed,
> Who gives food to the hungry.
> The LORD gives freedom to the prisoners.
>
> The LORD opens the eyes of the blind
> The LORD raises those who are bowed down;
> The LORD loves the righteous [*tsadiq*, a noun closely related to *tsedeq*, righteousness]. (vv. 1–8)

Again we see the many attributes describing God, attributes that are the basis of the psalmist's hope. God is the creator who also keeps truth, does justice, and loves the righteous. God also gives food to the hungry, frees prisoners, and restores sight to the blind—characteristics of a future messianic eschatological age (Isa. 61:1–2), and characteristics fulfilled in Christ's ministry (Matt. 11:2–6; Luke 4:8–9).

Conclusion

The psalmists of Israel express hope in all genres of their psalms. Of the many occurrences of the word *hope* in the Old Testament, most are in Psalms, Job, and Proverbs. These three poetic and wisdom books contain more than two-thirds of the Old Testament occurrences of the word *hope*. We can rightly say the psalmists express their hope far more explicitly than other Old Testament writers. Their hope permeates every type of psalm. Their hope is in God alone, never in humans or human institutions. They clearly state that such misplaced hope always ends in futility and failure. The faith of the psalmists is a model for us. Their praises, prayers, laments, and petitions provide good examples for us to follow. Their hope in God alone is our hope as well. Even though we have a fuller vision of hope in the death and resurrection of Christ, it is the same hope. Thanks be to God for the hope of the psalmists!

Proverbs

The book of Proverbs is one of the Wisdom books of the Old Testament. In Proverbs 1:1, authorship is attributed to Solomon, son of David, although several other headings in the book refer to different authors in addition to Solomon: Agur son of Jakeh (30:1), King Lemuel (31:1), and sayings of the wise men (24:23). The book of Proverbs describes the way of wisdom: instructions from an older teacher to a young person (especially chs. 1–9) and short, often single-verse sayings, or aphorisms, (chs. 10–29). Though numerous parallels can be drawn between Israelite wisdom and wisdom across the ancient Near East, Israelite wisdom is specifically Yahwistic or God-oriented wisdom: "The fear [*yir'ah*] of the LORD is the beginning of wisdom" (9:10 KJV).

The Hebrew word *yir'ah* means not only "fear, being afraid, terror" but also includes the sense of "awe, respect, honor, reverence." In reference to God, it is a synonym for worshiping and obeying him. This concept of fear-reverence of God is stated repeatedly in Proverbs as a basis for right living:

> The fear of the LORD is the beginning of knowledge. (1:7)
>
> The fear of the LORD is hatred of evil. (8:13)
>
> The fear of the LORD prolongs life. (10:27)
>
> In the fear of the LORD one has strong confidence. (14:26)
>
> The fear of the LORD is a fountain of life. (14:27)
>
> The fear of the LORD is instruction in wisdom. (15:33)
>
> By the fear of the LORD a man avoids evil. (16:6)
>
> The fear of the LORD leads to life. (19:23)
>
> The reward for humility and fear of the LORD
> is riches and honor and life. (22:4)

Proverbs offers numerous contrasts between the wise person and the fool, the righteous and the wicked. A few examples illustrate this:

> The fear of the LORD is the beginning of knowledge,
> But fools despise wisdom and instruction. (1:7)

> The curse of the LORD is on the house of the wicked,
> But He blesses the home of the just. . . .
> The wise shall inherit glory,
> But shame shall be the legacy of fools. (3:33, 35)

> The tongue of the righteous is choice silver;
> The heart of the wicked is worth little.
> The lips of the righteous feed many,
> But fools die for lack of wisdom.
> The blessing of the LORD makes one rich,
> And He adds no sorrow with it.
> To do evil is like sport to a fool,
> But a man of understanding has wisdom.
> The fear of the wicked will come upon him,
> And the desire of the righteous will be granted.
> When the whirlwind passes by, the wicked is no more,
> But the righteous has an everlasting foundation. (10:20–25)

The contrast of the wise and the foolish also provides the contrast between hope and hopelessness in Proverbs. The righteous, the wise, have hope in God. Their trust in God and his grace and mercy provides them with hope. The foolish, the wicked, have no such hope. Their situation is hopeless:

> The hope [*tochelet*, from *yachel*, hope, expectation]
> of the righteous will be gladness,
> But the expectation [*tiqvah*, hope] of the wicked will perish (10:28).

> The righteousness [*tsedaqah*] of the upright [*yashar*]
> will deliver [*natsal*] them,
> But the unfaithful will be caught by their lust.

> When a wicked man dies, his expectation [*yiqvah*, hope] will perish,
> And the hope [*tochelet*] of the unjust perishes. (11:6–7)

These two passages show the clear contrast in the fate of the righteous and the wicked. The hope—and outcome—of the righteous is joy and gladness of heart. But the hope—the expectation—of the wicked dies, as the wicked die. The righteous are delivered; the wicked die in their wickedness.

A couple of the proverbs describe those who are not wise. For them, fools have more hope than they do:

> Do you see a man wise in his own eyes?
> There is more hope [*tiqvah*] for a fool than for him. (26:12)
>
> Do you see a man hasty in his words?
> There is more hope [*tiqvah*] for a fool than for him. (29:20)

The instructions in Proverbs also suggest the proper discipline of children: "Correct [*yasar*, discipline, admonish] your children while there is still hope [*tiqvah*]; / do not let them destroy themselves" (19:18 NCV). While children are still young, there is the hope—hope that they will respond to the discipline, hope that when they are old, they will not depart from the right way (22:6).

But what does one say when hope is delayed, when it does not come as one had hoped? Such delay makes one heartsick (13:12a). However, a delay in the coming of hope does not mean a situation is hopeless. Job hoped for God to answer his cries throughout his dialogue with his friends. God did answer—not on Job's timetable, but on God's timetable. The proverb continues—when one's desire (hope) comes, it is a tree of life (13:12b). The tree of life image is a reminder of creation and the garden of Eden (Gen. 2:9). When one's hope is realized, hope brings life. While the Old Testament has few references to life after death, this passage and the following offer a possible hope of life beyond death for the righteous.

> The wicked is driven away in his wickedness:
> but the righteous hath hope
> [*chasah*, finds refuge] in his death. (14:32 KJV)
>
> For surely there is a hereafter [*'acharit*, literally "a future"],
> And your hope will not be cut off. (23:18)

The words of this latter proverb are exactly the same as Jeremiah's words to exiles, that God has in store for them a future and a hope (Jer. 29:11). While both may refer to hope in terms of posterity, these three verses from Proverbs may also suggest life beyond death. Two more passages from Proverbs speak of a future in terms of possible life after death for the righteous, but not for the evil or wicked:

> So shall the knowledge of wisdom be to your soul;
> If you have found it, there is a prospect
> ['*acharit*, literally "a future"],
> And your hope [*tiqvah*] will not be cut off. (24:14)
>
> For there will be no future ['*acherit*] for the evil;
> the lamp of the wicked will be extinguished.
> (v. 20, author's translation)

In Proverbs, following the way of wisdom gives one hope. That hope is not in oneself or even in wisdom itself. The hope is in God, fearing and obeying him. God is the source of wisdom (2:6). He created the heavens and earth with wisdom and understanding (3:19). True hope comes from him:

> Trust [*batach*] in the LORD with all your heart,
> And lean not on your own understanding. (3:5)
>
> For the LORD will be your confidence [*kesel*, confidence, hope],
> And will keep your foot from being caught. (v. 26)

The hope expressed by Israel's sages thousands of years ago remains our hope today. The sages expressed a few glimmers of hope in life beyond death with God their primary focus of hope. We Christians live on this side of Christ's death and resurrection. We have a hope in atonement accomplished in the Christ event. God is also our hope. His love and mercy for all humankind in Christ gives us immeasurable hope.

ECCLESIASTES AND *Song of Songs*

These two books are being treated together because both are traditionally ascribed to Solomon. However, the two are quite different works.

Ecclesiastes

The book of Ecclesiastes, also called Qoheleth, is one of the Wisdom books of the Old Testament along with Job and Proverbs. The title of the book comes from the first verse. The Hebrew word is *Qoheleth*; the Greek word is *Ecclesiastes*—the English translation of the word is usually "Preacher" or "Teacher." The book of Ecclesiastes is ascribed to Solomon although Solomon is never mentioned explicitly. However, the preacher-teacher is called "the son of David, king in Jerusalem" (1:1) and "king over Israel in Jerusalem" (v. 12). The book is likely ascribed to Solomon because of Solomon's association with wisdom and proverbs (1 Kings 4:29–34). Most critical scholars ascribe the book to a much later postexilic period because of the presence of late Hebrew words and Aramaic and Persian loanwords (words from these languages used in the book).

The book of Ecclesiastes is noted for its generally skeptical and pessimistic outlook on life. The preacher-teacher who narrates the book seems to be an older person giving instruction, or the fruit of his life search for meaning, to a younger person. The best known word from the book is "vanity," which occurs thirty-eight times in the book—twice the phrase "Vanity of vanities, all is vanity" occurs and serves as bookends to the book (1:2; 12:8). The Hebrew word *hevel*, translated commonly as "vanity," means "vapor, breath, ephemeral, something empty or worthless"; in Ecclesiastes it means something meaningless or fruitless. The preacher-teacher tries to find happiness and meaning in every possible situation—but finds only vanity, meaninglessness.

Another theme in the book is "there is nothing new under the sun" (1:9). The phrase "under the sun" occurs twenty-eight times in Ecclesiastes and the related phrase "under heaven" occurs three times. The book opens with examples of cycles of life and nature: generations come and go, the sun rises and sets to rise again, the wind blows and comes round again, streams flow to the sea, but the sea is never filled, and streams keep flowing, what has been will be again. There is nothing new under the sun (vv. 4–11).

The preacher-teacher tries to apply his wisdom to the human condition. He concludes all human work, labor, is meaningless and like chasing the wind (v. 14). He decides to search for wisdom and folly and contrast them—but finds this also is meaningless More wisdom and knowledge bring only more sorrow and grief (vv. 17–18). He tries pleasure and laughter, but those also are meaningless (2:1–2). He tries all the great works wealth and power permit: building houses, making gardens and orchards and vineyards, purchasing many servants, having large herds and flocks, getting gold and silver and royal treasure, acquiring many musicians and musical instruments; whatever he desires he gets. However, once he finishes his work and acquisitions, he deems it was all meaningless, like chasing the wind (vv. 3–11). He does decide wisdom is better than folly, but also sees that the wise and foolish alike have the same final fate—death (vv. 12–15). Moreover, the wise man or king cannot know what sort of person will succeed him—will his son or successor be wise and prudent or foolish? He decides this, too, is futile and meaningless (vv. 16–23). So he concludes there is nothing better than to eat and drink and enjoy the good from his work—for this is a gift from God (vv. 24–26). We must note that despite his pessimism and continual statements on the meaninglessness and futility of life, the preacher-teacher always affirms the existence of God and God's control over all creation. However, he also affirms that humans cannot discern God's ways or purposes.

The preacher-teacher continues his observation by noting there is a time and a season for everything under heaven and gives examples by using pairs of opposites (a time to be born, a time to die, a time to plant, a time to pluck up what is planted, and so on; 3:1–8). His conclusion is that God is the one who controls all destiny:

> He has made everything beautiful in its time. Also He has put eternity in their hearts, except that no one can find out the work that God does from beginning to end. I know that nothing is better for them than to rejoice, and to do good in their lives, and also that every man should eat and drink and enjoy the good of all his labor—it is the gift of God.
>
> I know that whatever God does,
> It shall be forever.
> Nothing can be added to it,
> And nothing taken from it.
> God does it, that men should fear before Him. (vv. 11–14)

The preacher-teacher does acknowledge God and that God's work is eternal, unlike humans' temporal works. Humans cannot add to or take away from God's works. Furthermore, the preacher-teacher recognizes a purpose in God's work—humans are to fear, worship, reverence, and stand in awe of him. As repeatedly stated in Proverbs, a major wisdom premise is that the fear, worship, reverence, awe of God is the beginning of wisdom. For all his pessimism and sense of the meaninglessness of his experiences of life, the preacher-teacher never loses faith in God or the assurance that God is in control. He bemoans the fact that he cannot know, indeed no human can know, the mind of God or what human destiny will be.

The preacher-teacher then focuses on the end of all creation, humans and animals alike—all die. All are dust and all return to dust (vv. 18–22). He asks: "Who knows if the spirit of the humans goes up, and if the spirit of the animals goes down into the earth?" (v. 21, author's translation). He does not answer, but the implication is that no human can know. However, from what he already has said about God, God knows the destiny of humans, animals, and all creation.

The preacher-teacher does note some advantage to having friends and companions who can help one another (4:8–12). He also provides some prudent advice about worship practices: come to the sanctuary to hear and listen rather than bringing a fool's sacrifice—sacrifices without proper preparation of one's heart. Don't speak long, meaningless speeches to God, make no rash vows, and be sure to fulfill your vows. Above all, fear, worship, reverence, and stand in awe of God (5:1–7).

As he has previously determined that all his human works to seek greatness and power do not give him happiness (2:3–11), the preacher-teacher also determines that silver—money and wealth—does not satisfy. Those seeking riches never have enough, find no happiness with what they have, and cannot rest worrying about whether they will keep it or lose it—this also is futility and meaninglessness (5:10–17). Instead, he has determined one thing is good:

> Here is what I have seen: It is good and fitting for one to eat and drink, and to enjoy the good of all his labor in which he toils under the sun all the days of his life which God gives him; for it is his heritage. As for every man to whom God has given riches and wealth, and given him power to eat of it, to receive his heritage and rejoice in his labor—this is the gift of God. For he will not dwell unduly on the days of his life, because God keeps him busy with the joy of his heart. (vv. 18–20)

The preacher-teacher exhorts all to eat and drink and enjoy their work all the days of their lives, recognizing that God has given it all—the food, the drink, the work, and especially all the days. Those to whom God has given wealth should rejoice in their work because it is a gift of God. None should dwell on the days of their lives, on the work or the length of the days, because God will fill the hearts and minds of all with joy.

The preacher-teacher again notes the futility and meaninglessness of a person's life who has wealth but cannot enjoy it and one who has long life but is not satisfied with the goodness he has received. All go to the same place—the grave (6:1–6). He then again raises the questions. First, "For who knows what is good for man in life, all the days of his vain life which he passes like a shadow? Who can tell a man what will happen after him under the sun?" (v. 12). Who knows what is good for people during their lives? From the human perspective, no one knows. No one has a perfect formula for success. But from another perspective, even one that the preacher-teacher acknowledges at times, God knows what is good. Likewise to the second question, no human can tell another person what will transpire after death. Only God can tell what will occur in the future and beyond the grave. Already the preacher-teacher has affirmed that God, and only God, is eternal. Only from a faith this side of the Christ event can we experience that hope of life eternal in God's presence.

The preacher-teacher returns to his theme of enjoying life as one experiences it, recognizing God appoints both prosperity and adversity:

> In the day of prosperity be joyful,
> But in the day of adversity consider:
> Surely God has appointed the one as well as the other,
> So that man can find out nothing that will come after him.
>
> I have seen everything in my days of vanity:
>
> There is a just man who perishes in his righteousness,
> And there is a wicked man who prolongs life in his wickedness.
>
> Do not be overly righteous,
> Nor be overly wise:
> Why should you destroy yourself?
> Do not be overly wicked,
> Nor be foolish:
> Why should you die before your time?
> It is good that you grasp this,
> And also not remove your hand from the other;
> For he who fears God will escape them all. (7:14–18)

But notice how the focus shifts. First he reiterates that no one can find out what will come after death. He then mentions cases of the just who die, apparently young, in their righteousness, and the wicked who live long lives despite their wickedness. This is followed by the strange negative commands: Don't be overly righteous or overly wise. Don't be overly wicked or foolish. It is possible the passage refers to those who are self-righteous, who are wise in their own eyes. Viewed this way the passage makes good sense and fits the final statement that those who fear, worship, reverence, and stand in awe of God will escape dying before their time.

There is only one explicit word of hope in the book of Ecclesiastes:

> But for him who is joined to all the living there is hope [*bittachon*, from *batach*, trust, hope], for a living dog is better than a dead lion.
>
> For the living know that they will die;
> But the dead know nothing,
> And they have no more reward,
> For the memory of them is forgotten. (9:4–5)

The passage reminds all that as long as there is life, there is hope. The dead have no hope. That truth holds for all time. The decisions one makes in this life, the faith or lack of faith, determine whether a person has any genuine hope, hope of eternal life.

In the closing chapter of Ecclesiastes, the preacher-teacher calls on youth to remember God, the Creator of all: "Remember now your Creator in the days of your youth, / Before the difficult days come, / And the years draw near when you say, / 'I have no pleasure in them'" (12:1). To remember does not mean merely to recall a fact but instead to call to mind, to think of, to commemorate, to bring past experiences into the present. The call to youth is to build that experience with the Creator, with God, while they are still young, recalling the words of Proverbs: "Train up a child in the way he should go, and when he is old he will not depart from it" (22:6). The imagery of Ecclesiastes 12:2–6 describes the aging process and old age. It is quite possible the preacher-teacher would extend the call to remember to all ages, calling on all to remember and celebrate God throughout our lives.

The preacher-teacher still sees death as the end: "Then the dust will return to the earth as it was, / And the spirit will return to God who gave it. / 'Vanity of vanities,' says the Preacher, all is vanity'" (vv. 7–8). Humans are dust (Gen. 2:7) and at death return to dust. The spirit or breath returns to God—but this is no real belief in life beyond death because the preacher-teacher returns to his opening assessment—all is futility, meaninglessness. Nonetheless, futility and meaninglessness are not his final words:

> Let us hear the conclusion of the whole matter:
>
> Fear God and keep His commandments,
> For this is man's all.
> For God will bring every work into judgment,
> Including every secret thing,
> Whether good or evil. (12:13–14)

In his closing words, the preacher-teacher reminds us of his earlier injunction—fear, worship, reverence, stand in awe of God, and in addition, keep his commandments. This is all humans can do, and this is all humans are called upon to do.

What hope do we find in Ecclesiastes? Despite his pessimism and focus on the futility and meaninglessness of life, the preacher-teacher affirms several points about God that can give hope. He affirms the existence of God as Creator of all. He affirms that God, and only God, is eternal. He also affirms all life as a gift of God. He calls on humans to enjoy the life and the sustenance God gives to all. He affirms that humans should fear, worship, reverence, and stand in awe of God. He affirms that humans cannot know anything beyond death—but God does know. The only direct reference to hope affirms the possibility of hope as long as one has life. He asks a question repeatedly: "Who knows?" usually referring to human destiny. His answer implies that no human can know the answer to ultimate questions. But he also implies that God does have a plan, a purpose, and the answer to all life's ultimate questions. So the hope of the preacher-teacher, though not stated explicitly, appears to rest in God. God is his hope, as God is our hope.

The perspective of the preacher-teacher is life under the sun or under heaven—the perspective from the human point of view. As Christians we have the additional perspective, the heavenly God-given perspective, based on the death and resurrection of Christ and the hope we have through Christ's atonement for us. No longer is our hope futile and meaningless. Our hope is an eternal hope in God and his salvation offered to all in Christ.

Song of Songs

The Song of Songs, also called the Song of Solomon, is in several regards the most unusual book in the Old Testament. The book is ascribed to Solomon, and his name appears seven times in the book. The date of composition has been argued from the time of Solomon at the earliest to the Persian period at the latest. The unusual aspect is that the book is a series of love songs between a man and a woman, with possibly a third speaker or chorus. The book has been described as a drama or even a musical production. God is never mentioned in the text. Nor is there any explicit mention of hope in the book. It is a celebration of human love and of intimate expressions of human love. The majority of verses of the book are words of the woman to the man and words of the man to the woman. Also unusual is that in Song of Songs we have more words of the woman expressing her love for the man than words of the man.

What elements of hope can one find in a book of love songs between a man and a woman? In Jewish tradition the book has been interpreted traditionally as an allegory of God's love for Israel and in Christian tradition as an allegory for Christ's love for the church. With the rise of modern critical scholarship, the book has been interpreted primarily as human love poetry. Seen in this manner, Song of Songs affirms the beauty and goodness of human love.

Genesis 1–2 describes the goodness of creation. Looking over his creation, God pronounces it all as very good (1:31). A part of that goodness includes humans and human sexuality and love. In creation, God blesses humans and tells them to be fruitful and multiply and fill the earth (1:28). That blessing puts God's approval on human love and sexuality. The church has tended to view human sexuality in a negative sense because of some of Paul's comments (1 Cor. 7:8–9). But in creation, marriage is seen as good, and human sexuality is affirmed (Gen. 2:24–25). Song of Songs provides an example of the celebration of the goodness of human love and sexuality. In Ecclesiastes, the preacher-teacher states that there is hope as long as there is life (9:4). Song of Songs affirms hope for humankind exists as long as there is love between man and woman. As Christians we also affirm the God-given gift of human love and sexuality. We take hope in that love and recognize the existence of human love as evidence of God's continual blessing on humans. Thanks be to God for the hope human love and sexuality affirm.

Isaiah

Isaiah is an eighth-century BC prophet to Judah. He is a contemporary with Amos and Hosea who prophesy to the Northern Kingdom, Israel, and Micah who also prophesies to Judah. Isaiah is apparently a native of Jerusalem, the primary locale for his messages. According to Jewish tradition in the Talmud, Isaiah is related to the royal house of David, and Uzziah is his cousin. He has access to the kings of Judah. His father's name is Amoz. Isaiah is married and his wife is a prophetess in her own right (ch. 8). They have at least two children, each of whom is given a symbolic name, Shear-yashub, "a remnant will return," and Maher-shalal-hash-baz, "the spoil speeds, the prey hastens."

Isaiah's Call and Mission

There is considerable scholarly debate about the authorship of the book of Isaiah, especially of the later chapters. Many scholars hold the position that later disciples of Isaiah are responsible for chapters 40–66 and several others, such as 34–35. This position is based partly on the different perspectives in the later chapters. Most of chapters 1–39 presume an eighth-century BC context when Assyria is the primary foreign power. The messages predominantly are warnings of judgment unless the people repent. In chapters 40–66, the context is that of sixth or fifth century BC. Jerusalem has been destroyed, and many leaders are carried into exile to Babylon, the new foreign power. The messages are of comfort and hope of restoration. In chapters 40–55, the exile is about to end, and restoration is about to occur; chapters 56–66 speak of a partial return and restoration. For this study of hope in Isaiah, the unity of the message of Isaiah will be assumed; the date of composition and single or multiple authorship will not be addressed. The prophet Isaiah himself clearly belongs in an eighth-century BC context.

Isaiah's call comes in the year King Uzziah dies, 642 BC. It comes as a vision set in the Jerusalem temple. Describing his call at a later time in his life, he records:

> In the year that King Uzziah died, I saw the Lord sitting on a very high throne. His long robe filled the Temple. Heavenly creatures of fire stood above him. Each creature had six wings: It used two wings to cover its face, two wings to cover its feet, and two wings for flying. Each creature was calling to the others:
>
> "Holy, holy, holy is the LORD All-Powerful.
> His glory fills the whole earth." (Isa. 6:1–3 NCV)

Isaiah responds to this vision with a cry of his own sinfulness and unworthiness (v. 5). Then one of the creatures takes a hot coal from the altar, touches Isaiah's lips, and says Isaiah's sins are forgiven (v. 7), and Isaiah hears God's call and accepts it: "Then I heard the Lord's voice, saying, 'Whom can I send? Who will go for us?' So I said, 'Here I am. Send me!'" (v. 8 NCV).

Isaiah's mission is not easy to accomplish, nor is God's message readily accepted by the people. Looking back at his call, Isaiah says the people would not heed God's message (vv. 8–10). As a result, their continuing sinfulness in response to God's message will bring judgment to the nation:

> Then I asked, "Lord, how long should I do this?"
> He answered,
>
> "Until the cities are destroyed
> and the people are gone,
> until there are no people left in the houses,
> until the land is destroyed and left empty.
> The LORD will send the people far away,
> and the land will be left empty.
> One-tenth of the people will be left in the land,
> but it will be destroyed again.
> These people will be like an oak tree
> whose stump is left when the tree is chopped down.
> The people who remain will be like a stump that will sprout again." (vv. 11–13 NCV)

It sounds almost hopeless—empty, destroyed cities, only a tenth remain, and then the land destroyed again. The people are like a tree chopped down with only a stump remaining. Nevertheless, even with the judgment there remains an element of hope. The stump *will* sprout again. It may be only a sprout, but in the sprout is hope and life. Isaiah and other prophets often repeat this image of hope.

Warnings of Judgment

From the beginning, Isaiah's message focuses on the sins of the people and warnings of judgment. An overview of the warnings in Isaiah 1 presents a good summary of impending judgment unless the people repent and follow God's law:

> Hear, O heavens, and give ear, O earth!
> For the LORD has spoken:
> "I have nourished and brought up children,
> And they have rebelled against Me;
> The ox knows its owner
> And the donkey its master's crib;
> But Israel does not know,
> My people do not consider."
>
> Alas, sinful nation,
> A people laden with iniquity,
> A brood of evildoers,
> Children who are corrupters!
> They have forsaken the LORD,
> They have provoked to anger
> The Holy One of Israel,
> They have turned away backward. (1:2–4)

The message is clear: judgment will come unless the people repent and turn back to God.

> Your country is desolate,
> Your cities are burned with fire;
> Strangers devour your land in your presence;

> And it is desolate, as overthrown by strangers. . . .
> Unless the LORD of hosts
> Had left to us a very small remnant,
> We would have become like Sodom,
> We would have been made like Gomorrah. (vv. 7, 9)

Even repentance may not turn aside God's judgment for the people's sin. What is especially abhorrent to God is religiosity and continued sinfulness—going through all the outward motions of worship while practicing iniquity:

> Hear the word of the LORD,
> You rulers of Sodom;
> Give ear to the law of our God,
> You people of Gomorrah:
> "To what purpose is the multitude of your sacrifices to Me?"
> Says the LORD.
> "I have had enough of burnt offerings of rams
> And the fat of fed cattle.
> I do not delight in the blood of bulls,
> Or of lambs or goats. . . .
>
> Bring no more futile sacrifices;
> Incense is an abomination to Me.
> The New Moons, the Sabbaths, and the calling of assemblies—
> I cannot endure iniquity and the sacred meeting." (vv. 10–11, 13)

What God commands is repentance and following the covenant laws of justice and righteousness:

> Wash yourselves, make yourselves clean;
> Put away the evil of your doings from before My eyes.
> Cease to do evil,
> Learn to do good;
> Seek justice,
> Rebuke the oppressor;
> Defend the fatherless,
> Plead for the widow. (vv. 16–17)

Repentance can bring the hope of forgiveness; indeed, God promises good if the people are obedient:

If you are willing and obedient,
You shall eat the good of the land;
But if you refuse and rebel,
You shall be devoured by the sword";
For the mouth of the LORD has spoken.

How the faithful city has become a harlot!
It was full of justice;
Righteousness lodged in it,
But now murderers. (vv. 19–21)

But God finds sinfulness, the worship of other gods, and even murder. As a result, his judgment will come on Judah and Jerusalem:

Therefore the Lord says,
The LORD of hosts, the Mighty One of Israel,
"Ah, I will rid Myself of My adversaries,
And take vengeance on My enemies.
I will turn My hand against you,
And thoroughly purge away your dross,
And take away all your alloy.
I will restore your judges as at the first,
And your counselors as at the beginning.
Afterward you shall be called the city of righteousness,
the faithful city."

Zion shall be redeemed with justice,
And her penitents with righteousness.
The destruction of transgressors and of sinners shall be together,
And those who forsake the LORD shall be consumed. (vv. 24–28)

God *will* bring judgment on enemies, and the people of Judah and Jerusalem are God's enemies because of their iniquity, but there is hope beyond judgment. God promises not only judgment but also restoration. After the judgment and restoration, Zion-Jerusalem will be called the city of righteousness and faithfulness.

Hope for the Future

Lest one think the message of judgment is Isaiah's last word, this oracle of warning and judgment is followed immediately with a strong message of hope for the future:

> Now it shall come to pass in the latter days
> That the mountain of the LORD'S house
> Shall be established on the top of the mountains,
> And shall be exalted above the hills;
> And all nations shall flow to it.
> Many people shall come and say,
> "Come, and let us go up to the mountain of the LORD,
> To the house of the God of Jacob;
> He will teach us His ways,
> And we shall walk in His paths."
> For out of Zion shall go forth the law,
> And the word of the LORD from Jerusalem.
> He shall judge between the nations,
> And rebuke many people;
> They shall beat their swords into plowshares,
> And their spears into pruning hooks;
> Nation shall not lift up sword against nation,
> Neither shall they learn war anymore. (2:2–4)

This eschatological picture of a glorious future depicts God's reign and the people's obedience. It will be a future filled with hope as God teaches all people—not just Judah and Jerusalem but *all* nations—his ways, and they live according to his will. This dual message of Isaiah 1–2 is repeated often throughout the book—warnings of judgment and messages of future hope.

While many passages in Isaiah are filled with hope, there are relatively few direct references to *hope* in the book. The passages that do use a word for *hope* in some instances speak of hopelessness.

Several of Isaiah's messages include symbolic actions, messages that are visual as well as spoken. In one symbolic action message, Isaiah walks about naked for three years to depict the hopelessness of trusting in foreign nations rather than God (Isa. 20:1–3) during the Assyrian attack on Judah. Isaiah's spoken message accompanying his symbolic action warns:

> People who looked to Cush for help will be afraid, and those who were amazed by Egypt's glory will be shamed. People who live near the sea will say, "Look at those countries. We trusted [*mabbat*, expect] them to help [*'ezer*] us. We ran to them so they would save [*natsal*, deliver] us from the king of Assyria. So how will we be able to escape?" (20:5–6 NCV)

The leaders of Judah look to foreign powers such as Egypt for help. They hope for help through treaties and alliances. But those countries are of no help; Assyria will ravage them, so Judah's situation seems hopeless.

Isaiah warns against trusting in Egypt for help:

> "Woe to the rebellious children," says the LORD,
> "Who take counsel, but not of Me,
> And who devise plans, but not of My Spirit,
> That they may add sin to sin;
> Who walk to go down to Egypt,
> And have not asked My advice,
> To strengthen themselves in the strength of Pharaoh,
> And to trust [*chasah*, seek refuge] in the shadow of Egypt!
> Therefore the strength of Pharaoh
> Shall be your shame,
> And trust [*chasah*, seek refuge] in the shadow of Egypt
> Shall be your humiliation. (30:1–3)

Hope placed in Pharaoh or Egypt is hopeless. Only if Judah trusts or seeks refuge in God will Judah be delivered.

It is possible for a message to include hopelessness and hope at the same time. King Hezekiah is seriously ill. He calls for Isaiah who tells him he is about to die. Hezekiah then cries out to God professing his faithfulness. God grants him another fifteen years of life. In response, Hezekiah writes a hymn of praise to him. He says:

> People in the place of the dead cannot praise you;
> those who have died cannot sing praises to you;

those who die don't trust [*savar*, wait] you
to help [*'emet*, show faithfulness] them.
The people who are alive are the ones who praise you.
They praise you as I praise you today.
A father should tell his children
that you provide help [*'emet*, faithfulness].

The LORD saved [*hoshe'a*] me,
so we will play songs on stringed instruments
in the Temple of the LORD
all the days of our lives. (38:18–20 NCV)

Hezekiah's song relates that the dead have no hope of help from God. Hezekiah is alive thanks to God; his message is one of hope because God saves him.

Hope in Isaiah is often expressed with the Hebrew word *qavah*, usually translated as "wait for, await." The word has the sense of waiting expectantly. And that expectant waiting is itself hope. But the word can also describe an unrealized hope, a seemingly hopeless situation. In Isaiah's parable message of the vineyard, the vineyard owner

. . . dug it up and cleared out its stones,
And planted it with the choicest vine.
He built a tower in its midst,
And also made a winepress in it;
So He expected [*qavah*, hoped for] it to bring forth good grapes,
But it brought forth wild grapes. (5:2)

The interpretation God gives for the parable is that the vineyard represents Israel and Judah, and God is the owner of the vineyard:

For the vineyard of the LORD of hosts is the house of Israel,
And the men of Judah are His pleasant plant.
He looked for [*qavah*, hoped for] justice, but behold, oppression;
For righteousness, but behold, a cry for help. (v. 7)

The warning from the parable is that because of the people's faithlessness God is about to bring severe judgment on the people, their homes, and their fields, including exile and death (vv. 8–30).

The First Messianic Messages

There is much hope in Isaiah, even if the word *hope* is not present. Indeed, the messianic passages in Isaiah are among the most eloquent in the Old Testament. Isaiah includes two streams of messianic messages: one is a royal messianic figure, a future ruler of the house of David; the other is a servant figure, a servant messiah who is a suffering servant. The two streams are not mutually exclusive; instead they may be viewed as complementary. The royal figure may also be the humble servant of God. David is frequently referred to by God as "My servant David" (2 Sam. 3:18; 7:5; 2 Kings 19:34), but the focus of those passages is on the royal stream. The servant passages in Isaiah emphasize the humble nature of the servant. Among the significant messianic passages from early chapters of Isaiah are parts of chapters 7, 9, and 11.

Isaiah 7:14, "Therefore the Lord Himself will give you a sign: Behold, the virgin shall conceive and bear a Son, and shall call His name Immanuel," is undoubtedly the most quoted verse in the book, primarily from its use in the gospel of Matthew. In the New Testament context, the verse expresses the messianic hope fulfilled in the birth of Jesus. In its context in Isaiah 7, the passage offers significant hope to the original audience. The time frame of the message is 734–732 BC. Ahaz is king of Judah. Israel and Aram-Syria have formed a coalition to fight against the Assyrian army that is threatening to take their countries. Ahaz does not want to join the coalition, so the kings of Israel and Aram-Syria try to attack Judah, depose Ahaz as king, and place on the throne a ruler who will join their coalition (vv. 1–3). God sends Isaiah and his son to Ahaz with a message of hope. The child's name, Shear-yashub, is itself a sign of hope, "a remnant will return" (v. 3). The message from God is: "But I, the Lord GOD, say, 'Their plan will not succeed; / it will not happen'" (v. 7 NCV). God then gives a further sign (*'ot*), an additional symbolic-action message:

> Behold, the young woman is pregnant and about to give birth to a son and she will call his name Immanuel (With-us-God). Curds and honey he will eat when he knows to reject the evil and to choose the good. Indeed before the child knows to reject the evil and to choose the good, the land whose two kings you fear will be abandoned. (vv. 14–16, author's translation)

This sign (Hebrew *'ot*; Septuagint, *semeion*) is of immediate significance to Ahaz. The sign is not just the birth of the child, but that before the child is old enough to choose good from evil the lands of Israel and Aram-Syria will be deserted. Many biblical scholars suggest the reference may be to a young woman who is present when the sign is announced, possibly Ahaz's wife or some other member of the royal court. The sign and the immediate hope of the message is that the threat Ahaz is experiencing will cease to exist in just a few years. Damascus itself is captured by the Assyrians in 732, and Aram-Syria is completely under Assyrian control. Israel falls to the Assyrians in 721 BC. The sign is fulfilled within a short time of its original delivery.

The New Testament takes this passage from Isaiah as a prophecy of the coming of Christ, offering the fulfillment of promise over seven hundred years after Isaiah's day. Therefore, Isaiah's message has an immediate fulfillment in Isaiah's and Ahaz's day, as well as a second fulfillment in Jesus' birth.

The message of Isaiah 7 is followed immediately by another message, this one addressed to Isaiah. God instructs Isaiah to get a large tablet and write on it the name Maher-shalal-hash-baz ("the spoil speeds, the prey hastens") and have witnesses attest to the inscription. Isaiah does so, and then goes in to his wife, the prophetess. She conceives and has a son. God instructs Isaiah to name the child Maher-shal-hash-baz. The message is that before the child can say "my father, my mother"—more likely intending "daddy, mommy"—the king of Assyria will carry off the wealth of Damascus and Samaria, the capitals of Aram-Syria and Israel (8:1–4). Since the message specifies Damascus and Samaria, it clearly belongs to the same time frame. As mentioned above in reference to chapter 7, the events of the next few years fulfill the message-sign.

These two message-signs give hope that within a few years Israel and Aram-Syria will no longer be a threat to Judah. However, the second message also warns that Assyria will invade Judah for Judah's sins. Isaiah warns the people, but they do not repent (vv. 5–15). Nevertheless, Isaiah remains hopeful. His hope is not in the city of Jerusalem or the temple, but in God alone:

> And I will wait on [*chakah*] the LORD,
> Who hides His face from the house of Jacob;
> And I will hope [*qavah*, waited expectantly] in Him.
> Here am I and the children whom the LORD has given me!
> We are for signs [*'ot*] and wonders in Israel
> From the LORD of hosts,
> Who dwells in Mount Zion. (vv. 17–18)

In this passage Isaiah and his children are the message-signs. The names of the two sons, Shear-yashub ("a remnant will return") and Maher-shalal-hash-baz ("the spoil speeds, the prey hastens"), are significant. Maher-shalal-hash-baz is a message-sign that judgment is imminent for Israel and Aram (and will also come on Judah and Jerusalem if they do not repent). Shear-yashub is a message-sign that the judgment is not the last word: a remnant will return from a future judgment and exile. Shear-yashub is living hope for the future.

Isaiah 9 is another of the royal messianic passages:

> For unto us a Child is born,
> Unto us a Son is given;
> And the government will be upon His shoulder.
> And His name will be called
> Wonderful, Counselor, Mighty God,
> Everlasting Father, Prince of Peace.
> Of the increase of His government and peace
> There will be no end,
> Upon the throne of David and over His kingdom,

> To order it and establish it with judgment and justice
> From that time forward, even forever.
> The zeal of the LORD of hosts will perform this. (vv. 6–7)

As in Isaiah 7, the birth of a child lies at the heart of the message. This child is identified as a prince, an heir to the throne. His rule is described as a hope-filled future event. But note that the child-ruler does not accomplish this peaceful rule—God's zeal accomplishes all. Once again all hope rests in God.

Chapter 11 describes a royal messianic figure and a future eschatological reign:

> There shall come forth a Rod from the stem of Jesse,
> And a Branch shall grow out of his roots.
> The Spirit of the LORD shall rest upon Him,
> The Spirit of wisdom and understanding,
> The Spirit of counsel and might,
> The Spirit of knowledge and of the fear of the LORD..
>
> But with righteousness He shall judge the poor,
> And decide with equity for the meek of the earth;
>
> Righteousness shall be the belt of His loins,
> And faithfulness the belt of His waist.
> "The wolf also shall dwell with the lamb,
> The leopard shall lie down with the young goat,
> The calf and the young lion and the fatling together;
> And a little child shall lead them.
>
> The nursing child shall play by the cobra's hole,
> And the weaned child shall put his hand in the viper's den.
> They shall not hurt nor destroy in all My holy mountain,
> For the earth shall be full of the knowledge of the LORD
> As the waters cover the sea."
>
> For the Gentiles shall seek Him,
> And His resting place shall be glorious."
> It shall come to pass in that day
> That the Lord shall set His hand again the second time
> To recover the remnant of His people who are left,
> From Assyria and Egypt.

And will assemble the outcasts of Israel,
And gather together the dispersed of Judah
From the four corners of the earth.
(vv. 1–2, 4a, 5–6, 8–9, 10b–11a, 12b)

The chapter definitely depicts a future royal messianic figure. In addition to ideal rule, there is perfect peace in nature. The king will be filled with God's spirit, and all the earth will be filled with experiential knowledge of him. All people will seek this ruler and his God. As positive as the message is in the earlier verses, the greatest hope is found in verses 11–12. God will restore a remnant of his people from Assyria and Egypt, a remnant from Israel and Judah, and return them from all over the world where they have been dispersed.

These hopeful messianic passages are surrounded with chapters warning of imminent judgment that will occur before the future restoration. After chapter 39, however, the warnings of impending judgment on Israel and Judah almost completely stop.

Chapter 40 opens with hopeful words of comfort. Jerusalem has been judged, convicted, and sentenced, and now has completed her sentence. The message describes God leading his people back from exile to Jerusalem like a shepherd leading his sheep. The message is one of hope to those remaining in Jerusalem and to those in exile in Babylon. The exile is about to end; the exiles and their descendants are about to return home. The time context is just before Cyrus and the Persian army defeat Babylon in 539 BC.

Isaiah 44:24–45:8 is a very significant passage in several ways. It is filled with hope for the return of the people from exile. The passage focuses on the incomparability of God. He is the creator of everything and is the only God—there is no other. God is Israel's redeemer (*go`el*) who will cause Judah and Jerusalem to be rebuilt. God will use Cyrus the Persian ruler as his anointed (*meschie`ach*, "messiah"), his agent, to bring about the return of the people to their land. Cyrus is not the redeemer; God is. Cyrus may not know God, but God knows Cyrus and has raised him up. This good news of imminent return and restoration strengthens the people's belief that God is Lord of all. The people's hope does not depend on a foreign power or ruler; their hope is God—there is no other God, and there is no other hope.

The Second Messianic Messages

Chapters 40–66 of Isaiah include the second kind of messianic passages, those of the servant messiah. The servant image is used both of a messianic figure and of Jacob/Israel, the people. Both are to be God's servants. The servant messiah is described in Isaiah 42 as God's chosen one who will bring justice to the nations (vv. 1–4) in a hope-filled future: "He will not lose hope or give up until he brings justice to the world. / And people far away will trust [*yachal*, wait expectantly] his teachings" (v. 4 NCV).

God then addresses this servant and describes the mission of the servant:

> I, the LORD, have called You in righteousness,
> And will hold Your hand;
> I will keep You and give You as a covenant to the people,
> As a light to the Gentiles,
> To open blind eyes,
> To bring out prisoners from the prison,
> Those who sit in darkness from the prison house.
> I am the LORD, that is My name;
> And My glory I will not give to another,
> Nor My praise to carved images.
> Behold, the former things have come to pass,
> And new things I declare;
> Before they spring forth I tell you of them. (vv. 6–9)

This servant is given by God as a covenant to the people—to all the people, not only Israel and Judah but also to the Gentiles, the nations. This covenant language calls to mind the Davidic covenant in which David and his descendants are to rule over God's people. However, here the language is not royal or dynastic; it is servant language. God describes his chosen leader not as a conquering warrior but as a humble servant in whom all people can hope, trust, and await expectantly.

The severity of the warnings of judgment in the earlier chapters of Isaiah is matched by the assurance of God's comfort and restoration in these latter chapters:

> Listen to Me, My people;
> And give ear to Me, O My nation:
> For law will proceed from Me,
> And I will make My justice [*mishpat*] rest
> As a light of the peoples.
> My righteousness [*tsedeq*] is near,
> My salvation [*yesha`*] has gone forth,
> And My arms will judge the peoples;
> The coastlands will wait upon [*qavah*, hope)] Me,
> And on My arm they will trust [*yachal*, wait expectantly].
> Lift up your eyes to the heavens,
> And look on the earth beneath.
> For the heavens will vanish away like smoke,
> The earth will grow old like a garment,
> And those who dwell in it will die in like manner;
> But My salvation [*yeshua`*] will be forever,
> And My righteousness [*tsedeq*] will not be abolished. (51:4–6)

God addresses the people in first person as "My people"—the relationship is personal and covenantal. But the message also concerns "the peoples"—all nations. The trust or hope of all nations in God and his salvation will last forever. Heaven and earth may pass away, but God's salvation and righteousness will never end.

In Isaiah 61 an unnamed person, quite likely the servant figure, speaks of God's anointing and his mission:

> The Spirit of the Lord GOD is upon Me,
> Because the LORD has anointed [*mashach*] Me
> To preach good tidings to the poor;
> He has sent Me to heal the brokenhearted,
> To proclaim liberty to the captives,
> And the opening of the prison to those who are bound;
> To proclaim the acceptable year of the LORD,
> And the day of vengeance of our God;

> To comfort all who mourn . . . .
> And they shall rebuild the old ruins,
> They shall raise up the former desolations,
>
> And they shall repair the ruined cities,
> The desolations of many generations. (vv. 1–2, 4)

The anointing recalls the royal messianic figure, anointed as a king. But the mission of this person is to preach the good news, to heal, to proclaim liberty, to comfort and console. There is no royal terminology here. The message is of rebuilding and repairing, but the servant is not doing it. The servant proclaims the message; God accomplishes the healing, setting free and comforting; and those whom God has blessed finish the task of rebuilding and repairing. The servant delivers God's message to those who are still hurting, mourning, in bondage, such as the exiles in Babylon. The hope is what God is about to do.

Isaiah's message of hope to God's people in eighth-century BC Judah and Jerusalem warns and then assures of hope beyond judgment. The message speaks to sixth- and fifth-century BC exiles in Babylon and those who remain in Jerusalem and Judah. The message is of hope in an imminent action by God to allow displaced ones to return home. It is a message of restoration and rebuilding.

But Isaiah's message also speaks of a more distant hope, an eschatological hope of full restoration of an ideal Davidic king; of rule under God's guidance with perfect justice, righteousness, and peace for all people; and of Edenic peace and harmony in nature. Christians look to Jesus as the royal-servant messiah who both embodies and proclaims that hope. The final realization of that vision lies in the future, as it did for the original audience.

Jeremiah

The opening lines from Charles Dickens's novel *A Tale of Two Cities* could have been written by the prophet Jeremiah as he looks back over his life and ministry.

> It was the best of times, it was the worst of times, it was the age of wisdom, it was the age of foolishness, it was the epoch of belief, it was the epoch of incredulity, it was the season of Light, it was the season of Darkness, it was the spring of hope, it was the winter of despair . . . .

Jeremiah is often called the "weeping prophet," in part due to his laments to God, his so-called "confessions," and his traditional ascription as the author of Lamentations. Jeremiah, like many of the Old Testament prophets, delivers strong messages of judgment if the people do not repent, as well as messages of hope if they do repent. Unlike most of the other prophets, Jeremiah lives through the very judgment he proclaims. He is often physically attacked and persecuted for his messages by those he seeks to bring to repentance—the people and the political and religious leaders of his land. The "best of times" he experiences include Josiah's short-lived religious reforms and Judah's expansion into parts of the former Northern Kingdom, Israel. The "worst of times" certainly include the destruction of Jerusalem and the temple, the exile of many citizens to Babylon, not once but twice (597 BC and 587/86 BC), and his own forced relocation to Egypt.

Jeremiah receives his call from God in the thirteenth year of Josiah, 627/26 BC, and he continues to proclaim God's message at least until several years after 587 BC. His call is to be God's mouthpiece ("I have put My words in your mouth," 1:9). He considers that call to have come even before he was conceived in his mother's womb (v. 5), and he faithfully carries out the commission throughout his life. His messages, as described in his call, are twofold: judgment ("To root out and to pull down, / To destroy and to throw down") unless the people repent, and hope ("To build and to plant") even after judgment, if there is repentance (v. 10). But people refuse to heed the messages to repent, and so the judgment comes. Even after the destruction of Jerusalem and the exile, the people do not repent or heed his word, so Jeremiah's message to his fellow exiles in Egypt is of judgment (ch. 44). According to Jewish tradition, Jeremiah dies in Egypt as a martyr.

God promises to be with Jeremiah (1:8). That promise of God's presence gives Jeremiah strength to face trials and persecutions and also to cry out in despair, with the assurance that God hears his cries.

Early Messages

Judgment

Jeremiah's early messages are of strong judgment unless the people repent. One primary metaphor Jeremiah uses is that of Israel (or Israel and Judah) as the bride or wife of God. The Sinaitic covenant is the marriage covenant between God and the people. He is their God and they are his people. But Israel proves faithless (3:6–10, for example). As a result:

> Judah saw that I divorced unfaithful Israel because of her adultery, but that didn't make Israel's wicked sister Judah afraid. She also went out and acted like a prostitute! And she didn't care that she was acting like a prostitute. (vv. 8–9 NCV)

That divorce of Israel refers to the fall of the Northern Kingdom to the Assyrians in 722–21 BC. However Judah does not learn from that judgment and is just as faithless as Israel. Even so, God still offers mercy. Even after Israel falls, the situation is not hopeless; judgment need not be the final word. God says:

> Go and proclaim these words toward the north, and say:
>
> "Return [*shuv*, return, repent], backsliding Israel," says the LORD;
> "I will not cause My anger to fall on you.

> For I am merciful [*chasid*, kind, a word closely related to *chesed*,
> steadfast love]," says the LORD;
> "I will not remain angry forever." (v. 12)

God's call for Israel to return and repent is the frequently used prophetic word *shuv*, which includes the meanings of turning (from sin) and returning (to God)—the essence of repentance. Even after the fall of Israel, *if* the remnant of Israel repents, God will be merciful. If Israel repents, God will show *chasid* or *chesed*, steadfast love, lovingkindness—the Hebrew word closest to the New Testament, Greek word, *agape* love.

Judgment comes on Israel. The Southern Kingdom, Judah, also endures an Assyrian invasion during Hezekiah's reign as king. But Hezekiah and the people repent; Hezekiah institutes religious reforms, and God delivers the nation. By Jeremiah's day, Hezekiah's reforms were distant history. Hezekiah's son Manasseh undoes his father's religious reforms by allowing pagan worship and even setting up altars to pagan gods. Despite a later account of Manasseh's repentance (2 Chron. 33:10–13), Manasseh's sins and the sins of the people of Judah in following him are given as the reasons for the ultimate destruction of Judah fifty-five to fifty-six years after his death. Both 2 Kings and Jeremiah state that the sins of Manasseh lead to the destruction of Judah and Jerusalem (2 Kings 21:11–12; Jer. 15:4).

> Truly, in vain [*sheqer*, lie] is salvation hoped for from the hills,
> And from the multitude of mountains;
> Truly, in the LORD our God
> Is the salvation [*teshu`ah*, salvation,
> a word closely related to *yasha`*] of Israel. (3:23)

Hope and Blessing

Jeremiah's temple sermon (recorded in both 7:1–15 and 26:1–19) is one example of public messages that offer hope if the people will heed the call to repent. The sermon, dated to the beginning of King Jehoiakim's reign (609 BC, 26:1), warns the people of Jerusalem that the temple and the city will be destroyed just as Shiloh was destroyed (7:12–15). Shiloh, the central sanctuary of Israel at the time of Eli and Samuel, housed the ark of the covenant. The city was destroyed apparently by the Philistines after they captured the ark in battle (1 Sam. 5–6). The beginning of Jeremiah's temple sermon holds the promise of hope if the people will repent:

> This is what the LORD All-Powerful, the God of Israel, says: Change your lives and do what is right! Then I will let you live in this place. Don't trust the lies of people who say, "This is the Temple of the LORD. This is the Temple of the LORD. This is the Temple of the LORD!" You must change your lives and do what is right. Be fair to each other. You must not be hard on strangers, orphans, and widows. Don't kill innocent people in this place! Don't follow other gods, or they will ruin your lives. If you do these things, I will let you live in this land that I gave to your ancestors to keep forever. (7:3–7 NCV)

This is a tremendous promise, clearly tied, however, to obedience and repentance. Many of the people apparently rely on the promise—made to a previous generation at the time of Isaiah and Hezekiah—that Jerusalem would not fall to the Assyrians in 701 BC. Hezekiah and the people repented then and instituted religious reforms, and God delivered them. But the repentance of that generation will not save the people in Jeremiah's day. They cannot repeat old clichés, "This is the Temple of the LORD," and think that is what God desires. Their hope can rest only in him and in their repentance and right living.

Jeremiah 17:5–8 is a wisdom poem that contrasts those who trust in humans and human resources with those who trust in God. Those who trust in humans are cursed; their situation is hopeless. In contrast: "Blessed is the man who trusts [*batach*] in the LORD, / And whose hope [*mibtach*] is the LORD" (v. 7). Those who put their trust and hope in God will be blessed. In this verse, hope and trust are from the same Hebrew word; the first is a verb, the second a noun. God will fulfill their hope according to their actions and deeds (v. 10).

Jeremiah then relates hope to the temple and the ark of the covenant as a visible symbol of God's presence:

> A glorious high throne from the beginning
> Is the place of our sanctuary.

> O LORD, the hope [*miqveh*] of Israel,
> All who forsake You shall be ashamed.
> "Those who depart from Me
> Shall be written in the earth,
> Because they have forsaken the LORD,
> The fountain of living waters." (vv. 12–13)

The blessing of verse 7 will come to those who trust in God. The temple and ark, though wonderful symbols of his presence and the covenant between God and his people, are not themselves hope. God alone is their hope, as Jeremiah continually reminds the people.

Jeremiah then addresses God, seeking understanding and assurance of his presence in the face of the people's lack of repentance and the suffering and persecution Jeremiah has personally endured:

> Heal me, O LORD, and I shall be healed;
> Save [*hoshe'a,* deliver] me, and I shall be saved,
> For You are my praise. . . .
> Do not be a terror to me;
> You are my hope [*machseh*, refuge] in the day of doom. (vv. 14, 17)

Jeremiah's faith remains strong. He calls on God as the only one who can heal and save him. He affirms God as his hope, or refuge, when God brings judgment on Judah, Jerusalem, and the temple. Jeremiah is not spared from the destruction of Jerusalem and the temple, nor does he ask to be spared. God is his hope and refuge at the time Jerusalem falls and the temple is destroyed.

Jeremiah deals with the refusal of the people to heed God's word, and the hopelessness of realizing judgment will be inevitable. Symbolic actions add a visual aspect to a number of his messages. For example, Jeremiah is directed by God to visit a potter's shop and observe the potter at work (ch. 18). The potter is making a vessel on his wheel: "He was using his hands to make a pot from clay, but something went wrong with it. So he used that clay to make another pot the way he wanted it to be" (v. 4 NCV).

The message from this scene is that nations or people are like the clay in God's hand. The potter can make and shape the pot as he desires—so God can make and shape nations and people. More importantly, the message relates to the judgment or blessing God proposes for nations and people. If God pronounces judgment on a nation and that nation repents, he will not bring that judgment; likewise, if God pronounces blessing on a nation and the nation sins and turns away from him, he will bring judgment rather than blessing (vv. 6–11). The message warns of judgment on a sinful nation but offers hope if the people repent. But the people do not repent. "And they said, 'That is hopeless! So we will walk according to our own plans, and we will every one obey the dictates of his evil heart'" (v. 12).

Despair and Hope

The next chapter has a related symbolic action message. Jeremiah, by God's direction, purchases a pottery vessel from the potter. He then gathers some of the elders and priests and goes to the valley of Hinnom, just outside the city. There he announces impending judgment on the city and nation:

> Hear the word of the Lord, O kings of Judah and inhabitants of Jerusalem. Thus says the Lord of hosts, the God of Israel: "Behold, I will bring such a catastrophe on this place, that whoever hears of it, his ears will tingle.
>
> "Because they have forsaken Me and made this an alien place, because they have burned incense in it to other gods whom neither they, their fathers, nor the kings of Judah have known, and have filled this place with the blood of the innocents (they have also built the high places of Baal, to burn their sons with fire for burnt offerings to Baal, which I did not command or speak, nor did it come into My mind), therefore behold, the days are coming," says the Lord, "that this place shall no more be called Tophet or the Valley of the Son of Hinnom, but the Valley of Slaughter. . . .
>
> "Then you shall break the flask in the sight of the men who go with you, and say to them, 'Thus says the Lord of hosts: "Even so I will break this people and this city, as one breaks a potter's vessel, which

cannot be made whole again; and they shall bury them in Tophet till there is no place to bury.'" (19:3–6, 10–11)

In chapter 18, opportunity still exists for judgment to be averted, if the people repent. By chapter 19 the situation and the message change radically: judgment is inevitable. The vessel that has been fired is no longer pliable; the potter can't remake it. If the nation has become so set in its sins, judgment will come—the vessel will be shattered. The message sounds hopeless. Jerusalem and Judah will be destroyed. The hope possible in chapter 18 is gone. But is all hope gone?

The people do call on God in times of despair and destruction. They do profess their hope in him. But their current situation seems hopeless:

> God, the Hope [*miqveh*, hope] of Israel,
> you have saved Israel in times of trouble.
> Why are you like a stranger in the land,
> or like a traveler who only stays one night? . . . .
>
> LORD, have you completely rejected the nation of Judah?
> Do you hate Jerusalem?
> Why have you hurt us so badly
> that we cannot be made well again?
> We hoped [*qavah*, waited expectantly for] for peace,
> but nothing good has come.
> We looked for a time of healing,
> but only terror came. . . .
> Do foreign idols have the power to bring rain?
> Does the sky itself have the power to send down showers?
> No, it is you, LORD our God.
> You are our only hope
> [*qavah*, literally, we waited expectantly for you],
> because you are the one who made all these things.
> (14:8, 19, 22 NCV)

Their final word is not despair. Even as the people experience devastation all around them, they affirm that foreign idols and deities have no power or authority. Their hope is in God alone. In their despair, they address their prayers and petitions to God in whom they still hope.

Even after the exile of 597 BC, when King Jehoiachin and many of the leaders of Judah are taken to Babylon; the situation is not hopeless—not for those in exile, and not for those remaining in the land. Jeremiah has words of comfort and hope for both groups, but only if they trust in God. The message of hope to King Zedekiah, placed on the throne by Nebuchadnezzar after Jehoiachin is deported to Babylon, calls for Zedekiah to submit to the yoke of Babylon, accepting that as God's judgment for Judah's sins (ch. 27). In another symbolic action message, Jeremiah comes into the assembly of leaders from several nations, including Zedekiah, wearing a wooden yoke on his shoulders and speaks God's message: "I also spoke to Zedekiah king of Judah according to all these words, saying, 'Bring your necks under the yoke of the king of Babylon, and serve him and his people, and live!'" (v. 12). There is hope, life, *if* Zedekiah and the people submit to Babylon, and *if* they repent and serve God.

Later Messages

Exile and Hope

Jeremiah communicates with the first exiles sent to Babylon in 597 BC (ch. 29). Unlike many of the false prophets who keep telling exiles that captivity will be short, Jeremiah tells them the exile will be lengthy but, even in exile, they can find hope.

> Thus says the LORD of hosts, the God of Israel, to all who were carried away captive, whom I have caused to be carried away from Jerusalem to Babylon: Build houses and dwell in them; plant gardens and eat their fruit. Take wives and beget sons and daughters; and take wives for your sons and give your daughters to husbands, so that they may bear sons and daughters—that you may be increased there, and not diminished. And seek the peace [*shalom*] of the city where I have caused you to be carried away captive, and pray to the LORD for it; for in its peace you will have peace. (vv. 4–7)

> For thus says the LORD: After seventy years are completed at Babylon, I will visit you and perform My good word toward you, and cause you to return to this place. For I know the thoughts that I think toward you, says the LORD, thoughts of peace and not of evil, to give you a future and a hope. Then you will call upon Me and go and pray to Me, and I will listen to you. And you will seek Me and find Me, when you search for Me with all your heart. I will be found by you, says the LORD, and I will bring you back from your captivity; I will gather you from all the nations and from all the places where I have driven you, says the LORD, and I will bring you to the place from which I cause you to be carried away captive. (vv. 10–14)

First, the people must realize that the exile will last a long time, and second, they are to make the most of their exile—build houses, plant crops, and raise families. Third, they are to pray for Babylon and Babylon's peace or well-being (*shalom*), because in Babylon's peace they will find peace. Fourth, and most important, they are to remain full of hope. For when the years of exile are completed, God promises to bring the exiles back home. The promise is one of peace and restoration and a promise to give the exiles both "a future and a hope" (v. 11). God's judgment in the exile is not the final word; God's final word is hope.

Jeremiah 30 and 31 have a concentration of messages of hope. These two chapters are part of the larger "Book of Consolation" or "Book of Comfort" (chs. 30–33). The passages focus on God's promise of a future restoration of the people—of Israel and Judah.

> The word that came to Jeremiah from the LORD, saying, "Thus speaks the LORD God of Israel, saying: 'Write in a book for yourself all the words that I have spoken to you. For behold, the days are coming,' says the LORD, 'that I will bring back from captivity My people Israel and Judah,' says the LORD. 'And I will cause them to return to the land that I gave to their fathers, and they shall possess it.'" (30:1–3)

The passage speaks of the captivity of both Israel and Judah—so it presupposes either the exile of 597 BC or the later one of 587–86 BC. The central message is that God will bring both Israel and Judah back from captivity, back to the promised land. The Hebrew word used here is *shuv*, the same word used regularly in the Prophets meaning to turn, return, and repent.

The word of warning calling the people to repent is also a word of hope in that God will bring them back from exile and cause them to return to their land.

> Alas! For that day is great,
> So that none is like it;
> And it is the time of Jacob's trouble,
> But he shall be saved out of it.
>
> "For it shall come to pass in that day,"
> Says the LORD of hosts,
> "That I will break his yoke from your neck,
> And will burst your bonds;
> Foreigners shall no more enslave them.
> But they shall serve the LORD their God,
> And David their king,
> Whom I will raise up for them.
>
> "Therefore do not fear, O My servant Jacob," says the LORD,
> "Nor be dismayed, O Israel;
> For behold, I will save you from afar,
> And your seed from the land of their captivity.
> Jacob shall return, have rest and be quiet,
> And no one shall make him afraid.
> For I am with you," says the LORD, "to save you;
> Though I make a full end of all nations where I have scattered you,
> Yet I will not make a complete end of you.
> But I will correct you in justice,
> And will not let you go altogether unpunished." (vv. 7–11)

The message continues, speaking of the destruction of both Israel and Judah as the time of Jacob's trouble. Yet again, this judgment is not the final word. There will come a time when Jacob will be saved, delivered beyond the judgment. God places a yoke on Judah, a yoke of servitude to Babylon (ch. 27). However, God will break that yoke, and the people will serve him.

He will save Jacob/Israel. Jacob will return (*shuv*). God again promises his divine presence: "I am with you to save you" (30:11).

The future message of hope continues: "'At the same time,' says the LORD, 'I will be the God of all the families of Israel, and they shall be My people'" (31:1). The language is reminiscent of Hosea 1–2 and Jeremiah 7:23: "I will be their God and they will be my people." The language offers the hope that all Israel (Israel and Judah) will acknowledge God as God, and they will be restored into right relationship with him as his people.

Rebuilding and Replanting

Despite the judgment Jeremiah experiences alongside the people of Judah and Jerusalem, despite living through the invasions of 597 BC and 587–86 BC, despite witnessing the exile of two kings and thousands of citizens to Babylon, despite seeing his city and his beloved temple ransacked and burned, despite his being forcibly taken to Egypt by well-intentioned but misguided zealots, judgment and exile are not the final words of God through the mouth of Jeremiah. The final word is still of hope, restoration, and return to the land.

Thus says the LORD:

> "A voice was heard in Ramah,
> Lamentation and bitter weeping,
> Rachel weeping for her children,
> Refusing to be comforted for her children,
> Because they are no more."

Thus says the LORD:

> "Refrain your voice from weeping,
> And your eyes from tears;
> For your work shall be rewarded, says the LORD,
> And they shall come back from the land of the enemy.
> There is hope in your future, says the LORD,
> That your children shall come back
> to their own border." (31:15–17)

Rachel was the mother of Joseph and Benjamin: the tribe of Benjamin and the half-tribes of Ephraim and Manasseh. The message is one of future hope for those tribes of the Northern Kingdom of Israel, hope for their return and restoration. Matthew cites this passage in reference to Herod's killing of the infants in Bethlehem (2:18). In Jeremiah, however, the message is not of grief; instead it is a message of great hope. Rachel is to take hope in the ultimate return of her children to their land. Jacob's children, the people of Israel, will be restored; Rachel's children will return. Indeed this is a future with hope!

The message of hope in Jeremiah 31 continues:

> Behold, the days are coming, says the LORD, that I will sow the house of Israel and the house of Judah with the seed of man and the seed of beast. And it shall come to pass, that as I have watched over them to pluck up, to break down, to throw down, to destroy, and to afflict, so I will watch over them to build and to plant, says the LORD. (vv. 27–28).

This message of future hope (days are coming—they are not here yet) includes both Israel and Judah. In this message of hope, God's words through Jeremiah recall the words of Jeremiah's initial call experience. The very words of judgment and hope that God placed in Jeremiah's mouth (1:9–10) become the basis for hope for Israel and Judah. In the original call, God said he had set Jeremiah over nations and kingdoms. In Jeremiah's lifetime, the judgment of at least two of those nations has been determined: Israel and Judah. They have already experienced and are experiencing the judgments; now God is watching over (*shaqed*, to watch over, either in judgment or blessing as in Jeremiah 1:11–12) them to bless, restore, and build them. The Hebrew words for "plant" and "build" can have the connotation of replanting and rebuilding, which fits the context in chapter 31. Envisioned is a future rebuilding of Jerusalem and replanting of gardens and vineyards in Judah and Israel.

The new covenant passage of 31:31–34 is one of the best known and often-quoted passages from Jeremiah.

> Behold, the days are coming, says the LORD, when I will make a new covenant with the house of Israel and with the house of Judah—not according to the covenant that I made with their fathers in the day that I took them by the hand to lead them out of the land of Egypt, My covenant which they broke, though I was a husband to them, says the LORD. But this is the covenant that I will make with the house of Israel after those days, says the LORD: I will put My law in their minds, and write it on their hearts; and I will be their God, and they shall be My people. No more shall every man teach his neighbor, and every man his brother, saying, "Know the LORD," for they all shall know Me, from the least of them to the greatest of them, says the LORD. For I will forgive their iniquity, and their sin I will remember no more.

This is also among the most hopeful passages in the book, although no specific word for hope appears in the passage. Several very important statements or promises are made here. First, the covenant itself is new or renewed. Normally, the newness of the covenant is emphasized. However, there is also a definite sense in which this new covenant is a renewal of the original covenant. The content of the new covenant is the same as the original covenant—the law God gave in Sinai. The newness relates to the personal aspect of the covenant. This covenant will not be written on tablets of stone; it will be written on the heart of each person. Although the people remain the same—the house of Israel and Judah—the emphasis is individual rather than national. The new/renewed covenant is between God and each individual as part of the community—God will put his law in all of their minds and write it on all of their hearts. All people, from the least to the greatest, will know (*yada`*, to know personally, intimately) him. Although we typically end our reference to Jeremiah's new covenant passage at verse 34, the passage actually continues for three more verses. These describe the impossibility of the new/renewed covenant being rescinded or revoked:

> Thus says the LORD,
>
> > Who gives the sun for a light by day,
> > The ordinances of the moon and the stars for a light by night,
> > Who disturbs the sea,

And its waves roar
(The LORD of hosts is His name):

"If those ordinances depart
From before Me, says the LORD,
Then the seed of Israel shall also cease
From being a nation before Me forever."

Thus says the LORD:

"If heaven above can be measured,
And the foundations of the earth searched out beneath,
I will also cast off all the seed of Israel
For all that they have done, says the LORD. (vv. 35–37)

The prophets often describe the incomparability of God ("To whom then will you liken Me, or to whom shall I be equal?" says the Holy One [Isa. 40:25]; Isa. 40:12–26; 46:5; and others). Here Jeremiah uses the image of God's incomparable authority over nature to say that Israel will cease to be a nation before God only if the natural order comes to an end. These verses add a time dimension to the hope of the new/renewed covenant. When those future days of the new/renewed covenant come to pass, they will last as long as the natural order endures—forever.

Our hope today is the same as Jeremiah's hope—with one addition. Jeremiah's hope is not in armies, fortifications, or weapons of mass destruction. It is not in religion, in temples, or even in the temple in Jerusalem. Just as Jeremiah's hope is in God alone, we, too, hope only in God. The additional hope we have today is the hope based on his supreme act of love and grace in Christ's life, atoning death, and resurrection. These give additional substance to our faith and to our hope.

Lamentations

The book of Lamentations, as its title suggests, is a series of laments especially related to the fall of Jerusalem and destruction of the temple by the Babylonians in 587–86 BC. Traditionally the book is associated with Jeremiah the prophet. Chapters 1–4 are all alphabetic acrostics, a type of Hebrew poetry in which each verse (three verses in ch. 3) starts with a successive letter of the Hebrew alphabet.

Anguish and Hope Then

The book clearly describes the anguish of the writer and the other survivors at the loss of Jerusalem, the temple, and the nation. The laments describe the conditions eyewitnesses who survived the catastrophe experience in the aftermath of the devastation. The laments express bitter complaints at times, depicting a situation that seems hopeless. The siege and fall of Jerusalem brought not only death but also exile of many of the citizens. The aftermath includes more suffering and death from hunger and starvation.

> The stones of the Temple are scattered
>   at every street corner. . . .
> The babies are so thirsty
>   their tongues stick to the roofs of their mouths.
> Children beg for bread,
>   but no one gives them any.
> Those who once ate fine foods
>   are now starving in the streets.
> People who grew up wearing nice clothes
>   now pick through trash piles. . . .
> Their skin hangs on their bones;
>   it is as dry as wood.
> Those who were killed in the war were better off
>   than those killed by hunger.
> They starve in pain and die,
>   because there is no food from the field.

With their own hands kind women
cook their own children.
They became food
when my people were destroyed. (4:1–10 NCV)

Even in the midst of the hopelessness of lament, despair, and anguish, Lamentations offers a message of hope, which forms the center of the book, in 3:21–33. Anguish and grief surround this section in the two chapters before and the two chapters after, and also in the twenty verses of chapter 3 before and the thirty-three verses after. But at the very center of the book we find hope. The reasons for God's judgment are stated clearly—the sins and rebellion of the people. They rejected God, his covenant, and his commandments (1:8, 18). Their priests and prophets led them astray with false prophecies and teaching (2:14). The situation seems hopeless: "And I said, 'My strength and my hope (*yachal*, hope, waiting expectantly) / Have perished from the LORD'" (3:18).

But still the author finds hope! Not hope in the people themselves, not hope in any human agency or deliverer, but hope in God, in his mercy and grace. In the midst of despair, the author remembers God's steadfast love and mercy:

This I recall to my mind,
Therefore I have hope [*yachal*, hope, waiting expectantly].
Through the LORD's mercies we are not consumed,
Because His compassions fail not.
They are new every morning;
Great is Your faithfulness.
"The LORD is my portion," says my soul,
"Therefore I hope [*yachal*, hope, waiting expectantly] in Him!"
The LORD is good to those who wait [*qavah*, hope, wait] for Him,
To the soul who seeks Him.
It is good that one should hope
[*yachal*, hope, waiting expectantly] and wait quietly
For the salvation of the LORD. (vv. 21–26)

Despair is overcome by the awareness of God's grace. The lament shifts to praise and hope as the writer realizes the situation is not hopeless. Even in suffering, God has still given him life and a new day. Therein lies hope. Every day can bring hope as well as despair. Hope derives not from the author's situation or condition; hope derives from God's compassion, mercy, and faithfulness. Even in the midst of suffering: "there is still hope (*tiqveh*, hope). . . . / The Lord will not reject his people forever. / Although he brings sorrow, he also has mercy and great love" (vv. 29b, 31–32 NCV).

Anguish and Hope Today

What does Lamentations say to us today? Most of us have never faced anything like what the author of Lamentations is facing. He lives through and personally witnesses the destruction of his nation, the death of hundreds or thousands of friends and relatives, the exile of many more to a foreign land as prisoners of war, and the suffering and starvation of ones left behind. The Holocaust of World War II and the more recent wars of genocide and ethnic cleansing are recent reminders of such widespread suffering and despair. One might also consider those widespread areas devastated by natural disasters, such as earthquakes, tsunamis, or tornados. More often we think of personal situations that can seem so hopeless—a diagnosis of cancer, loss of a loved one, loss of a job or home. At those times we may feel the kind of despair the author of Lamentations describes.

Yet we also affirm the hope of the author of Lamentations, and more. Because we live on this side of the cross, our hope is grounded in all the hope of the Old Testament and the atonement completed in Christ's death and resurrection. Our hope has that additional evidence of God's mercy and love. His love and mercy are indeed new and renewed every day. Every new day brings the promise and assurance of his presence with us, his creation. God's presence with us is the very basis of our hope. It is not the simplistic hope of enjoying the "good life" all the time. It is instead the hope and assurance of God being with us in the midst of every aspect of life and death—God-with-us in the happiness of life and God-with-us in the tragedies—just as God was found and affirmed by the author of Lamentations in the center of his grief and lament over the loss of family, friends, capital city, temple, and nation.

Ezekiel

Ezekiel is a priest living in Jerusalem who is taken captive to Babylon with the exiles in 597 BC. He lives among a community of Jewish exiles at Tel Abib on the River Chebar. Ezekiel's father's name is Buzi; he is also a priest. Ezekiel is married; his wife dies in Babylon. There is no mention of them having any children. The exiles in Babylon are not persecuted severely. They are able to practice their occupations. They build homes—Ezekiel mentions that he lives in a house (3:24). They even have some communication with those remaining in Jerusalem (33:21).

In the fifth year of the exile, 593 BC, Ezekiel has a call vision. The book of Ezekiel opens with the call experience using another date formula, the thirtieth year, probably referring to Ezekiel's age at the time of his call. In his call experience, Ezekiel has a vision of the glory of God on a chariot throne. Through this vision, God calls Ezekiel to prophesy to the house of Israel. God gives Ezekiel a scroll filled with words to eat. The eating of the scroll is the metaphor for God giving his word to Ezekiel.

The book of Ezekiel is divided into three parts. Chapters 1–24 are primarily oracles against Judah and Jerusalem. These oracles belong mainly to the period before 587 BC, before the fall of Jerusalem. They warn of the judgment to come upon Judah and Jerusalem for their sins. Chapters 25–32 are primarily oracles of judgment against foreign nations. These belong to the period after the fall of Judah and Jerusalem in 587 BC. The foreign nations are judged because they took advantage of the fall of Judah to enlarge their borders or because they assisted Babylon in the destruction of Jerusalem. Chapters 33–48 are oracles concerning the deliverance of the house of Israel and the restoration of the temple and the land. Most of the hope in the book of Ezekiel is found in the third part, the focus for this study.

Part one gives the justification for God's judgment on Judah and Jerusalem due to their continued rebellion and sinfulness after the first exile in 597 BC. Chapters 8–11 are a series of visions in which Ezekiel is transported to Jerusalem and observes abominable practices by the priests and leaders taking place in the temple. In the visions Ezekiel also sees the glory of the Lord that was over the cherubim in the holy of holies in the temple. The glory departs in stages from the holy of holies to the porch of the temple, then through the east gate of the temple, and finally to the Mount of Olives east of Jerusalem. The vision depicts God leaving the temple and Jerusalem because of the sinfulness of the people. The message is that he has abandoned the temple and city before it falls to the Babylonians. He does so because of the idolatry of the people. God then allows the Babylonians to capture the city. The situation seems to be absolutely hopeless. How can the people of Jerusalem have any hope if God abandons them to the consequences of their sinfulness? As hopeless as God's abandonment is, it is not his final word through Ezekiel.

Rebellion and Restoration

Ezekiel 20 is an oracle that recounts Israel's history—past sinfulness and rebellions against God. The present generation is no different from previous ones. They remain sinful and rebellious. God now brings the full brunt of his judgment on his people, but judgment is still not his final word:

> "For on My holy mountain, on the mountain height of Israel," says the Lord GOD, "there all the house of Israel, all of them in the land, shall serve Me; there I will accept them. . . . I will accept you as a sweet aroma when I bring you out from the peoples and gather you out of the countries where you have been scattered. . . . Then you shall know that I am the LORD, when I bring you into the land of Israel, into the country for which I raised My hand in an oath to give to your fathers. . . . Then you shall know that I am the LORD, when I have dealt with you for My name's sake, not according to your wicked ways nor according to your corrupt doings, O house of Israel," says the Lord GOD. (20:40–44)

Alongside the judgment is restoration and forgiveness. At a future time, God will bring back the exiles from all the lands where they have been scattered. He will bring back all the house of Israel; they will all serve God, and he will accept them all. God will deal with them not as they deserve because of their wicked ways but mercifully for his name's sake.

God speaks against the human leaders of Israel, shepherds who have been feeding themselves on the sheep rather than feeding the sheep (34:1–10). Now God himself will be the shepherd for his people:

> For thus says the Lord God: "Indeed I Myself will search for My sheep . . . and deliver them from all the places where they were scattered. . . . And I will bring them out from the peoples . . . and will bring them to their own land. . . . I will feed My flock, and I will make them lie down," says the Lord God. "I will seek what was lost and bring back what was driven away, bind up the broken and strengthen what was sick." (vv. 11–16)

This message speaks of a hopeful future that includes deliverance and restoration of exiles to the land. God himself will feed them and make them lie down to rest (Ps. 23). Moreover God will search for lost sheep and bring them back; he will bind up the injured and heal the sick. Hope trumps judgment! The message of hope continues:

> "I will make a covenant of peace [*shalom*] with them. . . . I will make them and the places all around My hill a blessing; and I will cause showers to come down in their season; there shall be showers of blessing. Then the trees of the field shall yield their fruit, and the earth shall yield her increase. . . . Thus they shall know that I, the Lord their God, am with them, and they, the house of Israel, are My people," says the Lord God. "You are My flock, the flock of My pasture; you are men, and I am your God," says the Lord God. (34:25–31)

This hope includes a restoration of nature as well. God will establish a covenant of *shalom* with the people, a covenant of peace or well-being. In this new covenant relationship, all the house of Israel will know that God is with them—the promise of his presence, of Immanuel, God-with-us. They will also know that they are God's people and he is their God. That is a promise of great hope.

The message of hope continues in Ezekiel 36:

> I will give you a new heart and put a new spirit within you; I will take the heart of stone out of your flesh and give you a heart of flesh. I will put My Spirit within you and cause you to walk in My statutes, and you will keep My judgments and do them. Then you shall dwell in the land that I gave to your fathers; you shall be My people, and I will be your God. . . . And I will multiply the fruit of your trees and the increase of your fields, so that you need never again bear the reproach of famine among the nations. . . . Thus says the Lord GOD: "On the day that I cleanse you from all your iniquities, I will also enable you to dwell in the cities, and the ruins shall be rebuilt. . . . So they will say, 'This land that was desolate has become like the garden of Eden; and the wasted, desolate, and ruined cities are now fortified and inhabited.'" (36:26–28, 30, 33, 35)

The hope is God's promise to put a new heart and spirit in the people. With this new heart and spirit, the people will faithfully worship God and follow all of his commandments. This restoration will include a renewal of nature as well as a rebuilding of the cities. The land will become like the garden of Eden. The future restoration is almost like a return to God's original creation—people and nature as it was before the fall. Such is the hope of Ezekiel's vision!

Dry Bones

One of the more famous visions in Ezekiel is that of the valley of dry bones. During a vision, Ezekiel is taken to a valley or plain filled with bones, most likely unburied bodies on a battlefield. God asks him if the bones can live again. Ezekiel responds that only God knows. God tells Ezekiel to prophesy to the bones, and he does. God then says:

> "Thus says the Lord GOD to these bones: 'Surely I will cause breath [*ruach*, wind, spirit] to enter into you, and you shall live. I will put sinews

> on you and bring flesh upon you, cover you with skin and put breath [*ruach*, wind, spirit] in you; and you shall live. Then you shall know that I am the LORD.'" . . . Also He said to me, "Prophesy to the breath [*ruach*, wind, spirit], prophesy, son of man, and say to the breath [*ruach*, wind, spirit], 'Thus says the Lord GOD: "Come from the four winds [*ruach*, breath, wind, spirit—here plural], O breath [*ruach*, wind, spirit], and breathe on these slain, that they may live.'" So I prophesied as He commanded me, and breath [*ruach*, wind, spirit] came into them, and they lived, and stood upon their feet, an exceedingly great army. Then He said to me, "Son of man, these bones are the whole house of Israel. They indeed say, 'Our bones are dry, our hope [*tiqvah*] is lost, and we ourselves are cut off'! Therefore prophesy and say to them, 'Thus says the Lord GOD: . . ."I will put My Spirit [*ruach*, breath, wind, spirit)] in you, and you shall live, and I will place you in your own land. Then you shall know that I, the LORD, have spoken it and performed it," says the LORD.'" (37:5–6, 9–12, 14)

This passage has one of the explicit references to hope in Ezekiel—the people say "our hope is lost" (v. 11)—but the passage expresses tremendous hope. The people are described as being like the sun-bleached bones—without any life. But the hope of new life is described by the Hebrew word *ruach* that means breath, wind, or spirit. In this passage the Hebrew word is translated by all three words. The passage is not primarily about resurrection, though some commentators interpret it in that manner. Instead, it describes God restoring the people to the land—a message filled with hope of new life in the land.

Hope in God's Presence

Chapters 40–42 describe a vision of the new temple in Jerusalem, with detailed dimensions of the buildings, gates, and courts. Chapter 43 is a vision describing the return of the glory of God, which reverses the description of the departure of God's glory in Ezekiel 11. This vision has the glory coming from the east and entering the temple grounds through the eastern gate:

> Behold, the glory of the God of Israel came from the way of the east. His voice was like the sound of many waters; and the earth shone with His glory. It was like the appearance of the vision which I saw—like the vision which I saw when I came to destroy the city. . . . And the glory of the LORD came into the temple by way of the gate which faces toward the east. The Spirit lifted me up and brought me into the inner court; and behold, the glory of the LORD filled the temple. (vv. :2–5)

God then describes the Holy of Holies in the new temple: "He said to me, 'Son of man, this is the place of My throne and the place of the soles of My feet, where I will dwell in the midst of the children of Israel forever'" (v. 7). The new temple is God's dwelling place; the Holy of Holies houses his throne and footstool. He promises to dwell in the temple in the midst of his people forever. This new temple is not one God will abandon. His presence in the temple is further symbolized:

> Then He brought me back to the outer gate of the sanctuary which faces toward the east, but it was shut. And the LORD said to me, "This gate shall be shut; it shall not be opened, and no man shall enter by it, because the LORD God of Israel has entered by it; therefore it shall be shut." (44:1–2)

The hope of the new temple vision is God's eternal presence in the temple and in the midst of the people. As Christians, we share in that hope on an even more personal level. Our hope is not on a new temple in Jerusalem. Our hope is in the indwelling of God's Spirit through Christ within us—our bodies are the new temple (1 Cor. 6:19).

Ezekiel 47 describes a spring flowing eastward from the threshold of the temple, becoming a river as it flows to the Dead Sea. Trees are all along the banks of the river. When the river reaches the Dead Sea, the waters of the sea are healed—the sea becomes fresh water and is filled with fish. On the banks of the river grow all kinds of trees. The trees bear fruit every month; the leaves do not wither. The fruit is for food, and the leaves are for medicinal uses (vv. 1–12). This river flowing from the temple is further evidence of God's presence. The fruitfulness is another Edenic image. Like the goodness of God's creation in Eden, so is the goodness of the new temple in a restored Jerusalem.

To exiles in Babylonia after the fall of Jerusalem in 587 BC, the visions of the new temple in a new city of Jerusalem is a most hopeful message. Hope resides in God's presence in the temple in the midst of his people. The last verse of Ezekiel closes on that same hope: "and the name of the city from that day shall be: THE LORD IS THERE" (48:35).

Daniel

Obedience and Hope

The book of Daniel can be divided into two parts: narratives about Daniel and his friends (chs. 1–6) and Daniel's visions (chs. 7–12). Daniel is among the youths carried into exile to Babylon by Nebuchadnezzar in the third year of King Jehoiachim's reign (1:1–2; see also 2 Chron. 36:5–7). No other information about Daniel or his family is given in the book.

Nebuchadnezzar orders his chief attendant to select some of the brightest youths from the elite of Judah and Jerusalem. The chief attendant is charged with educating and preparing these young men to serve in Nebuchadnezzar's palace. Daniel and three of his friends are among those chosen. They are to be educated for three years and then appear before the king. The young men receive royal rations of food and wine. Daniel proposes that he and his three friends—known by their Babylonian names as Shadrach, Meshach, and Abed-Nego—be allowed to eat only vegetables and drink water rather than the royal delicacies and wine. As faithful Israelites, Daniel and his friends do not want to defile themselves. After a ten-day test period, Daniel and his friends look better than all the others in training. So Daniel and his friends continue to eat the vegetables and drink only water. At the end of the training period, when the king interviews them, he finds Daniel and his three friends exceed all the magicians and astrologers in the kingdom (ch. 1). The narrative is an encouragement for the readers/hearers of the book of Daniel to keep pure in diet and behavior even in difficult situations, such as living as exiles in a foreign land.

In chapter 2, Nebuchadnezzar has a dream and commands his astrologers, magicians, and sorcerers to tell him his dream and its interpretation. They all claim that no one can tell him his dream and ask him to tell them the dream so they can interpret it. Nebuchadnezzar then commands they all be killed if they cannot tell him his dream. Daniel learns of the situation and asks his friends to pray for him. The dream is given to Daniel in a night vision. He tells Nebuchadnezzar both the dream and its interpretation. Nebuchadnezzar confesses God as the God of gods, and promotes Daniel over all the province of Babylon and also promotes the three friends. The narrative demonstrates God's power and control over foreign rulers and his blessing on his faithful followers.

In chapter 3, Nebuchadnezzar sets up a gold image and commands everyone to bow down and worship it. The three friends, Shadrach, Meshach, and Abed-Nego, refuse (Daniel is not mentioned in this narrative). The king commands them to bow down and worship the image or be thrown into a fiery furnace. They still refuse:

> If that is the case, our God whom we serve is able to deliver us from the burning fiery furnace, and He will deliver us from your hand, O king. But if not, let it be known to you, O king, that we do not serve your gods, nor will we worship the gold image which you have set up. (vv. 17–18)

Nebuchadnezzar then has the furnace heated seven times hotter than usual, and the three are thrown into the furnace. The furnace is so hot it kills the men who throw the friends in the furnace, but the friends are unharmed. Nebuchadnezzar sees a fourth one in the furnace: "and the form of the fourth is like the Son of God" (v. 25). Nebuchadnezzar calls for the three to come out and blesses God:

> Nebuchadnezzar spoke, saying, "Blessed be the God of Shadrach, Meshach, and Abed-Nego, who sent His Angel and delivered His servants who trusted in Him, and they have frustrated the king's word, and yielded their bodies, that they should not serve nor worship any god except their own God!" (v. 28)

He orders that anyone who speaks against God be killed, and he promotes the three friends. The message encourages people to remain faithful to God even under dire threats. Shadrach, Meshach, and Abed-Nego place their hope and faith in God. They remain obedient to God, refusing to compromise their faith even under death threat.

In chapter 6 Darius has become the king. He has made Daniel one of three officials over the whole kingdom. The governors of the provinces try to find some charge to bring against Daniel. The only way they find to charge him is in his religion, his faith. They have Darius sign a decree that requires the death of anyone who prays to any god or any person except Darius for thirty days. Any person who defies the decree will be thrown into a lions' den. Daniel continues his practice of praying to God three times a day, even though he knows of the king's decree. The men report Daniel's disobedience to Darius. Darius does not want to have Daniel thrown into the lions' den, but even he must follow his own edict.

> So the king gave the command, and they brought Daniel and cast him into the den of lions. But the king spoke, saying to Daniel, "Your God, whom you serve continually, He will deliver you." Then a stone was brought and laid on the mouth of the den, and the king sealed it with his own signet ring and with the signets of his lords, that the purpose concerning Daniel might not be changed. Now the king went to his palace and spent the night fasting; and no musicians were brought before him. Also his sleep went from him. Then the king arose very early in the morning and went in haste to the den of lions. And when he came to the den, he cried out with a lamenting voice to Daniel. The king spoke, saying to Daniel, "Daniel, servant of the living God, has your God, whom you serve continually, been able to deliver you from the lions?" Then Daniel said to the king, "O king, live forever! My God sent His angel and shut the lions' mouths, so that they have not hurt me, because I was found innocent before Him; and also, O king, I have done no wrong before you." Now the king was exceedingly glad for him, and commanded that they should take Daniel up out of the den. So Daniel was taken up out of the den, and no injury whatever was found on him, because he believed in his God. (vv. 16–23)

Darius orders those who had accused Daniel and their families be thrown into the lions' den. They are immediately killed by the lions.

> Then King Darius wrote:
>
> > To all peoples, nations, and languages that dwell in all the earth:
> >
> > Peace be multiplied to you.

I make a decree that in every dominion of my kingdom men must tremble and fear before the God of Daniel.

For He is the living God,
And steadfast forever;
His kingdom is the one which shall not be destroyed,
And His dominion shall endure to the end.

He delivers and rescues,
And He works signs and wonders
In heaven and on earth,
Who has delivered Daniel
from the power of the lions. (vv. 25–27)

Daniel remains faithful to God despite the threat of death, and God honors Daniel's faithfulness with protection and deliverance. Darius confesses that God is the living God, just as Nebuchadnezzar had done earlier. The message is: remain steadfast in faithfulness even in very difficult situations and God will deliver. That is the hope consistently indicated in the narratives of Daniel 1–6.

The Future and Hope

Daniel 7–12 is a series of visions Daniel receives and narrates in first person. The visions depict an apocalyptic future in which the righteous face great persecution from evil powers. Several of the visions point to the rise of Antiochus Epiphanes and his desecration of the temple in 167 BC. Other visions may refer to the coming of the Romans. In the end God will defeat the evil powers and establish his kingdom. The righteous will ultimately reign with God. The book closes with a promise to Daniel that he, too, will share in the promises of the kingdom of God: "But you, go your way till the end; for you shall rest, and will arise to your inheritance at the end of the days" (12:13). That promise of God's kingdom at the end of days is Daniel's hope. For those who endure the great persecutions, such as those under Antiochus Epiphanes, their hope also lies in God's ultimate victory and reign and in their participation in that kingdom in the resurrection. In both the narratives and visions, hope is in God.

Hosea

The prophet Hosea is considered to be a contemporary of the prophet Amos. Hosea's ministry would be sometime in the middle of the eighth century, 750 BC or a little later than Amos. Hosea is the only prophet native to the Northern Kingdom of Israel and whose ministry is specifically to the Northern Kingdom. Amos, on the other hand, is from Judah, the Southern Kingdom, but is called to go and prophesy to Israel, specifically at Bethel, one of the sanctuaries of the Northern Kingdom.

The Family of Hosea; the Family of God

The entire book of Hosea is organized around the dual theme of judgment and hope. The first three chapters use Hosea's family situation as a parallel or analogy to Israel's religious situation. God calls Hosea to marry a prostitute, Gomer, and he does so. The interpretation that Gomer is faithful when they are first married and becomes a prostitute later is followed here. This interpretation fits the analogy the book of Hosea presents in depicting Israel's relationship with God. Israel was faithful in the wilderness but turned to the Baals and other gods when they entered the promised land.

Gomer has three children during the time she and Hosea are married. All three children are given symbolic names reflecting Israel's unfaithfulness and the judgment God will bring on Israel if they do not repent. The first child is clearly Hosea's child—"she conceived and bore him a son" (1:3). The symbolic name *Jezreel* is to be a place where God brings judgment on Jehu's dynasty for its bloodguilt and on Israel for Israel's sinfulness (vv. 4–5). The second child is named *Lo-Ruhamah* ("Not-pitied" or "Not-loved," vv. 6–7). The name may indicate Hosea has some question about being the father of the child. The prophetic message is that God will no longer pity or forgive Israel for her sinfulness. Gomer conceives a third time and has another son. The name of that third child, *Lo-Ammi*, means "Not-my-people" or "Not-mine." The name indicates Hosea is not the father of this child, Gomer has been unfaithful, and this is a child born to another man. God declares concerning Israel, "You are not My people, and I will not be your God" (vv. 8–9).

Despite this situation within Hosea's family setting and God's message of judgment on Israel, a message of hope follows:

> Yet the number of the children of Israel
> Shall be as the sand of the sea,
> Which cannot be measured or numbered.
> And it shall come to pass
> In the place where it was said to them,
> "You are not My people,"
> There it shall be said to them,
> "You are sons of the living God."
> Then the children of Judah and the children of Israel
> Shall be gathered together,
> And appoint for themselves one head;
> And they shall come up out of the land,
> For great will be the day of Jezreel!
> Say to your brethren, "My people,"
> And to your sisters, "Mercy is shown." (1:10–2:1)

The hope is in the new names given to the children. Jezreel will be a place of celebration and joy, not judgment. Not-pitied, Not-loved will be called Pitied, Loved; and Not-my-people will be called My-people. God will show mercy and forgiveness to his people.

The rest of chapter 2 is a word of judgment spoken against the people of Israel, using the analogy of the unfaithful wife or unfaithful mother. It describes the unfaithfulness of Israel as "she" runs after other lovers and pursues them and does not recognize that God, her true husband, provides all she needs. So judgment will come upon Israel because of "her" sinfulness.

The very end of chapter 2 gives a message of hope again. God says he will bring Israel into the wilderness and speak tenderly and give back her vineyards, and he will make the Valley of Achor, a place of sin and judgment in the earlier books of the Old Testament, a door of hope (vv. 14–15). Judgment can lead to hope. The hope is that Israel will respond to God as in the days of her youth when she came out of the land of Egypt.

> "And it shall be, in that day,"
> Says the LORD,
> "That you will call Me 'My Husband,'
> And no longer call Me 'My Master'
> [literally "My Baal" *Baali* in Hebrew],
> For I will take from her mouth the names of the Baals,
> And they shall be remembered by their name no more.
> In that day I will make a covenant for them
> With the beasts of the field,
> With the birds of the air,
> And with the creeping things of the ground.
> Bow and sword of battle I will shatter from the earth,
> To make them lie down safely
> I will betroth you to Me forever;
> Yes, I will betroth you to Me
> In righteousness and justice,
> In lovingkindness and mercy;
> I will betroth you to Me in faithfulness,
> And you shall know the LORD." (vv. 16–20)

The hope is a covenant God will make (a "marriage" covenant) with Israel and with all nature. The covenant will bring peace: Israel will be betrothed, "married," to God in righteousness, justice, steadfast love, mercy, and faithfulness. The covenant will be eternal.

Chapter 3 returns to the narrative of Hosea and his wife. God tells Hosea to go and show his love for his adulterous wife, just as God loves Israel despite Israel's unfaithfulness. Hosea purchases Gomer to remove her from her adulterous affairs. Hosea tells her she must remain with him for many days and have no relations with any man, including him. Likewise

God will purify Israel; the people will live for many days without kings, leaders, and objects of worship. But there is a message of hope for Israel at the end of the chapter: "Afterward the children of Israel shall return and seek the LORD their God and David their king. They shall fear the LORD and His goodness in the latter days" (3:5).

We are not told the rest of Hosea's story. Did Gomer remain with Hosea after the period of her purification? Did they "live happily ever after"? We are not told because the outcome of Hosea's family situation is not the relevant message. The relevant message is Israel's response to God. God offers hope to Israel if the people will return to him.

Calls for Repentance; Messages of Hope

Chapters 4–10 bring more warning of impending judgment on the people and calls for repentance. Chapter 11 provides another message of hope. God uses the family metaphor again to describe his relationship with Israel.

> When Israel was a child [*na'ar*, youth], I loved him,
> And out of Egypt I called My son.
> As they called them,
> So they went from them;
> They sacrificed to the Baals,
> And burned incense to carved images.
> I taught Ephraim to walk,
> Taking them by their arms;
> But they did not know that I healed them.
> I drew them with gentle cords,
> With bands of love,
> And I was to them as those who take the yoke from their neck.
> I stooped and fed them. (vv. 1–4)

God describes his relationship with Israel when Israel was a youth—God called them out of Egypt. When Israel was a toddler, God taught Israel to walk—and healed their hurts when the people fell. When Israel was an infant, God stooped down to feed the people. That's God and his loving care. But Israel has turned away from God. The people worship Baals; they do not recognize that God is the one healing them. Because of Israel's refusal to repent, God will allow Assyria to conquer them (vv. 5–7).

Nevertheless, this judgment is not God's final word.

> How can I give you up, Ephraim?
> How can I hand you over, Israel?
> How can I make you like Admah?
> How can I set you like Zeboiim?
> My heart churns within Me;
> My sympathy is stirred.
> I will not execute the fierceness of My anger;
> I will not again destroy Ephraim.
> For I am God, and not man,
> The Holy One in your midst;
> And I will not come with terror. (vv. 8–9)

These verses show us the heart of God, who will not fully destroy the people—even though they deserve no mercy. Israel can find hope in God's mercy—if the people will repent and return to him.

Chapters 12 and 13 continue to record the sinfulness of Israel and the judgments God will bring on the people. Because Israel has forgotten God, God says:

> So I will be to them like a lion;
> Like a leopard by the road I will lurk.
> I will meet them like a bear deprived of her cubs;
> I will tear open their rib cage,
> And there I will devour them like a lion.
> The wild beast shall tear them. (13:7–8)

The utter hopelessness of Israel's situation is made clear when God states:

> I will ransom them from the power of the grave;
> I will redeem them from death.
> O Death, I will be your plagues!
> O Grave, I will be your destruction!
> Pity is hidden from My eyes. (v. 14)

God threatens to destroy Israel personally, not to let death or the grave do so. He will cast off all pity.

However, this verse of seeming hopelessness is not God's last word to Israel through Hosea:

> O Israel, return [*shuv*, turn, return, repent] to the LORD your God,
> For you have stumbled because of your iniquity;
> Take words with you,
> And return [*shuv*] to the LORD.
> Say to Him,
> "Take away all iniquity;
> Receive us graciously,
> For we will offer the sacrifices of our lips.
> Assyria shall not save us,
> We will not ride on horses,
> Nor will we say anymore to the work of our hands,
> 'You are our gods.'
> For in You the fatherless finds mercy."
> I will heal their backsliding,
> I will love them freely,
> For My anger has turned away from him. (14:1–4)

God's final word is an offer of forgiveness, healing, and love—*if* Israel will truly repent. Israel's only hope comes through repentance and seeking God's mercy. The New Testament provides further evidence of God's final word and work of atonement in Christ. God is Israel's hope and our hope.

Joel

The book of Joel has few indicators of time or place. All that is known of the prophet is that he is the son of Pethuel (1:1). Scholars date the book from the ninth to the fourth century BC. Jerusalem has often been suggested as the locale for the book because of the many references to Jerusalem, Zion, and the temple.

The book of Joel can be divided into two parts. The first part of the book, 1:1–2:17, uses warlike imagery to describe a series of locust plagues and the results of the plagues. It is not clear from the oracle whether the plagues have already occurred or the oracle is a warning of plague if the people do not repent. The message may also be a metaphor describing a military invasion of the land. The second part of the book, 2:18–3:21, describes the day of the Lord as a day of judgment followed by a word of hope beyond the judgment.

Judgment

The book opens with a description of waves of locusts destroying the land:

> What the chewing locust left, the swarming locust has eaten;
> What the swarming locust left, the crawling locust has eaten;
> And what the crawling locust left,
> the consuming locust has eaten. (1:4)

In response to this natural disaster that decimates the land, the people are told to call a fast and a convocation in the temple and to cry out to God (v. 14). The purpose of this solemn assembly is not to offer sacrifices and offerings to God but to:

> So rend [*qar`a*, tear, rend] your heart, and not your garments;
> Return [*shuv*, turn, repent] to the LORD your God,

> For He is gracious [*channun*] and merciful [*rachum*]
> Slow to anger, and of great kindness
> [*chesed*, steadfast love, lovingkindness];
> And He relents [*nicham*, have compassion, repent]
> from doing harm.
> Who knows if He will turn [*shuv*, return, repent]
> and relent [*nicham*, have compassion, repent],
> And leave a blessing behind Him—
> A grain offering and a drink offering
> For the LORD your God? (2:13–14)

The message of Joel is for the people to rend their hearts, to repent to God. The Hebrew *shuv* is the common prophetic call to turn, to return, and to repent. The description of God as gracious, merciful, slow to anger, having great steadfast love, and relenting from doing harm is a message of hope—hope that if the people repent, then God may not bring the disaster being described or may show mercy after judgment. It calls to mind the Sinaitic covenant description of God in Exodus 34:6.

The Day of the Lord

Much of the remainder of Joel 2 describes how God will respond if the people repent and call on him. God will show mercy and restore the devastated crops and vineyards, and they will have abundance (vv. 17–25). As a result:

> You shall eat in plenty and be satisfied,
> And praise the name of the LORD your God,
> Who has dealt wondrously with you;
> And My people shall never be put to shame.
> Then you shall know that I am in the midst of Israel:
> I am the LORD your God
> And there is no other.
> My people shall never be put to shame. (vv. 26–27)

The message is definitely one of hope. Even though God warns of judgment on the land, on all the produce of the land (or has brought such judgment already), hope is based on God's mercy when Judah repents and shows by their actions they are returning to him. God will graciously restore the productivity of the land. The additional hope Joel expresses is the promise of God's presence. In the restoration, the people will know through personal experience with God that he is in their midst. They will also know that God is their God, that there is no other (Isa. 45). Joel also speaks of Israel in this message of hope, indicating that Israel, too, may experience restoration and new hope.

The hope does not end with these promises. Joel next describes a future, eschatological time when God will pour out his spirit on all flesh, all humankind:

> It shall come to pass afterward
> That I will pour out My Spirit on all flesh;
> Your sons and your daughters shall prophesy,
> Your old men shall dream dreams,
> Your young men shall see visions
> And also on My menservants and on My maidservants
> I will pour out My Spirit in those days. (vv. 26–29)

This message of hope speaks of God pouring out his spirit on all: on all flesh, not just one race or ethnic group; on all, men and women, sons and daughters, not just one gender or age group; on all, servants and free, not just one social class or status. This is a tremendous message of hope for all people everywhere. This text is the passage Peter used on the day of pentecost (Acts 2) to describe the coming of the Holy Spirit on all people—pentecost was a fulfillment of Joel's message—inaugurated by the death and resurrection of Christ. Today we find great hope in Joel's message as well.

In describing a coming day of the Lord, Joel speaks of even more hope:

> It shall come to pass
> That whoever calls on the name of the LORD
> Shall be saved.
> For in Mount Zion and in Jerusalem there shall be deliverance,

> As the LORD has said,
> Among the remnant whom the LORD calls.
> "For behold, in those days and at that time,
> When I bring back the captives of Judah and Jerusalem. (2:32–3:1)

The message speaks of a future, eschatological time that will bring deliverance in Zion-Jerusalem. It describes a remnant—captives who will come back to Jerusalem. While Joel does indicate exile, he also speaks of return. Even those in or after Joel's time who experience exile can have hope in a promised return. Peter related the salvation and deliverance promised on the day of the Lord to the Christ event Joel prophesied.

For all the messages of hope in Joel, there is only one occurrence of a word for *hope* in the book, and that is in its closing paragraph:

> The LORD also shall roar out of Zion, and utter his voice from Jerusalem; and the heavens and the earth shall shake: but the LORD will be the hope [*machseh*, refuge, shelter] of his people, and the strength of the children of Israel. So shall ye know that I am the LORD your God dwelling in Zion, my holy mountain: then shall Jerusalem be holy, and there shall no strangers pass through her any more.
>
> And it shall come to pass in that day, that the mountains shall drop down new wine, and the hills shall flow with milk, and all the rivers of Judah shall flow with waters, and a fountain shall come forth of the house of the LORD, and shall water the valley of Shittim. . . . But Judah shall dwell for ever, and Jerusalem from generation to generation. For I will cleanse their blood that I have not cleansed: for the LORD dwelleth in Zion. (3:16–18, 20–21 KJV)

This hope serves as the climax of the book. Hope is explicit. God is and will be the hope and strength of Israel and Judah, and all God's people. The promise is repeated that they, and we, will know through personal experience that God is God.

Amos

Amos is considered the first of the classical or writing prophets. All we know about Amos is that he was a shepherd or sheepbreeder and a dresser of sycamore trees (1:1; 7:14). His ministry is usually set between 750 and 745 BC, near the end of the reigns Jeroboam II of Israel and Uzziah of Judah. Both these kings have long and successful reigns. The political and economic conditions in both kingdoms are the best since the time of David and Solomon. However, Amos calls the people back into a proper relationship with God. He reminds the people that they are not following God's commandments or God's law and, therefore, judgment is about to come on them. The warning of judgment appears to offer no hope. But the reality is that the message is intended to bring hope to the people.

The book of Amos has three primary parts. Chapters 1–2 present oracles against all the nations surrounding Israel and Israel itself. The second part of the book, chapters 3–6, is a series of oracles specifically directed against Israel because of her sinfulness and disobedience to God. The third part consists of five visions depicting God bringing judgment against the nation of Israel (7:1–9:10). At the end of the third part of the book are words of hope to those who hear God's word through Amos and respond to the message (9:11–15).

Oracles Against the Nations

The oracles against the nations in the first two chapters basically speak a word of judgment against each of the nations that surround Israel, all whose borders touch Israel or are very close to Israel, and finally against Israel itself. The oracles have a distinct pattern:

Thus says the LORD

For three transgressions of [nation] and for four,

> I will not turn away its punishment
> Because he/they [lists a major sin—sin against humanity]
> So I will send fire on [wall/house] of [city or dynasty]
> And it will destroy the fortresses of [dynasty]

Several of the oracles will include an additional sin and an additional judgment, and several add a closing, "says the LORD."

Amos's purpose with the pattern and repetition is to grab the attention of the audience with the message that each of Israel's neighbors (who were often Israel's enemies) will be destroyed for sinfulness. After listing six nations and their sins, the audience is in full agreement with Amos's message. God has every reason to judge these nations because of their sinfulness of being terrible, wicked people.

The seventh nation that Amos speaks God's judgment against is Judah. The sin of Judah is a sin against God—despising the law of God and not following his commandments (2:4). Then comes the climax to the oracles. The final oracle is against Israel:

> Thus says the LORD:
>
> "For three transgressions of Israel, and for four,
> I will not turn away its punishment,
> Because they sell the righteous for silver,
> And the poor for a pair of sandals.
> They pant after the dust of the earth
> which is on the head of the poor,
> And pervert the way of the humble.
> A man and his father go in to the same girl,
> To defile My holy name.
> They lie down by every altar on clothes taken in pledge,
> And drink the wine of the condemned
> in the house of their god." (vv. 6–8)

In the oracle against Israel, Amos mentions multiple sins, which include moral and ethical sins against fellow Israelites and against God. The pattern of the oracles is to convince Israel that, just as the other nations deserve God's judgment, Israel deserves God's judgment.

Rather than describing the judgment immediately as the other oracles do, however, God reminds Israel what he has done for the people:

> "Yet it was I who destroyed the Amorite before them,
> Whose height was like the height of the cedars,
> And he was as strong as the oaks;
> Yet I destroyed his fruit above
> And his roots beneath.
> Also it was I who brought you up from the land of Egypt,
> And led you forty years through the wilderness,
> To possess the land of the Amorite.
> I raised up some of your sons as prophets,
> And some of your young men as Nazirites.
> Is it not so, O you children of Israel?"
> Says the LORD. (vv. 9–11)

But Israel's response to God's acts of deliverance is not faithfulness. Instead Israel "gave the Nazirites wine to drink, / And commanded the prophets saying, 'Do not prophesy'" (v. 12). Amos may have been one of the prophets who were told not to prophesy by the people (see 7:15). As a result of the refusal to hear and heed God's word, God now speaks of impending judgment; God will bring an unnamed enemy force against Israel to destroy them:

> "Behold, I am weighed down by you,
> As a cart full of sheaves is weighed down.
> Therefore flight shall perish from the swift,
> The strong shall not strengthen his power,
> Nor shall the mighty deliver himself;
> He shall not stand who handles the bow,
> The swift of foot shall not escape,
> Nor shall he who rides a horse deliver himself.
> The most courageous men of might
> Shall flee naked in that day,"
> Says the LORD. (2:13–16)

"Hear this word"

Amos 3–6 is a series of messages warning Israel of God's impending judgment. Chapters 3–5 each open with the words "Hear this word":

> Hear this word that the LORD has spoken against you, O children of Israel, against the whole family which I brought up from the land of Egypt, saying:
>
> "You only have I known of all the families of the earth;
> Therefore I will punish you for all your iniquities." (3:1–2)

This first word sets the context for God's judgment. Because Israel has a special covenant relationship with God ("You only have I known"), God will judge Israel for her iniquities. God chose Israel to be a blessing for all people; Israel's faithlessness to that covenant relationship brings certain judgment.

However, God does not bring judgment without giving his people sufficient warning and opportunity for repentance:

> Surely the Lord GOD does nothing,
> Unless He reveals His secret to His servants the prophets.
> A lion has roared!
> Who will not fear?
> The Lord GOD has spoken!
> Who can but prophesy? (vv. 7–8)

God's prophets bring God's word and warning to the people. There is hope if they hear and heed God's word and repent. God may forgive, and judgment may be averted. Amos, God's prophet, has heard God's word and must proclaim that word. There is hope if the people hear and repent.

Amos's message preaches against societal sins of injustice and oppression. God calls for right relationship with him based on justice and righteousness, not just sacrifices and offerings (5:21–25). God offers the people of Israel hope if they seek him and live righteously:

> For thus says the LORD to the house of Israel:
> "Seek Me and live;
> But do not seek Bethel,
> Nor enter Gilgal,

Nor pass over to Beersheba;
For Gilgal shall surely go into captivity,
And Bethel shall come to nothing.
Seek the LORD and live,
Lest He break out like fire in the house of Joseph,
And devour it,
With no one to quench it in Bethel—
You who turn justice to wormwood,
And lay righteousness to rest in the earth!" (vv. 4–7)

God's message is that merely seeking religious sanctuaries and shrines—Bethel, Gilgal, and Beersheba—is not what he desires. He wants Israel to seek him. God's promise is *if* they seek him, they will live. They have hope in God, not in sanctuaries and shrines, not in sacrifices and offerings, but in right relationship with God based on right actions—justice and righteousness—and seeking God.

God also relates seeking God with seeking good rather than evil:

Seek good and not evil,
That you may live;
So the LORD God of hosts will be with you,
As you have spoken.
Hate evil, love good;
Establish justice in the gate.
It may be that the LORD God of hosts
Will be gracious to the remnant of Joseph. (vv. 14–15)

The seeking of good brings a double word of hope. First there is the hope, the promise, that Israel may live. Second is the hope expressed in God's presence with his people who seek him and seek good—God will be with them.

Visions of Judgment and Hope

The visions in Amos 7–9 present increasingly severe judgments on unrepentant Israel, culminating in God destroying the sanctuaries of Israel and seeking out all survivors from all places—to kill them (9:1–4). The message seems hopeless.

But God does not end his message through Amos with that hopeless word. The final word in Amos speaks of a future beyond God's judgment on the kingdoms of Israel and Judah.

> "On that day I will raise up
> The tabernacle of David, which has fallen down,
> And repair its damages;
> I will raise up its ruins,
> And rebuild it as in the days of old . . . .
>
> "Behold, the days are coming," says the LORD,
> "When the plowman shall overtake the reaper,
> And the treader of grapes him who sows seed;
> The mountains shall drip with sweet wine,
> And all the hills shall flow with it.
> I will bring back the captives of My people Israel;
> They shall build the waste cities and inhabit them;
> They shall plant vineyards and drink wine from them;
> They shall also make gardens and eat fruit from them.
> I will plant them in their land,
> And no longer shall they be pulled up
> From the land I have given them,"
> Says the LORD your God. (vv. 11–15)

Amos's hope speaks of rebuilding the temple after destruction, which occurs in 587 BC. It also speaks of captives and exiles returning to the land. On one level Amos's hope is rebuilding after judgment. On another level, Amos describes an eschatological day when all nature will be restored, all the exiles who are taken captive will be returned, and God himself will plant the people in the land—an image similar to God's original creation in the garden of Eden (Gen. 2). In creation, God planted the garden and Adam tended it; in Amos's final word God plants the people in the land and the people plant the gardens.

Amos's earlier messages found hope in seeking God and in seeking good as a way to life. Our hope is also found in seeking God and seeking good. Our affirmation and our hope is confirmed in the Christ event as the fulfillment of God's redemption for all humankind.

Obadiah

Obadiah is the shortest book of the Old Testament. The book is an oracle of judgment on Edom because of its participation in the destruction of Judah and Jerusalem at the time of the Babylonian conquest and exile (597 and 587 BC). Obadiah pronounces God's judgment on Edom for their complicity against Judah. No word of hope is offered to Edom. Only a couple of possible words of hope for Judah and Zion-Jerusalem are found in the book.

> But on Mount Zion there shall be deliverance,
> And there shall be holiness;
> The house of Jacob shall possess their possessions. (1:17)

> And the captives of this host of the children of Israel
> Shall possess the land of the Canaanites
> As far as Zarephath.
> The captives of Jerusalem who are in Sepharad
> Shall possess the cities of the South.
> Then saviors shall come to Mount Zion
> To judge the mountains of Esau,
> And the kingdom shall be the LORD's. (vv. 20–21)

Judgment is assured for Edom, but deliverance will come to Mount Zion-Jerusalem. So the hope is for a future restoration of Jerusalem. The latter two verses indicate a return of the captives or exiles to their land. In other words, judgment on Edom will be followed by exiles returning to their land. But the greatest word of hope is the closing word: "the kingdom shall be the LORD's." The restored nation-kingdom will not primarily be David's kingdom; it will be God's kingdom. The Old Testament has few other references to the kingdom of God; the phrase "kingdom of God" is mainly used in the New Testament in reference to God's reign, inaugurated in the Christ event, and to be consummated in God's eschatological reign. This exclamation is a great message of hope to those surviving after the destruction of Judah in 587 BC. The message equally offers hope for Christians living between Christ's resurrection and the final consummation of the kingdom of God. The kingdom *shall be* the Lord's.

Jonah

The book of Jonah differs from most of the classical prophets in that it is primarily a narrative about a prophet rather than words of the prophet. Many scholars interpret Jonah as a parable rather than a historical account. There is, however, one reference to Jonah in the historical books of the Old Testament that states Jonah was a prophet during the reign of Jeroboam II of Israel (2 Kings 14:25) in the mid-eighth century BC.

According to the narrative, God calls Jonah to go and preach to the people of Nineveh, calling them to repent of their evil ways. Instead, Jonah tries to flee from God and goes in the opposite direction, to Joppa, where he boards a ship headed for Tarshish. But Jonah doesn't have the last word. God sends a massive storm down over the boat. The sailors cry out to their gods, but the storm does not relent. They then question Jonah, who confesses what he has (or *has not*) done. Jonah tells them to throw him overboard. The sailors refuse and try to row back to shore. But the storm is so strong they cannot get back to land. So the sailors call out to God, asking that he not hold them guilty of murder, and they throw Jonah overboard. The storm immediately ceases, and the sailors then fear and worship God, making vows and offering sacrifices. Jonah's disobedience leads to the conversion of a boatload of sailors! Where there was the threat of death for all, a hopeless situation, now a response of faith brings hope and faith, deliverance and salvation to a shipload of former pagans. To his credit, Jonah does give testimony of his faith to the sailors—he tells them he worships the Lord who made the sea and the dry land. They know he is fleeing from God. That testimony leads to their conversion, their faith experience.

But what about Jonah? He has been thrown overboard, but he has given no evidence of repentance. Will Jonah drown? Is that what Jonah wants? Even though Jonah has been fleeing God, God is not through with him. God sends a big fish to swallow Jonah, and the prophet spends three days and three nights in the belly of the fish. God is merciful and protects Jonah even though Jonah is rebellious and fleeing from him. After three days and nights, Jonah finally decides to pray to God. But even in his prayer, Jonah blames God (reminiscent of Adam in the garden after the first sin): "You cast me into the deep. . . . / 'I have been cast out of Your sight'" (2:3–4). By the end of the prayer, Jonah reaffirms his faith in God, "You have brought up my life from the pit. . . . / I will sacrifice to You / With the voice of thanksgiving. . . . Salvation is of the LORD!" (vv. 6–9). Jonah recognizes his only hope is in God. He cannot get himself out of this mess; no one else can help him. God is his only help and only hope. In response to Jonah's prayer, God speaks to the fish and the fish spits Jonah out onto the dry land.

God commissions Jonah a second time to go to Nineveh and take God's message to the people there. This time Jonah goes. He goes part of the way into the city and proclaims his message: "Yet forty days, and Nineveh shall be overthrown!" (3:4b). The text indicates he speaks the words only once. The response of the Ninevites is unbelievable! The people repent, all of them. They proclaim a fast and put on mourning clothes. The king gets off his throne, takes off his royal attire, and puts on mourning clothes. The king and leaders proclaim a total fast for humans and animals, mourning for sins, and call on all to cry out to God, to turn from their evil ways and violence; and they do so. God sees this and decides not to destroy Nineveh because of their repentance. The people of Nineveh find hope in calling on God, in obeying him through repentance and putting an end to violence. A pagan city, hated oppressors of the Israelites, nevertheless find hope in God. God helps them as a result of their faith, obedience, and hope.

We might think that is the end of the story, but it isn't. We might think that Jonah, the reluctant prophet, rejoices at the unbelievable response to God's message that he delivered, but Jonah is not pleased. Instead, Jonah is angry. Jonah delivered the message of impending doom on Nineveh, happily. He wanted to see Nineveh destroyed. He even sat outside the city waiting to see God's destruction on the city. Jonah did not want the people to repent; he did not want to see the city spared. He wanted fire and brimstone.

However, God is still not through with Jonah. Jonah tried to excuse his earlier fleeing from God by saying God is "a gracious and merciful God, slow to anger and abundant in lovingkindness, One who relents from doing harm" (4:2). God tries to convince Jonah of the stronger power of mercy and grace. God causes a plant to grow up overnight to give shade and relief to Jonah, and Jonah is exceedingly happy for the relief. That night God sends a cutworm to destroy the plant. The next day he sends a massive heat wave to the area, and Jonah is sitting out in the blistering heat with a sultry wind. Jonah is angry over the loss of the plant's shade and relief. God asks Jonah:

> You have had pity on the plant for which you have not labored, nor made it grow, which came up in a night and perished in a night. And should I not pity Nineveh, that great city, in which are more than one hundred and twenty thousand persons who cannot discern between their right hand and their left—and much livestock? (vv. 10–11)

There the narrative ends. Did Jonah ever get it? We are not told. What we see is that God is a God of hope. He is a God of hope for a shipload of pagan sailors threatened with death in a storm on the high seas and delivered by their faith response. He is a God of hope to foreign empires—even the enemies of Israel, and the oppressors of Israel—and they are saved by calling on God and repenting of their evil ways. And Jonah—he knows his hope is in God. He acknowledged as much in his prayer from the belly of the fish. He acknowledged it again in describing God's nature as gracious, merciful, and abounding in steadfast love. God *is* Jonah's hope also, his only hope!

What do we learn about God in the book of Jonah?

God is the creator of seas and dry land—everything.

Even the winds, waves, and storms obey God's commands.

The animals and plants obey God—even cutworms!

God cares about all people and all his creation.

God is a God of hope who wants all of creation restored to right relationship with him—humans and animals, *all* of creation! That's amazing hope.

Micah

Micah is an eighth-century BC prophet contemporary of Amos, Hosea, and Isaiah. He lives in the town of Moresheth-Gath. Like Isaiah, Micah's prophecy is directed primarily to Judah. His message expresses a concern for social justice issues, much as Amos does. Micah is the first prophet to explicitly speak of the destruction of Jerusalem as judgment on the sins of the people. Micah specifically describes the destruction of both Samaria (1:6) and Jerusalem (3:12) as judgment for the sins of both Israel and Judah. Micah's message of judgment against Jerusalem is used a century later in defense of Jeremiah when he is charged with a capital offense for prophesying Jerusalem would fall (Jer. 26:1–19). The book of Micah may be divided into two parts, chapters 1–5 and chapters 6–7. Each part includes oracles of judgment and oracles of hope or salvation.

Wrongdoing, Judgment, and Hope

Chapter 1 describes the sin of both Israel and Judah, focusing on the sins of idolatry. For their sins, God will bring judgment on them that includes captivity. Chapters 2 and 3 describe the sins of the wealthy and powerful and their oppression of the poor. They confiscate land and throw the helpless out of their homes. They tell the prophets not to preach. The wealthy are now the enemy, so they will be judged. The people practice injustice and wickedness, bribery and violence. Therefore God will bring destruction on the people.

Along with the accusations and warnings of coming judgment, the book of Micah also has hope; Micah 2:12–13 depicts a surviving remnant that God will gather and lead. From the context, it is not clear whether God leads a remnant out before the destruction of the land or leads them to return from captivity in a foreign land. Hope is present in either case—God will preserve a remnant and will be present with that remnant.

Chapter 4 has a very strong message of hope. It does speak of a captivity to Babylon (v. 10), but it presents a picture of an eschatological future in which God's dwelling place on Zion-Jerusalem will be restored. The juxtaposition of Micah 3:12 and 4:1 shows the seriousness of Judah's sin and the severity of God's judgment alongside his mercy and grace.

> Therefore because of you
> Zion shall be plowed like a field,
> Jerusalem shall become heaps of ruins,
> And the mountain of the temple
> Like the bare hills of the forest.
> Now it shall come to pass in the latter days
> That the mountain of the LORD's house
> Shall be established on the top of the mountains,
> And shall be exalted above the hills;
> And peoples shall flow to it. (3:12–4:1)

The hope for that eschatological future includes the message also found in Isaiah 2:2–4. All nations will come to Zion-Jerusalem, seeking God and following his commandments. Furthermore:

> They shall beat their swords into plowshares,
> And their spears into pruning hooks;
> Nation shall not lift up sword against nation,
> Neither shall they learn war anymore.
> But everyone shall sit under his vine and under his fig tree,
> And no one shall make them afraid;
> For the mouth of the LORD of hosts has spoken. (4:3–4)

The hope is expressed as all people living securely in their homes under their vines and trees. God will bring back all—the lame and the outcast alike—in that future day.

In another passage of hope, Micah describes a future ruler like a new David:

> But you, Bethlehem Ephrathah,
> Though you are little among the thousands of Judah,

> Yet out of you shall come forth to Me
> The One to be Ruler in Israel,
> Whose goings forth are from of old,
> From everlasting. (5:2)

This passage is one of the key messianic passages cited in Matthew 2:5–6 and John 7:42.

God vs. the People: Judgment and Hope

Micah 6 is set as a court case. The prophet presents God's charges against the people. First he describes what God has done—God faithfully keeps his covenant with the people (vv. 3–5). In response, the people ask what God wants from them—does he want more sacrifices?

> With what shall I come before the LORD,
> And bow myself before the High God?
> Shall I come before Him with burnt offerings,
> With calves a year old?
> Will the LORD be pleased with thousands of rams,
> Ten thousand rivers of oil?
> Shall I give my firstborn for my transgression,
> The fruit of my body for the sin of my soul? (vv. 6–7)

Micah responds that it is not sacrifices, religiosity, that God wants. He wants right living, right relationship with God and fellow humans: "He has shown you, O man, what is good; / And what does the LORD require of you / But to do justly, / To love mercy, / And to walk humbly with your God?" (v. 8). The remainder of chapter 6 and much of chapter 7 recount the people's injustice, lies, and deceit. All the evidence points to a guilty verdict. The people are guilty and deserve the full judgment that is due those who break covenant, who break relationship with God—destruction and death.

Once again, judgment is not God's final word. Whether the cry of the prophet or of righteous ones in the land, a cry of hope is raised: "Therefore I will look to the LORD; / I will wait for [*yachel*, hope] the God of my salvation [*yesha'*]; / My God will hear me" (7:7). This is the one explicit use of a word for hope in Micah. The one speaking expresses the assurance that God, the God of his salvation, will hear him. Furthermore he calls God "my God"; he has a personal relationship with God.

The book of Micah closes with a description of God and God's mercy:

> Who is a God like You,
> Pardoning iniquity
> And passing over the transgression of the remnant of His heritage?
> He does not retain His anger forever,
> Because He delights in mercy [*chesed*, steadfast love].
> He will again have compassion [*racham*, love, show compassion] on us,
> And will subdue our iniquities.
> You will cast all our sins
> Into the depths of the sea.
> You will give truth [*'emet*, faithfulness] to Jacob
> And mercy [*chesed*, steadfast love] to Abraham,
> Which You have sworn to our fathers
> From days of old. (vv. 18–20)

This final word of Micah is a word of hope. God's nature, his character, is that he forgives sin and demonstrates faithfulness and steadfast love. Hope is cast in terms of the promises made to Abraham, Isaac, and Jacob. So Micah's last word on hope looks back to the covenant promises made to the patriarchs in Genesis and forward to a future when God will again have compassion and forgive, when God will give faithfulness and steadfast love to his people.

Our hope builds on Micah's hope and adds the hope of the messiah whose birth Micah foresaw. This hope has the fulfillment of the birth of Christ, the completion of God's plan of atonement in the death and resurrection of Christ, and a future element in the consummation of the kingdom at Christ's return.

Nahum

The only information we have concerning Nahum is his name and possibly his hometown, Elkosh. The book is called both an oracle (*massa'*, oracle, burden) and a vision (*chazon*) (1:1). The book alludes to only two historical events. The first is the sack of Thebes in Egypt, called by the Egyptian name No-Amon (3:8). Thebes was sacked by the Assyrians under Ashurbanipal in 663 BC. The other event is the fall of Nineveh, the capital of Assyria, in 612 BC (3:7, 14–19). Most scholars date the book to the period between 612 BC and the fall of Jerusalem in 587 BC.

Almost the entire book of Nahum is a series of oracles against Nineveh (1:1). Chapters 2 and 3 describe a war against Nineveh and taunts over the defeat of Nineveh. Perhaps one could find a measure of hope in oracles that describe the fall of one's enemy, the same nation God used to bring judgment on the Northern Kingdom of Israel.

Nahum 1 describes the nature of God—he is a jealous God who takes vengeance on his enemies. God is slow to anger and great in power, but he does not leave the guilty unpunished. God is Lord over nature, and further described as: "The LORD is good, / A stronghold [*ma`oz*, refuge] in the day of trouble; / And He knows those who trust [*chasah*, take refuge] in Him" (v. 7). This passage offers a message of hope—God is a refuge and knows those who take refuge in God. This hope is based on God's goodness.

Nahum includes at least two short oracles of salvation. Both offer hope to the ones addressed. The first oracle does not mention the people addressed, but one can presume it is Israel or Judah: "Though I have afflicted you, / I will afflict you no more; / For now I will break off his yoke from you, / And burst your bonds apart" (vv. 12–13). In this brief oracle, God promises restoration to those who have been afflicted. The yoke of oppression or captivity will be broken. The restoration of Israel-Judah will come when Nineveh is destroyed. Israel-Judah will experience deliverance after Assyria is destroyed. God used Assyria as an instrument to judge Israel and Judah for their sins. However, God also judges Assyria for its sins. Israel and Judah can wait expectantly for God to restore them.

The second oracle of salvation is addressed to Judah and Israel:

> Behold, on the mountains
> The feet of him who brings good tidings,
> Who proclaims peace!
> O Judah, keep your appointed feasts,
> Perform your vows.
> For the wicked one shall no more pass through you;
> He is utterly cut off.
> He who scatters has come up before your face.
> Man the fort!
> Watch the road!
> Strengthen your flanks!
> Fortify your power mightily.
> For the LORD will restore the excellence of Jacob
> Like the excellence of Israel. (1:15–2:2)

This oracle proclaims peace for Israel-Judah. It speaks of worship being restored when Israel-Judah is restored. God is the one who will restore Israel-Judah. The oracle offers hope. Isaiah has a similar oracle of salvation (Isa. 52:7–10). God is and will be their hope. Both Peter and Paul refer to this oracle either from Isaiah or Nahum (Acts 10:36; Rom. 10:15). Christ is the one who brings good tidings and peace. He is the one who brings ultimate restoration and ultimate hope for those who believe in him.

Habakkuk

As was the case with Nahum, no information is given about the prophet Habakkuk apart from his name. No dates or datable events are mentioned in the book. Most scholars date Habakkuk between 612 BC (the fall of Nineveh) and 587 BC (the fall of Jerusalem) and a little later than Nahum. The book, like Nahum, is called an oracle (*massa'*, oracle, burden).

The book opens with two laments by the prophet, raising the question of theodicy: Why is there so much injustice, and why doesn't God punish those responsible for the injustice (1:2–4, 12–17)? God answers each of the laments (1:5–11; 2:1–5). The rest of chapter 2 consists of five woes to all who practice injustice and wickedness.

Chapter 3 is called a prayer and accompanied on a musical instrument (3:1). It begins with a petition by Habakkuk (v. 2) followed by a theophanic description of God's past acts (vv. 3–7). The theophany changes to a battle scene in which God defeated his enemies in the past (vv. 8–15). The prayer (and book) closes with Habakkuk's response of faith that God will act in like manner in the future.

Questions and Answers

In response to Habakkuk's lament concerning the violence, injustice, and oppression of the righteous (1:2–4), God responds that he is about to raise up the Babylonians as instruments of judgment. The Babylonians think they are acting on their own power and the power of their god. God says in this they sin (vv. 5–11).

Habakkuk asks God more questions:

> Are You not from everlasting,
> O LORD my God, my Holy One?

We shall not die.
O LORD, You have appointed them for judgment;
O Rock, You have marked them for correction.
You are of purer eyes than to behold evil,
And cannot look on wickedness.
Why do You look on those who deal treacherously,
And hold Your tongue when the wicked devours
A person more righteous than he? (vv. 12–13)

Habakkuk starts by affirming the eternal nature of God. He also affirms that God has pure eyes and cannot tolerate evil. He affirms that the Lord is his God but questions why God does not take action against the wicked. Habakkuk says he will stand on his watchtower to see what God will say. God's response is for Habakkuk to write the vision on tablets, so one running can read it. God then says:

For the vision is yet for an appointed time;
But at the end it will speak, and it will not lie.
Though it tarries, wait for [*chakah*] it;
Because it will surely come,
It will not tarry.

Behold the proud,
His soul is not upright in him;
But the just [*tsadik*, righteous] shall live by his faith
['*emunah*, faithfulness]. (2:3–4)

God tells Habakkuk that the vision is for a future time and that Habakkuk must wait for it. The answer, God's response, will come on God's schedule, not on Habakkuk's. God does assure Habakkuk that justice will come. In that day, the just will live by God's faithfulness. This message is an exceedingly hope-filled word for Habakkuk and his audience who remain faithful to God. It is a passage Paul cites twice (Rom. 1:17; Gal. 3:11), as does the author of Hebrews (10:37–38). It is also one of the key Old Testament passages for the doctrine of justification by faith—Luther's *sola fide* or justification by faith alone.

The remainder of chapter 2 has five woe passages—passages that open with the word "woe" and speak judgment on the wicked. The woes close with a word of promise: "But the LORD is in His holy temple. / Let all the earth keep silence before Him" (v. 20). The wicked may commit every kind of wickedness. They may think God does not see them or is not going to punish their sins. But Habakkuk tells his audience and the wicked that God has not forgotten and has seen every sin. God is alive and active. He is resident in his temple, and all the earth is to keep silent before him.

A Prayer

In his prayer, Habakkuk asks God to remember God's past acts of grace and mercy as God performs his judgment on the wicked:

> O LORD, I have heard your speech and was afraid;
> O LORD, revive Your work in the midst of the years!
> In the midst of the years make it known;
> In wrath remember mercy.
>
> God came from Teman,
> The Holy One from Mount Paran. Selah
> His glory covered the heavens,
> And the earth was full of His praise. (3:2–3)

The prayer becomes a theophanic description of God's past acts of deliverance, very much like Moses's blessing in Deuteronomy 33:2. In the prayer, Habakkuk describes past actions of God over the forces of nature and over the enemies of God's people. Habakkuk tells how God acted to bring salvation: "You went forth for the salvation [*yesha`*] of Your people, / For salvation [*yesha`*] with Your Anointed" (3:13). Habakkuk closes his prayer with a word of praise to God and a word of assurance. God has addressed Habakkuk's laments. Habakkuk is certain God will judge the wicked and will act to deliver his people. The timetable is, indeed, in God's hands. Habakkuk has renewed hope in him:

> Yet I will rejoice in the LORD,
> I will joy in the God of my salvation [*yesha`*].

> The LORD God is my strength;
> He will make my feet like deer's feet,
> And He will make me walk on my high hills. (vv. 18–19)

The message of Habakkuk is hope for the faithful who face difficult times. The hope in no way downplays the present suffering, but the message does offer the encouragement that God hears and answers—as he answered Habakkuk. The hope assures those who suffer that God is the God of their salvation—they will be saved.

Zephaniah

Zephaniah has an unprecedented genealogy for Old Testament prophets (1:1). Including the prophet, five generations are given. We also are told he prophesies during the reign of Josiah. The book of Zephaniah offers no other information on the man Zephaniah or the time of his prophecy. Since the book gives no indication of knowing Josiah's reforms (2 Kings 22–23), most biblical scholars date Zephaniah's prophecies to the early years of Josiah's reign, before 622 BC.

Judgment on Creation

Zephaniah opens with an oracle declaring God's judgment on all creation, humans and nature (1:2–3). The initial oracle is followed by an oracle of judgment against Judah and Jerusalem, especially against all idolatry and syncretistic religious practices of those who worship God while also worshiping Baal, Milcom, and the host of heaven (vv. 4–6).

Zephaniah then describes a coming day of the Lord—a day with invited guests and a sacrifice God has prepared. All are to be silent in God's presence. The day is not going to be a time of feasting and rejoicing. It will be a day of judgment and wrath against all the enemies of God (1:7–2:3). Even so, the last verse of the oracle gives a glimmer of hope: "Seek the LORD, all you meek of the earth, / Who have upheld His justice. / Seek righteousness, seek humility. / It may be that you will be hidden / In the day of the LORD's anger" (2:3). After warning his hearers of the imminent judgment, Zephaniah calls on the meek and humble, those who do God's justice, to seek God, to seek righteousness and humility. The hope is that the meek and humble may be hidden in the day of God's judgment.

Judgment on the Nations

Zephaniah next gives four oracles against the foreign nations of Philistia, Moab and Ammon, Ethiopia, and Assyria (vv. 4–15). He then utters an oracle against Jerusalem.

> Woe to her who is rebellious and polluted,
> To the oppressing city!
> She has not obeyed His voice,
> She has not received correction;
> She has not trusted in the LORD,
> She has not drawn near to her God.
> Her princes in her midst are roaring lions;
> Her judges are evening wolves
> That leave not a bone till morning.
> Her prophets are insolent, treacherous people;
> Her priests have polluted the sanctuary,
> They have done violence to the law. (3:1–4)

Jerusalem's sins are so egregious that God will bring the same judgment on it that has been and will be brought on other nations (vv. 5–8).

Hope Beyond Judgment

The book closes with a message of great hope beyond judgment. The judgment must first come to remove all the wicked. Afterward:

> For then I will restore to the peoples a pure language,
> That they all may call on the name of the LORD,
> To serve Him with one accord. . . .
> I will leave in your midst
> A meek and humble people,
> And they shall trust in the name of the LORD.
> The remnant of Israel shall do no unrighteousness
> And speak no lies,
> Nor shall a deceitful tongue be found in their mouth;
> For they shall feed their flocks and lie down,
> And no one shall make them afraid. (vv. 9, 12–13)

God promises restoration and to leave a meek and humble people in the midst of Jerusalem (2:3). Those who are restored will live in peace, and no one will make them afraid.

The closing words of Zephaniah are a hymn of praise and hope:

> Sing, O daughter of Zion!
> Shout, O Israel!
> Be glad and rejoice with all your heart,
> O daughter of Jerusalem!
> The LORD has taken away your judgments. . . .
> The King of Israel, the LORD, is in your midst;
> You shall see disaster no more. . . .
> "The LORD your God in your midst,
> The Mighty One, will save [*yasha`*];
> He will rejoice over you with gladness,
> He will quiet you with His love [*'ahavah*],
> He will rejoice over you with singing." . . .
> I will save [*yasha`*] the lame,
> And gather those who were driven out . . . .
> At that time I will bring you back. (3:14–20)

Clearly God is their hope. In the restored Jerusalem, God is the king and is present in the midst of the people. God's presence brings hope; God's salvation brings hope; God's returning those who were driven out brings hope. This is a future hope for Zephaniah's audience, an eschatological future restoration. This hope is not limited to Jerusalem but is for all Israel.

Christians today can sing and rejoice, affirming all of Zephaniah's hope. Christians have the additional hope of God's indwelling presence, a presence not limited to Jerusalem. Christian hope is not only in a restoration or return to Jerusalem but also in a future new Jerusalem as part of a new heaven and new earth. This hope is based on the completion of the atonement in Christ and the hope of Christ's return.

Haggai

Haggai is mentioned twice in Ezra (5:1; 6:14), but the name of this author is all that is known about him. According to date formulas in the book, Haggai prophesies in Jerusalem for a period of about four months in 520 BC. The book is a series of oracles concerning the rebuilding of the temple in Jerusalem.

The book opens with an oracle chastising the people of Jerusalem for living in paneled homes while the temple lies in ruins. God says the people have little to eat, drink, and wear because they have neglected God and the temple. God calls for the people to procure wood and rebuild the temple (1:2–11). In response to this chastisement:

> Then Zerubbabel the son of Shealtiel, and Joshua the son of Jehozadak, the high priest, with all the remnant of the people, obeyed the voice of the LORD their God, and the words of Haggai the prophet, as the LORD their God had sent him; and the people feared the presence of the LORD. Then Haggai, the LORD's messenger, spoke the LORD's message to the people, saying, "I am with you, says the LORD." So the LORD stirred up the spirit of Zerubbabel the son of Shealtiel, governor of Judah, and the spirit of Joshua the son of Jehozadak, the high priest, and the spirit of all the remnant of the people; and they came and worked on the house of the LORD of hosts, their God. (vv. 12–14)

Zerubbabel the governor, Joshua the high priest, and all the people respond with obedience, fearing and worshiping God. Haggai then speaks a word of assurance to the people—the assurance of God's presence. The message is one of encouragement and hope. The people have responded to God with obedience—they began work on rebuilding the temple—and God assures them of his presence with them in their work.

Haggai follows with a further word of encouragement, specifically mentioning Zerubbabel and Joshua as well as all the people. The word for each is the same:

> "Yet now be strong, Zerubbabel," says the LORD; "and be strong, Joshua, son of Jehozadak, the high priest; and be strong, all you people of the land," says the LORD, "and work; for I am with you," says the LORD of hosts. "According to the word that I covenanted with you when you came out of Egypt, so My Spirit remains among you; do not fear!" (2:4–5)

All are called upon to be strong and work. Again God promises his presence, relating the promise to the exodus and the Sinaitic covenant. In that backward glance, God reminds the people of his past presence. He also gives the people hope that he and his spirit are still with them.

Some of the people who had seen the former temple describe the new temple as nothing compared to the former temple (v. 3). However, God responds to them:

> "I will fill this temple with glory," says the LORD of hosts. . . . "The glory of this latter temple shall be greater than the former," says the LORD of hosts. "And in this place I will give peace," says the LORD of hosts. (vv. 7, 9)

Notice the hope in God's words. The temple being built is as nothing compared to the former temple. God doesn't say that the new temple will be greater than the former temple. He promises to fill the new temple with glory—with his glory. The glory of the new temple will be greater than the former. Ezekiel describes the departure of God's glory from the former temple before it is destroyed (Ezek. 11). He also describes a new temple and a return of God's glory to the new temple (Ezek. 43). God now says the new temple will have greater glory, and in the temple God will give peace. This is the hope for Zerubbabel, Joshua, and all the people.

God has one more word of hope for all the people. Up to this day, God has struck the land with blight and mildew because of the people's inaction. But now, with the work on the new temple progressing, God promises: "But from this day I will bless you" (2:19). The hope is that God will restore the productivity of the land.

Haggai offers a word of hope to the generation of returnees to Jerusalem who rebuild the temple. God will bless them because they rebuild it. The entire message of Haggai is concerned with the temple—a building. Much of the hope of Haggai is centered in the building. Christian hope is not centered in a building, even if the building is a temple. Christian hope is centered in a person—in Jesus Christ—and in the atonement completed in his death and resurrection.

Zechariah

Zechariah is one of the most difficult and obscure books of the Old Testament. The book identifies Zechariah as the son of Berechiah. It also gives dates for the oracles in the second and fourth years of Darius, 520–518 BC. The book itself may be divided into two parts. Chapters 1–8 deal with the events surrounding the rebuilding of the temple and contain all the dated oracles. Chapters 9–14 have no dated oracles and appear to depict a context of insecurity and danger. The visions and oracles are often considered apocalyptic or the forerunners of apocalyptic oracles. These latter chapters express doubt about the future unless God intervenes to destroy and to rescue. Yet both parts of the book include some hope for the future.

Oracles of Warning and Hope

The opening oracle begins with a word of warning (1:2) but immediately has a message of hope if the people would repent:

> "Therefore say to them, 'Thus says the LORD of hosts: "Return [*shuv*, turn, return, repent] to Me," says the LORD of hosts, "and I will return [*shuv*, turn, return, repent] to you," says the LORD of hosts. (v. 3)

This is the clarion call of the Old Testament prophets—turn, return, repent. If the people do so, God will respond by returning to them. God will again be with them and bless them with his presence. The people can take hope in God's promise if, but only if, they repent.

That message is amplified later in a vision:

> "Therefore thus says the LORD:
> 'I am returning to Jerusalem with mercy [*rachamim*, compassion];
> My house shall be built in it,' says the LORD of hosts,
> 'And a surveyor's line shall be stretched out over Jerusalem.'"

> Again proclaim, saying, "Thus says the LORD of hosts:
> 'My cities shall again spread out through prosperity;
> The LORD will again comfort Zion,
> And will again choose Jerusalem.'" (vv. 16–17)

The promise is the very same—God will return—but here the promise and the hope are expanded. Not only will God return, but the cities of Judah will again be prosperous, and God will once again comfort Jerusalem and choose Jerusalem as his dwelling place. Another possible indicator of hope may be seen in the word translated as "surveyor's line." The Hebrew form is unclear. Most translations take the form as *qav*, the word for a cord or line. But the Hebrew consonants may also be understood as *qavah*, the word for hope. With that understanding, the verse reads "My house shall be built . . . and hope will be stretched out over Jerusalem." That is an exceedingly strong message of hope for the people.

In a vision concerning Jerusalem, God says:

> Jerusalem shall be inhabited as towns without walls, because of the multitude of men and livestock in it. "For I," says the LORD, "will be a wall of fire all around her, and I will be the glory in her midst." (2:4–5)

The message of hope here is that Jerusalem will have so many people living in it that there will be no walls, and there will be no need for walls because God's glory will be like a wall of fire all around the city. His presence will be the only protection the people need.

That same message of hope is reiterated in the same oracle with a call for Jerusalem to rejoice:

> "Sing and rejoice, O daughter of Zion! For behold, I am coming and I will dwell in your midst," says the LORD. "Many nations shall be joined to the LORD in that day, and they shall become My people. And I will dwell in your midst. Then you will know that the LORD of hosts has sent Me to you. And the LORD will take possession of Judah as His inheritance in the Holy Land, and will again choose Jerusalem." (vv. 10–12)

The hope is expanded even further. Not only will God be in the midst of Jerusalem, but also many nations will follow God in that day and become his people. This message of hope anticipates the conversion of many nations that is fulfilled in Christ. Zechariah sees that hope before Christ's coming.

The hope for a time of peace and security in the future spoken by Micah (Mic. 4:2–4) is repeated in Zechariah's vision of a future eschatological time: "'In that day,' says the LORD of hosts, / 'Everyone will invite his neighbor / Under his vine and under his fig tree'" (3:10).

Zechariah repeats this message of hope in chapter 8. Among the passages speaking of God's presence in Jerusalem and his return of the exiles are Zechariah 8:2, 7, 12, and 15. Each passage builds more hope. The chapter, and the first part of Zechariah, closes with one more hopeful word: "Yes, many peoples and strong nations / Shall come to seek the LORD of hosts in Jerusalem, / And to pray before the LORD" (v. 22). Once again Zechariah's vision of hope extends far beyond the Jewish community of Judah and Jerusalem—they are certainly included in the hope; the message is addressed to them. However, the hope is that many peoples, many strong nations, will seek God and pray in his presence in Jerusalem.

Oracles of Judgment, Purification, and Hope

The second part of Zechariah has many obscure passages and allusions that seem to defy interpretation. Nevertheless, there are some messages of hope. Without trying to interpret all of the second part of this book, the clear passages presenting hope to the hearers will be examined.

Chapter 9 contains one of the passages cited in the gospels at Christ's triumphal entry into Jerusalem on Palm Sunday:

> Rejoice greatly, O daughter of Zion!
> Shout, O daughter of Jerusalem!
> Behold, your King is coming to you;
> He is just [*tsadiq*, righteous] and having salvation [*yasha`*],
> Lowly and riding on a donkey,
> A colt, the foal of a donkey. (v. 9)

The message is of a future king the Gospels understand as being fulfilled in Christ. This king enters Jerusalem—not on a royal stallion, not in a horse-drawn chariot—humbly and riding on a donkey. This king has no royal regalia, no honor guard, no military weapons: he comes armed with righteousness and salvation. That hope expressed by Zechariah is a hope fulfilled in Christ's death and resurrection. Hope not in a royal king, although Jesus is of David's family, but in a humble servant king who enters triumphantly to die for people's sins, righteous and bringing salvation!

Zechariah 10 has a lengthy message of hope for Judah and Israel:

> I will strengthen the house of Judah,
> And I will save [*yasha`*] the house of Joseph.
> I will bring them back,
> Because I have mercy [*racham*] on them. . . .
> For I am the LORD their God,
> And I will hear them.
> Those of Ephraim shall be like a mighty man, . . .
> Their heart shall rejoice in the LORD.
> I will whistle for them and gather them,
> For I will redeem them;
> And they shall increase as they once increased. . . .
> And they shall remember Me in far countries;
> They shall live, together with their children,
> And they shall return.
> I will also bring them back from the land of Egypt,
> And gather them from Assyria.
> I will bring them into the land. (vv. 6–10)

The hope for Judah and Israel (Ephraim) is salvation, or deliverance and mercy. God will bring back all those sent into exile. God will be their God and they will be his people. Although many exiles have already returned, Zechariah describes a future day of a full return of God's people.

Zechariah 13 speaks of a massive judgment God will bring on the land as he removes all the sinners and uncleanness from the land. This is a massive purification that destroys two-thirds of the population:

> "And it shall come to pass in all the land,"
> Says the LORD,
> "That two-thirds in it shall be cut off and die,
> But one-third shall be left in it:
> I will bring the one-third through the fire,
> Will refine them as silver is refined,
> And test them as gold is tested.
> They will call on My name,
> And I will answer them.
> I will say, 'This is My people';
> And each one will say, 'The LORD is my God.'" (vv. 8–9)

The message is twofold. First God judges sin. Purification will be like that of a refiner's fire—the fire and heat remove all the slag and dross and leave behind the purified metal. Second, the remnant then has hope. They will all affirm the Lord as their God, and God will say they are his people. The message reiterates the message of Hosea and the metaphor he uses of marriage and children (Hos. 1–3).

The closing chapter of Zechariah depicts a future day of battle. In that battle the enemies of God will be destroyed, but in the midst of all the devastation of battle is a word of hope:

> It shall come to pass that everyone who is left of all the nations which came against Jerusalem shall go up from year to year to worship the King, the LORD of hosts, and to keep the Feast of Tabernacles. (14:16)

In that future eschatological day, in that day after great destruction, Zechariah sees hope of peace and of conversion among all the nations who fought against God and against Jerusalem. Everyone in all those nations will come every year to worship God and dwell in booths as they keep the Jewish Feast of Tabernacles. That future day has not yet arrived, but the hope remains for Christians—for an earth filled with peace and all its inhabitants worshiping God!

Malachi

The book of Malachi is the last book of the Old Testament prophets and the last book of the Old Testament following the Septuagint and English Bible order. Traditionally Malachi is taken as a name, although many critical scholars take it to be a title since the Hebrew literally means "My Messenger." Either way, it is an apt description for a prophet as God's messenger. There is also debate concerning the date of the book, which mentions no historical dates or events. It has been dated from the late seventh century BC to as late as the Maccabean period in the second century BC. Most scholars date it to the fifth century BC.

Most of the book is a series of oracles warning the people of judgment from God because of unacceptable worship practices and rejection of God. However, a number of passages promise the hope of God's blessing for faithful obedience. This hope and blessing is extended even to foreigners—Gentiles:

> "For from the rising of the sun, even to its going down,
> My name shall be great among the Gentiles;
> In every place incense shall be offered to My name,
> And a pure offering;
> For My name shall be great among the nations,"
> Says the LORD of hosts. (1:11)

In all places from east to west, God promises his name will be honored or revered even among the Gentiles. The nations will worship God with incense and pure offerings. This message of hope speaks of the spread of faith in God among all people.

Malachi 3:1 is another of the passages cited in the Gospels as speaking of the forerunner of the Messiah:

> "Behold, I send My messenger,
> And he will prepare the way before Me.

> And the Lord, whom you seek,
> Will suddenly come to His temple,
> Even the Messenger of the covenant,
> In whom you delight.
> Behold, He is coming,"
> Says the LORD of hosts.

Jesus quotes this passage as referring to John the Baptist (Matt. 11:10; Luke 7:27). So the Gospels definitely see the passage as one of great hope for a coming Messiah. Some interpret the messenger as Malachi since "my messenger" is identical in Hebrew to Malachi. However, the passage indicates a future context with someone other than Malachi as the messenger. The context of this passage further complicates a full understanding. This coming of the messenger heralds the coming of the Lord who will bring judgment—refining like a refiner's fire and coming in judgment (3:2–5), much like the judgment in Zechariah 13:8–9. For sinners, the coming means judgment; for the righteous, the coming is hope and blessing.

Another passage from Malachi offering hope calls for the people to bring all their tithes to the temple:

> "Bring all the tithes into the storehouse,
> That there may be food in My house,
> And try Me now in this,"
> Says the LORD of hosts,
> "If I will not open for you the windows of heaven
> And pour out for you such blessing
> That there will not be room enough to receive it." (3:10)

The hope expressed is God's promise to pour down blessing on the people in response to their faithfulness. The charge is that the people have been robbing God—they have not been bringing their tithes and offerings. So God has placed a curse on them. This passage offers the promise to remove the curse and replace it with blessing *if* the people are obedient and bring all the tithes to God. Faithful obedience brings the hope of blessing.

The last two verses of Malachi bring one more word of promise: God promises to send Elijah again before the day of the Lord:

> Behold, I will send you Elijah the prophet
> Before the coming of the great and dreadful day of the LORD.
> And he will turn [*shuv*, return, repent]
> The hearts of the fathers to the children,
> And the hearts of the children to their fathers,
> Lest I come and strike the earth with a curse. (4:5–6)

Stylistically, God sending Elijah seems to parallel God sending his messenger (3:1). The purpose of sending Elijah, and the hope of the passage, is that Elijah will cause fathers' hearts to turn to the children and the children's hearts to the fathers. If the people repent to one another and to God, God will bring blessing and not a curse. Elijah's coming is understood in Jewish tradition as being the forerunner of the Messiah. Thus the hope of Elijah's return that marks the close of the Old Testament, following the English Bible, connects the Old Testament with the New Testament and the ministry of John the Baptist as Elijah (Matt. 11:12–13) and Jesus as the Messiah, the Christ.

Summary on Hope in the Old Testament

We are now at the end of our study of hope in the Old Testament, and we have seen that hope is present throughout. The Old Testament opens with hope expressed in God's good creation. At the conclusion of Genesis 1, God pronounces the totality of creation as very good. The sin of humans results in the fall of all creation. The rest of the Bible, both Old and New Testaments, expresses the hope of humans and the efforts of God to redeem all creation. All major sections of the Old Testament end with the hope of future redemption.

English Bible order ends with the Prophets. The prophets were great proclaimers of hope. Their message warned of impending judgment, but judgment was never the final word. The hope is that blessing or restoration can come beyond judgment. Their message of hope included the hope of a coming Messiah, who we know as the Christ in the New Testament. All the hope looks to future fulfillment in the gracious, redemptive acts of God. All hope is in God's hands.

The hope includes an eschatological image of a redeemed creation in which all creation, humankind and nature, is redeemed and lives in peace and harmony under God (Isa. 11:1–9). The hope is that of a new heaven and a new earth (Isa. 65:17–25), a hope we still look forward to, a hope restated in Revelation 21–22, the closing chapters of the New Testament.

Hope in the *New Testament*

Introduction to Hope in the *New Testament*

Ancient and Modern Hope

In a significant way, the entire body of Christian scripture—our New Testament and its Hebrew predecessor—is a library of hope. Yet the biblical concepts of hope are not easily understood in light of our modern uses of the word. Consider the following:

"I hope it doesn't rain today." (A form of wishful thinking.)

"I hope I get the job I applied for." (A deep personal desire.)

"I hope I get a pony for Christmas." (Wishful thinking not grounded in probability or reality.)

"We're not counting on it, but we're hopeful." (Keeping a positive attitude.)

Each of these uses of *hope* is based fundamentally on wishes or desires not likely to happen. We hope for things we don't actually believe will occur. Hope is something of a last resort—what we hold on to when we run out of options. These definitions of hope have little to do with the concept of hope contained in the Old and New Testaments. The various words and phrases that we translate as "hope" all reflect expectation or anticipation of what those in biblical times trusted to be true. Hope was an act of faith, confirming that the believer trusted God's promises. For example, those living in oppression under Caesar could continue to live in hope because they knew God would one day liberate them and restore them to prominence. More than wishful or positive thinking, hope was a form of knowledge. Hope supported more than the possible: it claimed desired outcomes as probable. Hope was a form of trust.

The other primary use of the concept of *hope* was framed in the negative—not losing hope. To lose hope was evidence of lack of faith.

Losing hope meant people no longer trusted the promises of God to be true. "Hopelessness" was the worst possible fate for the people of God—it implied that they surrendered and admitted defeat.

Hope in the New Testament

These understandings of hope help to explain why the writings of Matthew, Mark, Luke, and John were called "gospels," or good news. These books did not contain wishful thinking, empty promises, or fantasy. The four Gospels presented the fulfillment of God's plan for humanity. Each gospel is "hope-full," filled with messages that assure readers and hearers that God is going to set all things right. No need for worry; no need for doubt—nothing but faith. The New Testament is a testament of hope.

The first-century audiences of the early Christian writings were very different from the twenty-first-century audience of today. The Jewish audiences were predominantly poor, uneducated, illiterate, and often of the lowest social classes. The gospels and letters intended for these audiences speak to both a personal and corporate hope—hope for the person and his or her family, as well as hope for the whole community. Modern Western audiences have a difficult time understanding the Bible from the perspective of first-century Jewish audiences, since our context is incredibly different. The Gentile audiences of the first century covered a wide spectrum, from rich to poor, educated to uneducated, sophisticated to simple, tradespeople, merchants, farmers, and a host of others. Most of the letters were written to newly forming Christian communities, so the messages of hope were twofold: (1) how Christ is the source of our hope; (2) as the body of Christ we become hope for the world.

While none of the authors of our New Testament intentionally focused on hope, the gift of hope is contained in every book. To survey the main points of each volume in the Christian library is to receive dozens of hopeful and hope-producing messages. Some redundancy and many complementary concepts exist, but the final word is clear: hope abounds!

Today's world is in need of hope. We face incredible challenges and insurmountable problems: terrorist attacks and natural disasters, wars and rumors of war, daily tales of cruelty and violence. The world's ways are not God's ways. The church has a unique and important role to play. It can be a beacon of hope, shining the light of God's grace into a dark and frightening world. As we read our sacred Scriptures, we need to look for the fundamental messages of hope. We need to share the vision of hope. We need to embrace the possibility of hope. We need to live in hope and be ready to give hope to others. Ours is a gospel of hope. We need to be a church of hope.

Matthew

The Gospel of Hope

Our gospels exist because time passed after the resurrection of Jesus Christ, and those who expected his imminent return were growing anxious. When the world kept on turning and generations passed, people needed a way to preserve the good news brought to earth by Jesus the Christ. The written gospels were the way the early church preserved hope for themselves and for the people who came after them.

Words that translate as *hope* are extremely rare in Matthew's gospel, but the concept of expectation and anticipation is prevalent throughout. It is reasonable to describe Matthew's gospel as a gospel of hope. One of the unique aspects of the gospel of Matthew is the recurrent message that Jesus is the fulfillment of Hebrew prophecy (for example, "So all this was done that it might be fulfilled which was spoken by the Lord through the prophet," Matt. 1:22). Jesus as the Christ is the one for whom the children of God have been waiting with longing. In Jesus, a new covenant is offered that redeems and completes all prior covenants. In a sense, there is nothing more to hope for—Jesus has come!

The Hope of Jesus' Teachings

Then He opened His mouth and taught them, saying:

> "Blessed are the poor in spirit,
> For theirs is the kingdom of heaven.
> Blessed are those who mourn,
> For they shall be comforted.
> Blessed are the meek,
> For they shall inherit the earth.

Blessed are those who hunger and thirst for righteousness,
For they shall be filled.
Blessed are the merciful,
For they shall obtain mercy.
Blessed are the pure in heart,
For they shall see God.
Blessed are the peacemakers,
For they shall be called sons of God.
Blessed are those who are persecuted for righteousness' sake,
For theirs is the kingdom of heaven.

"Blessed are you when they revile and persecute you, and say all kinds of evil against you falsely for My sake. Rejoice and be exceedingly glad, for great is your reward in heaven, for so they persecuted the prophets who were before you. . . . .

"Do not think that I came to destroy the Law or the Prophets. I did not come to destroy but to fulfill. For assuredly, I say to you, till heaven and earth pass away, one jot or one tittle will by no means pass from the law till all is fulfilled. Whoever therefore breaks one of the least of these commandments, and teaches men so, shall be called least in the kingdom of heaven; but whoever does and teaches them, he shall be called great in the kingdom of heaven. For I say to you, that unless your righteousness exceeds the righteousness of the scribes and Pharisees, you will by no means enter the kingdom of heaven.

"You have heard that it was said to those of old, 'You shall not murder, and whoever murders will be in danger of the judgment.' But I say to you that whoever is angry with his brother without a cause shall be in danger of the judgment. And whoever says to his brother, 'Raca!' shall be in danger of the council. But whoever says, 'You fool!' shall be in danger of hell fire. . . . .

"You have heard that it was said, 'An eye for an eye and a tooth for a tooth.' But I tell you not to resist an evil person. But whoever slaps you on your right cheek, turn the other to him also. If anyone wants to sue you and take away your tunic, let him have your cloak also. And whoever compels you to go one mile, go with him two. Give to him who asks you, and from him who wants to borrow from you do not turn away.

"You have heard that it was said, 'You shall love your neighbor and hate your enemy.' But I say to you, love your enemies, bless those who curse you, do good to those who hate you, and pray for those who spitefully use you and persecute you, that you may be sons of your Father in heaven; for He makes His sun rise on the evil and on the good, and sends rain on the just and on the unjust. For if you love those who love you, what reward have you? Do not even the tax collectors do the same? And if you greet your brethren only, what do you do more than others? Do not even the tax collectors do so? Therefore you shall be perfect, just as your Father in heaven is perfect.

"Take heed that you do not do your charitable deeds before men, to be seen by them. Otherwise you have no reward from your Father in heaven. Therefore, when you do a charitable deed, do not sound a trumpet before you as the hypocrites do in the synagogues and in the streets, that they may have glory from men. Assuredly, I say to you, they have their reward. But when you do a charitable deed, do not let your left hand know what your right hand is doing, that your charitable deed may be in secret; and your Father who sees in secret will Himself reward you openly.

"And when you pray, you shall not be like the hypocrites. For they love to pray standing in the synagogues and on the corners of the streets, that they may be seen by men. Assuredly, I say to you, they have their reward. But you, when you pray, go into your room, and when you have shut your door, pray to your Father who is in the secret place; and your Father who sees in secret will reward you openly. . . .

"Do not lay up for yourselves treasures on earth, where moth and rust destroy and where thieves break in and steal; but lay up for yourselves treasures in heaven, where neither moth nor rust destroys and where thieves do not break in and steal. For where your treasure is, there your heart will be also.

"The lamp of the body is the eye. If therefore your eye is good, your whole body will be full of light. But if your eye is bad, your whole body will be full of darkness. If therefore the light that is in you is darkness, how great is that darkness!

"No one can serve two masters; for either he will hate the one and love the other, or else he will be loyal to the one and despise the other. You cannot serve God and mammon.

"Therefore I say to you, do not worry about your life, what you will eat or what you will drink; nor about your body, what you will put on. Is not life more than food and the body more than clothing? Look at the birds of the air, for they neither sow nor reap nor gather into barns; yet your heavenly Father feeds them. Are you not of more value than they? Which of you by worrying can add one cubit to his stature?

"So why do you worry about clothing? Consider the lilies of the field, how they grow: they neither toil nor spin; and yet I say to you that even Solomon in all his glory was not arrayed like one of these. Now if God so clothes the grass of the field, which today is, and tomorrow is thrown into the oven, will He not much more clothe you, O you of little faith?

"Therefore do not worry, saying, 'What shall we eat?' or 'What shall we drink?' or 'What shall we wear?' For after all these things the Gentiles seek. For your heavenly Father knows that you need all these things. But seek first the kingdom of God and His righteousness, and all these things shall be added to you. Therefore do not worry about tomorrow, for tomorrow will worry about its own things. Sufficient for the day is its own trouble.

"Judge not, that you be not judged. For with what judgment you judge, you will be judged; and with the measure you use, it will be measured back to you. And why do you look at the speck in your brother's eye, but do not consider the plank in your own eye? Or how can you say to your brother, 'Let me remove the speck from your eye'; and look, a plank is in your own eye? Hypocrite! First remove the plank from your own eye, and then you will see clearly to remove the speck from your brother's eye. . . .

"Ask, and it will be given to you; seek, and you will find; knock, and it will be opened to you. For everyone who asks receives, and he who seeks finds, and to him who knocks it will be opened. Or what man is there among you who, if his son asks for bread, will give him a stone? Or if he asks for a fish, will he give him a serpent? If you then, being evil, know how to give good gifts to your children, how much more will your Father who is in heaven give good things to those who ask Him! Therefore, whatever you want men to do to you, do also to them, for this is the Law and the Prophets.

"Enter by the narrow gate; for wide is the gate and broad is the way that leads to destruction, and there are many who go in by it. Because narrow is the gate and difficult is the way which leads to life, and there are few who find it. . . .

"Not everyone who says to Me, 'Lord, Lord,' shall enter the kingdom of heaven, but he who does the will of My Father in heaven. Many

> will say to Me in that day, 'Lord, Lord, have we not prophesied in Your name, cast out demons in Your name, and done many wonders in Your name?' And then I will declare to them, 'I never knew you; depart from Me, you who practice lawlessness!'
>
> "Therefore whoever hears these sayings of Mine, and does them, I will liken him to a wise man who built his house on the rock: and the rain descended, the floods came, and the winds blew and beat on that house; and it did not fall, for it was founded on the rock.
>
> "But everyone who hears these sayings of Mine, and does not do them, will be like a foolish man who built his house on the sand: and the rain descended, the floods came, and the winds blew and beat on that house; and it fell. And great was its fall." (5:2–12, 17–22, 38–48; 6:1–6, 19–34; 7:1–5, 7–14, 21–27)

Hope is the leading theme of the beginning of the Sermon on the Mount (Matthew 5:1–7:29). The Beatitudes are words of comfort and a promise to those poor in spirit, meek, and marginalized that justice will one day soon be restored. However, the promises Jesus makes are not free. The people of God have a responsibility to live good and upright lives if they want to be beneficiaries of God's blessing. Obedience to the Law, love of neighbor (including enemies), unconditional love and kindness are not options from which we choose; they define who we are as followers of Jesus the Christ. Prayer, fasting, sharing, giving, and faith in God are the normal practices of God's people. Compassion, refusing to judge others, living by the golden rule, and remaining loyal to the teachings of Jesus are basic expectations. We live in the Spirit of God to become who God wants us to be. God gives us hope for the future to help us be faithful in the present.

Hope in the Parables

> "For the kingdom of heaven is like a landowner who went out early in the morning to hire laborers for his vineyard. Now when he had agreed with the laborers for a denarius a day, he sent them into his vineyard. And he went out about the third hour and saw others standing idle in the marketplace, and said to them, 'You also go into the vineyard, and whatever

> is right I will give you.' So they went. Again he went out about the sixth and the ninth hour, and did likewise. And about the eleventh hour he went out and found others standing idle, and said to them, 'Why have you been standing here idle all day?' They said to him, 'Because no one hired us.' He said to them, 'You also go into the vineyard, and whatever is right you will receive.'
>
> "So when evening had come, the owner of the vineyard said to his steward, 'Call the laborers and give them their wages, beginning with the last to the first.' And when those came who were hired about the eleventh hour, they each received a denarius. But when the first came, they supposed that they would receive more; and they likewise received each a denarius. And when they had received it, they complained against the landowner, saying, 'These last men have worked only one hour, and you made them equal to us who have borne the burden and the heat of the day.' But he answered one of them and said, 'Friend, I am doing you no wrong. Did you not agree with me for a denarius? Take what is yours and go your way. I wish to give to this last man the same as to you. Is it not lawful for me to do what I wish with my own things? Or is your eye evil because I am good?' So the last will be first, and the first last. For many are called, but few chosen." (20:1–16)

In the thirteenth chapter of Matthew, Jesus' teaching, particularly teaching in parables, becomes the focus of his ministry. Through parables, Jesus offers instruction and guidance in the proper thoughts, words, and actions of Christian disciples. He creates a vision of faithful living that is not only challenging, demanding, and difficult but also deeply rewarding and fulfilling. To offer a life of meaning and purpose, Jesus gives people hope. Feelings of futility and lack of direction are replaced by the opportunity to be part of something important.

Jesus uses parables to offer instruction for followers (for example, parable of the sower, 13:1–9, 18–23; parable of the lost sheep, 18:12–14; parable of the landowner, 21:33–40) and to explain what the kingdom of heaven is like (for example, parable of the wheat and tares, 13:24–30; parable of the laborers, 20:1–16; parable of the marriage feast, 22:1–14). The kingdom parables are truly parables of hope as they mainly focus on justice, fairness, equality, abundance, and reward. For a culture that historically has played the part of the underdog, a vision of restoration and final triumph is incredibly encouraging.

As a teacher, Jesus redefines spiritual instruction, using story and metaphor in ways formerly unknown in the Jewish faith. One way that Jesus does uphold traditional teaching methods was to offer instruction to groups of people rather than to individuals. Modern North American culture is individualistic, and we tend to read the Bible in a personal and private way, asking, "What does this passage or story mean to me?" In both the Hebrew and early Christian cultures, the core teachings were the guidelines, rules, and instructions for the community. When Jesus says "you," he is most often speaking in the plural rather than the singular. This distinction is significant in at least three crucial respects.

First, our faith is never exclusively a personal and private affair. We can be Christians only in relationship with others. God intends us to be "a people," and have responsibility, not just for our own needs and wants, but for the needs of others as well. The gift in this—the promise of hope—is that we never have to face life alone. God gives us one another as precious gifts.

Second, in the modern age we tend to define *sin* in terms of individual acts that violate a strict moral code rather than as a condition of brokenness and separation from God. Sin literally means "to miss the mark," and it originally had less to do with morality than with straying from the will of God. In the Jewish faith (of which Jesus was a part), if one member of the community sins, the whole community is affected. In ancient days, little could be done to avoid the condition of sin and the punishment it entailed. Jesus brings a message of forgiveness of sin and reconciliation with God. He instructs the community not to waste time focusing on individual transgressions, but to seek reconciliation with God. Jesus summarizes the hundreds of laws and rules from the Old Testament in a simple, concise teaching: "You shall love the LORD your God with all your heart, with all your soul, and with all your mind" (22:37) and "you shall love your neighbor as yourself" (v. 39b). Love displaces Law and provides the antidote to sin.

Third, God creates *synergy* in human community, the Greek concept of the whole being greater than the sum of the parts. God makes each of us to be good, but together God empowers us to be great. By the power of the Holy Spirit, God enables us to meet every challenge and to fill every need, that is, when we can learn to trust God and one another enough. True Christian discipleship is a hope-filled group activity.

The Hope of the Passion and Crucifixion

> Now when He came into the temple, the chief priests and the elders of the people confronted Him as He was teaching, and said, "By what authority are You doing these things? And who gave You this authority?" . . .
>
> Jesus said to them, "Assuredly, I say to you that tax collectors and harlots enter the kingdom of God before you. For John came to you in the way of righteousness, and you did not believe him; but tax collectors and harlots believed him; and when you saw it, you did not afterward relent and believe him.
>
> "Hear [a] parable: There was a certain landowner who planted a vineyard and set a hedge around it, dug a winepress in it and built a tower. And he leased it to vinedressers and went into a far country. Now when vintage-time drew near, he sent his servants to the vinedressers, that they might receive its fruit. And the vinedressers took his servants, beat one, killed one, and stoned another. Again he sent other servants, more than the first, and they did likewise to them. Then last of all he sent his son to them, saying, 'They will respect my son.' But when the vinedressers saw the son, they said among themselves, 'This is the heir. Come, let us kill him and seize his inheritance.' So they took him and cast him out of the vineyard and killed him.
>
> "Therefore, when the owner of the vineyard comes, what will he do to those vinedressers?"
>
> They said to Him, "He will destroy those wicked men miserably, and lease his vineyard to other vinedressers who will render to him the fruits in their seasons."
>
> Jesus said to them, "Have you never read in the Scriptures:
>
> > 'The stone which the builders rejected
> > Has become the chief cornerstone.

> This was the Lord's doing,
> And it is marvelous in our eyes'?
>
> "Therefore I say to you, the kingdom of God will be taken from you and given to a nation bearing the fruits of it." (21:23, 31–43)

The community of believers who travel with Jesus as disciples grow slowly in their understanding and acceptance of who Jesus really is. The disciples witness amazing miracles and healings (15:21–39), they receive direct instruction and revelation from Jesus (16:5–28; 17:14–20:28), and Peter, James, and John are present at the transfiguration (17:1–13). With each passing experience, the disciples grow in their certainty and confidence. They still have a long way to go, however, at the time of Jesus' triumphal entry into Jerusalem (21:1–11). One wonders how hopeful Jesus is as he contemplates entrusting the Christian movement into the hands of followers who do not seem fully prepared for the responsibility. Jesus faces his final days knowing that the unfolding of God's plan will continue through the ministry of the Twelve.

In Matthew's gospel, some of the most significant of all Jesus' teaching occur during the week preceding his crucifixion. The parable of the two sons (vv. 28–32), the parable of the landowner (vv. 33–46), and the parable of the marriage feast (22:1–15) are messages of hope, but only to those who are faithful and who understand the new covenant established through Jesus the Messiah. For the scribes, Pharisees, Herodians, and Sadducees, the message is anything but hopeful. Jesus details their hypocrisy and apostasy, and promises that "the kingdom of God will be taken from you and given to a nation bearing fruits of it" (21:43b). Jesus warns his followers of tribulations to come (24:4–26) but assures them that all will work out well, and that those who stand fast in their faith will receive the reward and blessing of God. Jesus encourages his followers to remain vigilant and prepared and to use their talents with integrity in his absence (25:1–30).

Perhaps the most powerful story of hope in human history is the triumph of Jesus over death through resurrection. The last hours and days of Jesus' life are an epic and classic drama. Following his triumphal entry into Jerusalem, Jesus confronts enemies who conspire to kill him, involving one of Jesus' own disciples in their plot. The disciples celebrate the Passover with Jesus—a religious tradition calling to remembrance God's deliverance of the chosen people from captivity in Egypt—and from that experience, Jesus institutes the first act of Holy Communion. Jesus takes common bread and table wine, transforming them into a keen symbol of hope, a daily and regular reminder of his place in the lives of his followers. No one present will ever be able to eat bread or drink wine again without calling Jesus to mind (26:26–29). Then, in the hours that follow, all hope seems lost (26:30–27:44). The forces of evil and darkness combine to extinguish the Light of the World (27:45–66). With the death of Jesus, hope ends, and for approximately thirty-six hours, the followers of Jesus exist in abject despair. But our hope rests not in what we see with our eyes, but in what we know in our hearts. Our God is an awesome God and has power over life and death. Our enduring hope is grounded in nothing less than the risen Christ (28:1–17).

The Promise of Hope

Matthew concludes his gospel with instruction and a promise. Jesus tells his followers and us today, "'All authority has been given to Me in heaven and on earth. Go therefore and make disciples of all nations, baptizing them in the name of the Father and of the Son and of the Holy Spirit, teaching them to observe all things that I have commanded you; and lo, I am with you always, even to the end of the age.' Amen" (28:18–20). We are given hope to share hope with everyone we meet.

Mark

The Gospel of Restoration

Each of the Gospels carries a central message of hope, yet each is also unique. Matthew frames his message of hope as fulfillment of Israelite prophecy—a religious hope. Mark frames his message of hope as a restoration of God's people—a political hope. Matthew constantly quotes Jewish scripture as evidence of Jesus' identity. Mark essentially ignores the Old Testament and instead focuses on the work and teaching of Jesus and proclaims a central message, that through Jesus justice will prevail.

Mark is the earliest of the four Gospels in the New Testament, but it dates to around 70 CE (Common Era). Scholars have long speculated about why the earliest gospel was written forty years after the life, ministry, and resurrection of Jesus. Mark's gospel promises that those who have lived in bondage for centuries—at the hands of Egyptians, Babylonians, Greeks, and Romans—may finally hope for freedom in Christ Jesus.

The gospel of Mark contains no Greek word that translates as *hope*. Yet, as in Matthew, teaching after teaching, healing after healing, and miracle after miracle lay a foundation of expectation and anticipation, hope for a very different future.

Mark does not begin his gospel with a genealogy or a birth narrative. Jesus' human family is unimportant to Mark. Mark establishes Jesus as the Son of God by beginning with Jesus' baptism. Mark defines Jesus' mission and ministry as preaching the gospel of the kingdom of God with the message: "The time is fulfilled, and the kingdom of God is at hand. Repent, and believe in the gospel" (1:14–15). The disciples are called, and immediately Jesus begins his miraculous acts, casting out demons, curing the sick, cleansing lepers, and healing the disabled (1:21–2:12). Such manifestations of power were compelling evidence that the poor and oppressed had reason to hope. All that made life difficult and hopeless was as nothing in the face of Jesus' power.

One of the most commonly used words in Mark's gospel is "immediately." In the first chapter alone, the word appears eight times (vv. 10, 12, 18, 20, 21, 28, 31, 42). The author of this gospel does not promise hope for the future, but a very real hope in the present moment. Common Jewish people had lived for centuries awaiting promises of restoration and justice in some future age; Mark proclaims that the time has come: immediately!

The gospel sets up conflict and controversy from the very early chapters. Mark makes clear that Jesus threatens those with worldly, human authority, and that those in power conspire from the outset to destroy him (3:1–12). In one confrontation with the scribes, Jesus proclaims, "Assuredly, I say to you, all sins will be forgiven the sons of men, and whatever blasphemies they may utter; but he who blasphemes against the Holy Spirit never has forgiveness, but is subject to eternal condemnation" (vv. 28–29). Only one sin is unpardonable in Mark's theology, and that is to reject the Holy Spirit manifest in the person of Jesus. Regardless of whether or not the Romans or the Jews rejected Jesus, both were guilty of this unpardonable sin.

Miracles of Hope

The miracles Jesus performs in Mark's gospel follow a simple, yet remarkable pattern. Rarely a chapter goes by in which Mark does not report the performance of a miracle: casting out an unclean spirit (1:23–28), healing Peter's mother-in-law (vv. 29–34), cleansing a leper (vv. 40–45), healing a paralyzed man (2:1–12), restoring a withered hand (3:1–6), stilling the storm (4:35–41), sending demons into the swineherd (5:1–20), healing the woman with the issue of blood (vv. 25–34), raising Jairus's daughter (vv. 35–43), feeding the five thousand (6:30–44), walking on water (vv. 45–52), curing the deaf mute (7:31–37), feeding the four thousand (8:1–10), casting out an evil spirit (9:14–29), healing blind Bartimaeus (10:46–52), and the cursing of the fig tree (11:12–14, 20–24). This continuous display of supernatural power gives hope to the sick, the disabled, the emotionally damaged, the powerless, the hungry, and those corrupted by evil. No earthly affliction can withstand the Spirit's power.

It is perhaps difficult for people living in the age of modern medicine and health care to understand the world at the time of Jesus. The average lifespan was little more than forty years, and no one had yet even imagined germs, genetics, viruses, bacteria, or basic hygiene. There were no corrective lenses for poor eyesight, no hearing aids to combat deafness, no antibiotics or painkillers. Many people suffered afflictions their entire lives with little or no relief. Imagine what it would be like to be blind or deaf and find out that a healer has come who can restore your sight or hearing. Those who were terrorized by seizures, psychological afflictions, and insanity (whether demonic or otherwise) suddenly could hope to live normal lives. Even the remotest possibility that a cure might exist would have been an incredible encouragement. Jesus offered hope of new life.

Mark emphasizes the importance of belief, hope as expectation that Jesus can do the wondrous acts he does. Jesus' power does not depend on the faith of the individual, however. Jesus exceeds all normal expectations—not only does he feed five thousand people, but twelve baskets of bread and fish are left over (6:32–44). He walks on water, defying natural physical laws (vv. 45–52). His power to heal is so great that he doesn't have to lay hands on the sick and disabled; a mere touch of the hem of his garment is sufficient (v. 56). One challenge the author of Mark highlights is the need to believe without being convinced by miracles. When the Pharisees seek a sign, Jesus laments, "Why does this generation see a sign? Assuredly, I say to you, no sign shall be given to this generation" (8:12b). When the disciples forget to take provisions with them (v. 14), they start to worry and quarrel, and Jesus grows annoyed with them. They have seen him feed crowds of five thousand and four thousand, and yet they doubt he will feed them. Jesus doesn't want people believing he is the Son of God simply because he can do amazing tricks; he wants them to believe because he is trustworthy and has authority. As evidence mounts through what Jesus does and says, all questions and doubt should disappear. In all the ways Jesus performs and behaves, he proves himself to be the hope of the children of God.

The Price of Hope

> Now as He was going out on the road, one came running, knelt before Him, and asked Him, "Good Teacher, what shall I do that I may inherit eternal life?"
>
> So Jesus said to him, "Why do you call Me good? No one is good but One, that is, God. You know the commandments: 'Do not commit adultery,' 'Do not murder,' 'Do not steal,' 'Do not bear false witness,' 'Do not defraud,' 'Honor your father and your mother.'"
>
> And he answered and said to Him, "Teacher, all these things I have kept from my youth."
>
> Then Jesus, looking at him, loved him, and said to him, "One thing you lack: Go your way, sell whatever you have and give to the poor, and you will have treasure in heaven; and come, take up the cross, and follow Me."
>
> But he was sad at this word, and went away sorrowful, for he had great possessions. (10:17–22)

The hope that Jesus offers is not cheap. The story of the rich young ruler (10:17–22) is an excellent illustration of the high value placed on God's gift of new life in Christ. The rich young man asks what he must do to inherit eternal life—to receive the greatest gift anyone could ever hope for—and Jesus reminds him that keeping the commandments is the place to start. But then he goes on to say, "One thing you lack: Go your way, sell whatever you have and give to the poor, and you will have treasure in heaven; and come, take up the cross, and follow Me" (v. 21). Often, we frame hope in one-sided terms; we want to win something, have a problem solved or a pain lifted, or receive an unexpected blessing. Few people hope to have to make a sacrifice, pay a price, or carry a burden. Christians cannot hope for cheap grace. Reward and blessing will come, but only when we are willing to make a commensurate commitment.

Mark draws an interesting comparison between greatness and humility. It is human to desire comfort, security, popularity, and safety. What God offers instead is a challenge to give, to serve, to risk, and to go where we might not wish to go. In many ways, Mark describes how Jesus asks us to hope for a harder life rather than an easier one. If Mark were to post a job description for a follower of Jesus, one wonders if anyone would apply. We are invited to leave home and family, loved ones and occupation, comfort and familiar surroundings, to go to strange places and meet strange people—many of whom will insult and reject us—and to put our lives in jeopardy on a daily basis. Oh yes, and this invitation includes no pay or tangible benefits in this life, just assurance of reward in the world to come. This is not the way we would normally describe *hope*.

The Hope of Faith

Speaking truth to power and confronting the worldly principalities is daunting at least and terrifying at best. Mark's description of Holy Week is an epic contest between the power of God and political power. The story of Jesus cleansing the temple of the moneychangers also occurs in Matthew and Luke, but with a significant difference in Mark's gospel. In Matthew and Luke, Jesus' reaction seems spontaneous and emotional, but in Mark's gospel the action is calculated and intentional: "And Jesus went into Jerusalem and into the temple. So when He had looked around at all things, as the hour was already late, He went out to Bethany with the twelve" (11:11); is followed by, "So they came to Jerusalem. Then Jesus went into the temple and began to drive out those who bought and sold in the temple, and overturned the tables of the money changers and the seats of those who sold doves" (v. 15). Money in first-century Israel was a symbol of power, and the money belonged to Rome. Jesus offends the sensibilities of Jewish religious leaders with his healings and his words, but when he lays hands on the moneychangers, he offends the legal sensibilities of Rome. Blasphemy against the Jewish faith means less than nothing to the Roman officials; a rebellious act against the Roman state garners much greater attention. Formerly, Jesus had been a nuisance and a Jewish problem; after his rash act of laying hands on Roman coin, he becomes a Roman problem. Though the gospel as we have it today may soften the blame the early church placed on Rome, it does not lessen the message of hope contained in the incident. The influence and control of Rome was increasing. Throughout Israel and Palestine people enjoyed fewer and fewer freedoms. Taxation was high and rising. More than 90 percent of the Judean people were impoverished and had limited privileges. The Caesars were viewed uniformly as forces of evil. The image of a courageous rebel taking on the Roman empire must have been an incredibly popular one. Just as we love the underdog in modern films and stories, so did first-century Judeans enjoy the humble Nazarene David taking on the Roman Goliath.

Yet this act of political defiance, more than any other, precipitates the drama that follows. In the week to come, Jewish and Roman leaders will combine to rob Jesus' followers of all hope. Jesus takes great pains to encourage his listeners, but the die is cast.

The contrast between the things of God and the things of the Roman empire come up once more when Jesus answers the question about paying taxes. Again affronting Rome, Jesus offers the famous line, "Render to Caesar the things that are Caesar's, and to God the things that are God's" (12:17). More than any of the other gospel writers, Mark paints the week between Palm Sunday and Good Friday as one of constant controversy, challenge, and conflict with various authority figures. Instructions to the disciples take the form of warnings and cautions. Tension and intrigue remain high in the final few chapters of Mark.

The story of the Passover meal and the institution of the Lord's Supper; the time spent in the Garden of Gethsemane; the betrayal, arrest, trial, and crucifixion of Jesus hold very little hope in Mark. Many incidents express a bleak finality, with little positive vision for the future. At the Last Supper Jesus says, "Assuredly, I say to you, I will no longer drink of the fruit of the vine until that day when I drink it new in the kingdom of God" (14:25). He tells the disciples they will stumble, betraying and rejecting him. He finds himself alone in Gethsemane as his close friends sleep. In his greatest need, Mark reports, "Then they all forsook Him and fled" (v. 50).

In none of the Gospels do we find deep hope in the crucifixion and the dark hours that follow. The miraculous gift of hope comes only through the Easter event, the resurrection of Jesus. Matthew, Luke, and John go to great lengths to recount how the earthly Jesus truly returned from death, earning the faith of followers that he was the true Christ. Mark's gospel contains a bit more ambiguity.

> Now when the Sabbath was past, Mary Magdalene, Mary the mother of James, and Salome bought spices, that they might come and anoint Him. Very early in the morning, on the first day of the week, they came to the tomb when the sun had risen. And they said among themselves, "Who will roll away the stone from the door of the tomb for us?" But when they looked up, they saw that the stone had been rolled away—for it was very large. And entering the tomb, they saw a young man clothed in a long white robe sitting on the right side; and they were alarmed.
>
> But he said to them, "Do not be alarmed. You seek Jesus of Nazareth, who was crucified. He is risen! He is not here. See the place where they laid Him. But go, tell His disciples—and Peter—that He is going before you into Galilee; there you will see Him, as He said to you."
>
> So they went out quickly and fled from the tomb, for they trembled and were amazed. And they said nothing to anyone, for they were afraid.
>
> Now when He rose early on the first day of the week, He appeared first to Mary Magdalene, out of whom He had cast seven demons. She went and told those who had been with Him, as they mourned and wept. And when they heard that He was alive and had been seen by her, they did not believe.
>
> After that, He appeared in another form to two of them as they walked and went into the country. And they went and told it to the rest, but they did not believe them either.

> Later He appeared to the eleven as they sat at the table; and He rebuked their unbelief and hardness of heart, because they did not believe those who had seen Him after He had risen. And He said to them, "Go into all the world and preach the gospel to every creature. He who believes and is baptized will be saved; but he who does not believe will be condemned. And these signs will follow those who believe: In My name they will cast out demons; they will speak with new tongues; they will take up serpents; and if they drink anything deadly, it will by no means hurt them; they will lay hands on the sick, and they will recover."
>
> So then, after the Lord had spoken to them, He was received up into heaven, and sat down at the right hand of God. And they went out and preached everywhere, the Lord working with them and confirming the word through the accompanying signs. Amen. (16:1–20)

Many scholars contend that Mark 16:9–20 is a much later addition to the original text, which ends abruptly at verse 8, when the women who visit the tomb "went out quickly and fled from the tomb, for they trembled and were amazed. And they said nothing to anyone, for they were afraid." Why would Mark not confirm the return of Jesus? In Mark, more than any other gospel account, faith is defined as trust in the person of Jesus and not as belief based in miracles or mighty acts of power. Mark reports that Jesus sometimes could not perform mighty acts (6:5) and that the unbelief of some people negated their ability to receive miracles. Mark proclaims an unconditional faith, and Jesus rebuffs people for needing or demanding signs. For Mark, there is no question of Jesus' resurrection, but he expects people to believe in this miracle without tangible proof. Faith, for Mark, is belief in things unseen. For the audience that reads Mark, seeing is not believing—believing is believing, and lack of tangible evidence is irrelevant to those who have ears to hear and eyes to see. Even when we don't see proof with our eyes, we can still trust God and know that Jesus continues to guide us through the power of the Holy Spirit. This is our hope, according to Mark.

Luke–Acts

Radical Hope

Matthew offered hope to the spiritually disenfranchised, using Hebrew scriptures to prove that Jesus was the true Messiah. Mark offered hope to the politically oppressed, contending that the kingdom of God revealed in Jesus Christ was superior to any earthly empire. Luke offers hope to the poor and marginalized, those on the fringes of society. We have in Luke's gospel a radical countercultural message of hope that he continues to unfold in the book of Acts. John's gospel physically separates Luke and Acts in our modern Bibles, but they belong together as two sides of one coin, and we will treat them as a unity here.

Only a small segment of our modern North American society can begin to imagine life in the first-century Middle East. The vast majority of the population was poor, living at a subsistence level. The norm was single-room huts with mud floors: no running water, no electricity, no refrigeration or air-conditioning. Large families lived in very small spaces with their livestock. Few households had enough food for more than two simple meals a day—generally bread, pottage, and wine—water, in most places, was not clean enough to drink. People worked from sunrise to sunset—including the elderly and children. Hygiene was minimal—bathing was infrequent, and people didn't understand the relationship of cleanliness to health. There was no dentistry or optometry, and medicine was primitive and unscientific. Most people lived with pain and affliction. The only education most people received came from their own families, so the opportunity to improve one's life was minimal at best. Taxation, paid in goods, trade, and services, kept most poor people locked in their poverty. In such a time and place, hope was a rare commodity.

Luke understands that Jesus offers more than a new Jewish sect or a grassroots movement. He lays the foundation for a new kind of world. The Christian Way is more than a continuation of an old faith tradition; it is a new beginning. Jesus is a fulfillment of the old (1:1), and he will reign over a kingdom of equity and equality that will never end (v. 33).

Hope for Society's Fringes

And Mary said:

"My soul magnifies the Lord,
And my spirit has rejoiced in God my Savior.
For He has regarded the lowly state of His maidservant;
For behold, henceforth all generations will call me blessed.
For He who is mighty has done great things for me,
And holy is His name.
And His mercy is on those who fear Him
From generation to generation.
He has shown strength with His arm;
He has scattered the proud in the imagination of their hearts.

He has put down the mighty from their thrones,
And exalted the lowly.
He has filled the hungry with good things,
And the rich He has sent away empty.
He has helped His servant Israel,
In remembrance of His mercy,
As He spoke to our fathers,
To Abraham and to his seed forever." (vv. 46–55)

Luke follows the pattern of Matthew by offering a genealogy to establish Jesus' lineage and place in the span of Jewish history (3:23–38), but he traces the line through Mary. Women, the lowest and most vulnerable members of Jewish society, play prominent roles throughout Luke's gospel. From lowly and humble beginnings, the Messiah comes in the form of a tiny baby. Angels visit simple and lowly people to announce the coming of John and Jesus—promises to ordinary people of extraordinary offspring (1:11–33). Luke sets the tone of his entire gospel in Mary's Magnificat (vv. 46–55), when Mary tells Elizabeth what God has done in the past and will continue through her Son: "He has put down the mighty from their thrones, / And exalted the lowly. / He has filled the hungry with good things, / And the rich He has sent away empty" (vv. 52–53). From before His birth, Jesus is identified as a champion for the poor and oppressed. Matthew has Magi come to visit the babe, bearing expensive gifts. Luke has poor and humble shepherds as the audience following the miracle of Jesus' birth (2:8–20). Luke validates through Simeon (vv. 25–35) and Anna (vv. 36–38) that Jesus is indeed the long-awaited Savior. Throughout the gospel, those from the fringes of society are the first to recognize Jesus for who he really is. Luke includes a unique story of the young boy Jesus sitting with the elders in the temple (vv. 41–50), establishing his special nature even as a child.

John the Baptist announces the coming of Jesus, as he does in the other three gospels, but it is interesting to note that in Luke he adds to his message, "He who has two tunics, let him give to him who has none; and he who has food, let him do likewise" (3:11). It is obvious that Luke sees economic and social justice as the heart of Jesus' life and teaching, reinforcing it even through the ministry of those around him.

As in all the Gospels, people come from all over to witness and receive the miracles of the Nazarene. Luke emphasizes how amazed and astonished people were, and how quickly word spread of this amazing teacher and healer (4:31–44).

Matthew and Mark contain the stories of Jesus eating with sinners and tax collectors, but Luke expands on these stories (5:29–32; 7:36–39; 19:1–10) and makes them more about acceptance of those whom society generally despises or rejects. In the book of Luke, we see Jesus' tolerance, acceptance, kindness, compassion, and inclusiveness for all people—hope for the hopeless.

Hope in the Beatitudes

Then He lifted up His eyes toward His disciples, and said:
"Blessed are you poor,
For yours is the kingdom of God.
Blessed are you who hunger now,
For you shall be filled.
Blessed are you who weep now,
For you shall laugh.
Blessed are you when men hate you,
And when they exclude you,
And revile you, and cast out your name as evil,
For the Son of Man's sake.
Rejoice in that day and leap for joy!
For indeed your reward is great in heaven,
For in like manner their fathers did to the prophets.
But woe to you who are rich,
For you have received your consolation.
Woe to you who are full,
For you shall hunger.
Woe to you who laugh now,
For you shall mourn and weep.
Woe to you when all men speak well of you,
For so did their fathers to the false prophets." (6:20–26)

A prime example of this is a simple contrast of the Beatitudes in Luke 6:20–26 with those contained in Matthew 5:1–12. Matthew offers conditions for each blessing. In Luke (6:20), Jesus says, "Blessed are you poor," while in Matthew (5:3) he says, "Blessed are the poor in spirit." Luke remembers Jesus speaking more personally and more directly. Jesus speaks to the physical condition in Luke, but Matthew interprets it in more emotional and spiritual terms. Luke 6:21a reads, "Blessed are you who hunger now, / For you shall be filled"; Matthew 5:6 says, "Blessed are those who hunger and thirst for righteousness, / For they shall be filled." Luke 6:21b proclaims, "Blessed are you who weep now, / For you shall laugh"; but Matthew 5:4 promises, "Blessed are those who mourn, / For they shall be comforted." Matthew reports that Jesus offered nine blessings in broad and inclusive terms—speaking a word of grace and hope to all, rich or poor, powerful or weak, those included in the community and those excluded as well. Luke reports four very direct and limited blessings to the poor, the weak, the hungry, the despairing, and the ostracized. He reinforces his intentions with four woes (absent from Matthew's gospel): woe to the rich, the full, the laughing, and the respected. Jesus preaches a message of justice, fairness, and impartiality. In Luke, Jesus is speaking a powerful message of hope to the poor, hungry, sad, and disrespected. Is it any wonder that multitudes traveled to hear him speak and witness his mighty works?

No Greater Hope

Jesus challenges the common teachings of the Pharisees, instructing followers to love enemies, share with even the undeserving, and lend with no expectation of return (6:27–36). He denounces judgment and condemnation (so prevalent in the temple and synagogue in Jesus' day), and commands instead forgiveness and mercy (vv. 37–38). Jesus contrasts doing what God expects with doing what human religious leaders expect (vv. 39–50). This affront to the religious status quo earned Jesus the wrath of the priests and teachers, but was a breath of fresh air to the common people.

Luke reports the many miraculous works shared in the other gospels: healing the centurion's servant (7:1–10), raising the widow's son (vv. 11–16), stilling the storm (8:22–25), sending the demons into the swine (vv. 26–40), healing the woman with the twelve-year hemorrhage (vv. 43–48), raising Jairus's daughter (vv. 49–56), and others. In a society where the poor had little access to any type of medical assistance or aid, these stories are particularly powerful. Luke reminds his audience that Jesus is Lord over illness and disease, insanity and demon possession, physical affliction and even death. No greater hope exists.

Luke tells some stories of Jesus that none of the others gospels report. Many contain significant messages of hope and encouragement. All of chapter 10 is unique to Luke. He begins with the mission and sending of seventy disciples, two-by-two, to teach, preach, and heal (vv. 1–16). When the seventy return (vv. 17–24), Jesus commends their effectiveness and offers a prayer to God thanking the Father that "You have hidden these things from the wise and prudent and revealed them to babes." The truth of God is not the private property of the learned religious leaders; through Jesus the Christ it is readily available to one and all. Luke records that anyone may be used to do the work of God.

A lawyer asks Jesus what absolutely must be done to inherit eternal life (v. 25). Jesus turns the question back to the lawyer (v. 26), and the lawyer wisely says, "You shall love the LORD your God with all your heart, with all your soul, with all your strength, and with all your mind, and your neighbor as yourself" (v. 27). This great commandment is certainly challenging, but it is equally available to all. It is not conditional on status, education, position in society, or a specially conferred blessing. Hope is not the province of the fortunate; it is a very real gift offered to all.

Hope from the Parables

> And behold, a certain lawyer stood up and tested Him, saying, "Teacher, what shall I do to inherit eternal life?"
>
> He said to him, "What is written in the law? What is your reading of it?"
>
> So he answered and said, " 'You shall love the LORD your God with all your heart, with all your soul, with all your strength, and with all your mind,' and 'your neighbor as yourself.' "
>
> And He said to him, "You have answered rightly; do this and you will live."
>
> But he, wanting to justify himself, said to Jesus, "And who is my neighbor?"

> Then Jesus answered and said: "A certain man went down from Jerusalem to Jericho, and fell among thieves, who stripped him of his clothing, wounded him, and departed, leaving him half dead. Now by chance a certain priest came down that road. And when he saw him, he passed by on the other side. Likewise a Levite, when he arrived at the place, came and looked, and passed by on the other side. But a certain Samaritan, as he journeyed, came where he was. And when he saw him, he had compassion. So he went to him and bandaged his wounds, pouring on oil and wine; and he set him on his own animal, brought him to an inn, and took care of him. On the next day, when he departed, he took out two denarii, gave them to the innkeeper, and said to him, 'Take care of him; and whatever more you spend, when I come again, I will repay you.' So which of these three do you think was neighbor to him who fell among the thieves?"
>
> And he said, "He who showed mercy on him."
>
> Then Jesus said to him, "Go and do likewise." (10:25–37)

The next story is the often misnamed parable of the "good Samaritan" (10:25–37). In this story, an unwary victim travels from Jerusalem to Jericho and is beset by robbers who beat him and leave him for dead. A priest and a Levite—two acknowledged "good" men in society—see the victim and intentionally ignore his distress. Then a Samaritan—an enemy of the man and a "bad" man by society's standards—comes along and, moved to compassion, offers exceptional aid and care. The common misreading of this parable places the reader in the role of the Good Samaritan—not a bad choice, but it ignores the literary structure and purpose of a parable. We readers of the story should put ourselves in the place of the subject of the opening sentence; therefore, we are not the Samaritan, but the victim. Think of what this means. How does it change the meaning of the parable? Instead of an instruction on how to behave, it becomes one more example of Luke's vision of true faith. In this journey of ours called "life," we will face many challenges, and we may even find ourselves victims of oppression, want, need, and violence. Our tendency is to rely on the religious and political institutions to rescue us and give us aid and hope. But in Jesus' day, some individuals in those institutions were corrupt, making the institutions ineffective. Where will our hope come from? Jesus says it is likely to come from the least likely places. The final challenge offered through this story is to consider who we would most like to encounter were we the victim. Following the ethos of the golden rule, we are charged to go and treat others as we would hope to be treated by others.

> And He said to them, "Which of you shall have a friend, and go to him at midnight and say to him, 'Friend, lend me three loaves; for a friend of mine has come to me on his journey, and I have nothing to set before him'; and he will answer from within and say, 'Do not trouble me; the door is now shut, and my children are with me in bed; I cannot rise and give to you'? I say to you, though he will not rise and give to him because he is his friend, yet because of his persistence he will rise and give him as many as he needs.
>
> "So I say to you, ask, and it will be given to you; seek, and you will find; knock, and it will be opened to you. For everyone who asks receives, and he who seeks finds, and to him who knocks it will be opened. (11:5–10)

One parable unique to Luke is that of the persistent friend (11:5–10), the man who will not leave his neighbor alone until he receives help. Finally, the neighbor gives in just to regain some peace and quiet. To a people losing hope, this is a very simple but important message: don't give up. Just because an answer has not come yet does not mean it will not come if we will hold fast to our faith.

Jesus faces his share of opposition in Luke, with priests, scribes, lawyers, Pharisees, and Sadducees challenging him at different times (11:37–54; 16:14–17; 20:1–8, 19–47). As in both Matthew and Mark, Luke presents many inspirational examples of Jesus speaking truth to power and challenging those in authority. The poor and marginalized lacked a voice; in fact, they lacked access to the seats of power to even attempt any kind of reform or change. How comforting it must have been to early audiences to hear the stories of the man from Nazareth not only confronting the powers and principalities of first-century Israel and Rome but summarily defeating them at almost every encounter.

One common affliction of the poor is to live in a constant state of desire for wealth and material comfort. Those who have very little, dream of having much. Those who go to bed hungry, long for a full belly. Those who live in fear of losing what they have, wish for the comfort and security that wealth provides. Jesus addresses this directly with his followers. He shares the parable of the rich fool (12:13–21), in which the man attempts to store up for himself reserves of food and goods to make sure all his needs are cared for. He dies, and all his best efforts are wasted. Jesus ends the tale by telling us there are more important things in life than storing up treasure on earth (v. 21). He proceeds to encourage his followers not to worry, but to trust that God will provide. Where are we to put our faith? If we value things, we will organize our lives to get more things and hold on to them. However, if we put our faith in God, we will direct all our energy to serving and pleasing God. "For where your treasure is, there your heart will be also" (v. 34). Jesus goes on to say that we simply do not have time to waste. Even more precious than gold or jewels, our time, energy, and gifts from God are all we have of real value. The parables of the watchful steward (vv. 35–40) and the faithful steward (vv. 41–48) are clear indicators that Jesus expects us to stay focused on doing good to honor and glorify God, and not to waste our time in pursuit of material wealth. Indeed, discipleship is extremely costly (vv. 49–59), but not nearly as costly as giving our lives to things of lesser importance. If God is first in our lives, every reward of true worth is promised to be ours. What a blessed and joyous word to those who have little or nothing.

Jesus teaches three parables unique to Luke that offer hope to the minority members of the Jewish culture. The parable of the lost sheep (15:1–7) says that every individual has special worth in the eyes of God—"there will be more joy in heaven over one sinner who repents than over ninety-nine just persons who need no repentance." Likewise, in the parable of the ten coins (vv. 8–10), the one that is found is a greater cause for joy than the ones safely in hand. The parable of the father and his two sons (vv. 11–32)—often referred to as the parable of the prodigal son—is a word of comfort and assurance that no matter how far we may stray, God awaits our return and rejoices when it occurs.

Hope for Those Who Believe

The encounters and teachings contained in Luke 16–18 challenge the authority of religious and political leaders and heighten the tension between Jesus and these authorities. In big and small ways, Jesus does the unexpected—reinterpreting conventional beliefs and giving them brand-new meanings. With each new teaching, each divine healing, each amazing miracle, Jesus' reputation and popularity increases with the common people, all the while plummeting with those whose power he challenges. The religious and political leaders launch an all-out campaign to try to discredit Jesus immediately following his triumphal entry into Jerusalem (20:1–47). As pressure increases, Jesus teaches about patience, confidence, steadfastness in prayer, trust, and faithfulness. He models a classic non-anxious presence in the face of constant assault (21:1–38). When every attempt to dishonor Jesus fails, the religious and political leaders conspire to destroy Jesus.

As with Matthew and Mark, the days and hours leading to Jesus' crucifixion are bleak, anxious, dark, and hopeless. To witness the Son of God treated with hostility and contempt, physically beaten and abused, mocked and spat upon, demoralized and debased, is almost too much to bear (22:63–23:49). How in the world could so much evil happen to someone so good?

Try to imagine, if you can, what it might have been like to live this story for the very first time; to not know how it all turns out. The greatest teacher and the most hopeful visionary you have ever met is killed, executed as a common criminal. You see the pain and agony of his slow, torturous death. You watch as his body is removed and placed in a grave. You see the tomb sealed. All hope is gone. What desolate and horrendous hours follow! A day and a half pass. Soon after sunrise on Sunday morning a rumor is heard—Jesus is alive! Jesus has come back from the dead. It is confirmed that the tomb is empty, and very soon stories begin to spread that people have seen him, including the disciples. Rumor changes into fact. The powers of evil and earthly values have killed the Son of God, but even killing him cannot defeat him. He conquers even death! Hope lives! The gospel of Luke ends with Jesus instructing those who believe in him and choose to follow him to bear witness to all they have seen and heard (24:47–48).

Hope After Jesus: The Acts of the Apostles

> The former account I made, O Theophilus, of all that Jesus began both to do and teach, until the day in which He was taken up, after He through the Holy Spirit had given commandments to the apostles whom He had chosen, to whom He also presented Himself alive after His suffering by many infallible proofs, being seen by them during forty days and speaking of the things pertaining to the kingdom of God.
>
> And being assembled together with them, He commanded them not to depart from Jerusalem, but to wait for the Promise of the Father, "which," He said, "you have heard from Me; for John truly baptized with water, but you shall be baptized with the Holy Spirit not many days from now." Therefore, when they had come together, they asked Him, saying, "Lord, will You at this time restore the kingdom to Israel?" And He said to them, "It is not for you to know times or seasons which the Father has put in His own authority. But you shall receive power when the Holy Spirit has come upon you; and you shall be witnesses to Me in Jerusalem, and in all Judea and Samaria, and to the end of the earth."
>
> Now when He had spoken these things, while they watched, He was taken up, and a cloud received Him out of their sight. And while they looked steadfastly toward heaven as He went up, behold, two men stood by them in white apparel, who also said, "Men of Galilee, why do you stand gazing up into heaven? This same Jesus, who was taken up from you into heaven, will so come in like manner as you saw Him go into heaven."

Then they returned to Jerusalem from the mount called Olivet, which is near Jerusalem, a Sabbath day's journey. And when they had entered, they went up into the upper room where they were staying: Peter, James, John, and Andrew; Philip and Thomas; Bartholomew and Matthew; James the son of Alphaeus and Simon the Zealot; and Judas the son of James. These all continued with one accord in prayer and supplication, with the women and Mary the mother of Jesus, and with His brothers.

And in those days Peter stood up in the midst of the disciples (altogether the number of names was about a hundred and twenty), and said, "Men and brethren, this Scripture had to be fulfilled, which the Holy Spirit spoke before by the mouth of David concerning Judas, who became a guide to those who arrested Jesus; for he was numbered with us and obtained a part in this ministry."

(Now this man purchased a field with the wages of iniquity; and falling headlong, he burst open in the middle and all his entrails gushed out. And it became known to all those dwelling in Jerusalem; so that field is called in their own language, Akel Dama, that is, Field of Blood.)

"For it is written in the Book of Psalms:

> 'Let his dwelling place be desolate,
> And let no one live in it';

and,

> 'Let another take his office.'

"Therefore, of these men who have accompanied us all the time that the Lord Jesus went in and out among us, beginning from the baptism of John to that day when He was taken up from us, one of these must become a witness with us of His resurrection."

And they proposed two: Joseph called Barsabas, who was surnamed Justus, and Matthias. And they prayed and said, "You, O Lord, who know the hearts of all, show which of these two You have chosen to take part in this ministry and apostleship from which Judas by transgression fell, that he might go to his own place." And they cast their lots, and the lot fell on Matthias. And he was numbered with the eleven apostles. (Acts of the Apostles 1:1–26)

The transition from the gospel of Luke to the Acts of the Apostles is the shift from Jesus' earthly ministry to the ministry of the disciples and apostles empowered by the Holy Spirit. Jesus brought hope; the church is to be an institution and movement of hope. The first chapter of Acts recounts the passing of the mantle from Jesus to his followers. In Luke, John the Baptist promised that Jesus would baptize with the Holy Spirit. In Acts 1:4–8, Jesus promises that this prophecy will be fulfilled within a few days. He also defines the work of the Twelve—to become apostles to the ends of the earth and witnesses to the good news of Jesus Christ.

In modern usage, the word *apostle* is often used synonymously with the words *disciple* or *follower.* This is inaccurate. Apostles are those sent out into the world to preach the good news and to teach and heal. Apostles take the gospel to new places and share it with people who have not heard or understood it. Disciples may follow and serve in a local setting; apostles are similar to missionaries, going out in the name of Jesus the Christ.

A Church of Hope

> But Peter, standing up with the eleven, raised his voice and said to them, "Men of Judea and all who dwell in Jerusalem, let this be known to you, and heed my words. For these are not drunk, as you suppose, since it is only the third hour of the day. But this is what was spoken by the prophet Joel:
>
> > 'And it shall come to pass in the last days, says God,
> > That I will pour out of My Spirit on all flesh;
> > Your sons and your daughters shall prophesy,
> > Your young men shall see visions,
> > Your old men shall dream dreams.
> > And on My menservants and on My maidservants
> > I will pour out My Spirit in those days;
> > And they shall prophesy.
> > I will show wonders in heaven above
> > And signs in the earth beneath:
> > Blood and fire and vapor of smoke.
> > The sun shall be turned into darkness,
> > And the moon into blood,

Before the coming of the great and awesome day of the LORD.
And it shall come to pass
That whoever calls on the name of the LORD
Shall be saved.'

"Men of Israel, hear these words: Jesus of Nazareth, a Man attested by God to you by miracles, wonders, and signs which God did through Him in your midst, as you yourselves also know—Him, being delivered by the determined purpose and foreknowledge of God, you have taken by lawless hands, have crucified, and put to death; whom God raised up, having loosed the pains of death, because it was not possible that He should be held by it. For David says concerning Him:

'I foresaw the LORD always before my face,
For He is at my right hand, that I may not be shaken.
Therefore my heart rejoiced, and my tongue was glad;
Moreover my flesh also will rest in hope.
For You will not leave my soul in Hades,
Nor will You allow Your Holy One to see corruption.
You have made known to me the ways of life;
You will make me full of joy in Your presence.'

"Men and brethren, let me speak freely to you of the patriarch David, that he is both dead and buried, and his tomb is with us to this day. Therefore, being a prophet, and knowing that God had sworn with an oath to him that of the fruit of his body, according to the flesh, He would raise up the Christ to sit on his throne, he, foreseeing this, spoke concerning the resurrection of the Christ, that His soul was not left in Hades, nor did His flesh see corruption. This Jesus God has raised up, of which we are all witnesses. Therefore being exalted to the right hand of God, and having received from the Father the promise of the Holy Spirit, He poured out this which you now see and hear.

"For David did not ascend into the heavens, but he says himself:

'The LORD said to my Lord,
"Sit at My right hand,
Till I make Your enemies Your footstool."'

"Therefore let all the house of Israel know assuredly that God has made this Jesus, whom you crucified, both Lord and Christ."

Now when they heard this, they were cut to the heart, and said to Peter and the rest of the apostles, "Men and brethren, what shall we do?"

> Then Peter said to them, "Repent, and let every one of you be baptized in the name of Jesus Christ for the remission of sins; and you shall receive the gift of the Holy Spirit. For the promise is to you and to your children, and to all who are afar off, as many as the Lord our God will call."
>
> And with many other words he testified and exhorted them, saying, "Be saved from this perverse generation." Then those who gladly received his word were baptized; and that day about three thousand souls were added to them. (2:14–41)

The second chapter of Acts is the story of the birth of the Christian church and the transformation of the Twelve, in the Holy Spirit, from disciples of Jesus Christ into the apostles to all the world. At the celebration of Pentecost (one of the significant Jewish festival days), the Holy Spirit baptizes the disciples and empowers them to speak in many languages to enable them to preach and teach the good news. This miraculous act, the true meaning of "speaking in tongues," expands the Christian movement from a provincial Jewish sect to a broad and far-reaching global phenomenon. The hope of the Jews, the hope of Israel, the hope of the poor become the hope of the world!

Not everyone reacts the same way to the Pentecost miracle. Some are deeply impressed, others are confused, and some are derisive and unimpressed (vv. 5–13). Most of the witnesses to the Pentecost event do not comprehend the greatest miracle and sign of hope: Peter finally living up to his designation as "Cephas" (the rock). Peter—who so frequently misunderstood what Jesus meant, who panicked and sank when he attempted to walk on water, who missed the point of the transfiguration, who argued with Jesus about his death, and who denied Jesus three times the night of his arrest—delivers a powerful and compelling invitation. The gift of God's Holy Spirit is offered to any and all who will repent of their sins and pledge to follow Jesus. The response to the testimony is amazing, with more than three thousand baptized in one day (v. 41). The church grows daily, as more and more people receive the word of hope and good news the apostles have to share (v. 47b). Following the example and model of Jesus, Peter and the rest of the apostles heal, teach, preach, and perform miracles. As Jesus predicted, they encounter resistance and persecution for their efforts (4:13–22).

Yet the power of the new movement is strong, and individuals find they are forever changed. A hopeful vision for a different kind of community and world, a different kind of church, arises from Luke's description in Acts 4:32–35:

> Now the multitude of those who believed were of one heart and one soul; neither did anyone say that any of the things he possessed was his own, but they had all things in common. And with great power the apostles gave witness to the resurrection of the Lord Jesus. And great grace was upon them all. Nor was there anyone among them who lacked; for all who were possessors of lands or houses sold them, and brought the proceeds of the things that were sold, and laid them at the apostles' feet; and they distributed to each as anyone had need.

This is a glorious fulfillment of the promises Jesus made when he walked the earth.

Hope in the Face of Persecution

Luke's story follows Peter's ministry in the early chapters (1–5, especially), the organization of leaders to make sure the ministry continues (chs. 6–7), and shifts focus to Saul (and his subsequent transformation and ministry, chapters 8–28). As Luke tells the story, the scope and reach of the Christian movement continues to stretch. The more the Jewish, Greek, and Roman provinces and communities resist the gospel message, the more momentum it generates. Even imprisonment, beatings, and plots to kill the apostles (4:3; 5:33, 40) result only in fueling the apostles' virtuous reputation. Stephen's martyrdom (6:8–7:60) offers the newly appointed church leader the opportunity to set the gospel of Jesus Christ in the context of Jewish history, claiming that Jesus the Christ fulfills all of Israel's hopes and that only the unenlightened can possibly miss the point. Outraged religious and political leaders increase their persecution of the Christian movement, unintentionally unleashing the greatest Christian force in history, second only to Jesus himself.

Saul was a brutal adversary to the early Christians. Luke writes, "As for Saul, he made havoc of the church, entering every house, and dragging off men and women, committing them to prison" (8:3). Saul kept the apostles on the run. It is difficult to imagine a more irritating and hostile opponent. Yet even the greatest forces of darkness on earth don't stand a chance when confronting the light of Christ. The ninth chapter of Acts provides one of the Bible's most dramatic stories of individual call. Saul, on a mission to hunt and capture followers of "the Way," travels the Damascus road. A bright light and a voice from heaven confront the unbeliever, leaving him blind and confused. The experience unnerves Saul, and opens him to a radical and total transformation. Ananias baptizes Saul with water and the Holy Spirit, and a new apostle is born. For many, baptism symbolizes new life in Christ. For Saul, the change was much more than symbolic—Saul became a completely different man.

The transformation of Saul has an immediate impact on the fledgling Christian movement. With their chief persecutor out of the way, "the churches throughout all Judea, Galilee, and Samaria had peace and were edified" (9:31).

Hope Despite Conflict

Luke shifts attention back to Peter at 9:32. The significance of this shift is vital to understanding Luke's intention. Saul takes the good news to people from cultural and social backgrounds that include Hellenistic Jews, Gentile converts to Judaism, and Gentiles—people who are unfamiliar with Jesus and the authority of the apostles. The audiences for the early ministry of the apostles include only Hellenistic Jews and estranged members of the various tribes of Israel. Paul calls these limitations into question, but Peter is still the cornerstone of the new movement, deciding where the church can go and where it will not go. The leaders of the early movement have to learn to work together for Jesus' message to spread to all people. Peter's vision in chapter 10 and his encounter with the centurion, Cornelius, challenge his limited understanding and cause him to expand his vision to include Gentiles.

The early Christian movement is a reinterpretation of traditional Judaism. Food laws, ritual circumcision, definitions of "clean" and "unclean" have been carried forward into the new Christian Way. To take the gospel to the Gentiles requires a fundamentally new openness to things formerly closed. Peter takes extreme criticism for his new approach (11:1–17), but once more proves himself a capable and competent leader, teaching the rest of the apostles, "When they heard these things they became silent, and they glorified God, saying, 'Then God has also granted to the Gentiles repentance to life'" (v. 18). The hope of God—the promise of salvation grounded in trust, expectation, and anticipation—is for everyone!

When focus shifts from Peter and the Twelve, one, simple little tossed-off phrase in Acts 13:9 has life-changing implications: "Then Saul, who is also called Paul . . ." From this point forward in the narrative, Paul is never again called Saul. His transformation is complete. He is filled with the Holy Spirit and has become a new creature in Christ. This is a wonderfully hopeful message. If someone with as heinous and hateful a history as Saul may be forgiven and redeemed, who among us is exempt from the transforming love of God? No one. Not one. No matter how dark and dismal our past might seem, exposed to the light of Christ and the power of the Holy Spirit, we can begin again.

The book of Acts paints parallel pictures of Paul and Peter. The two apostles, apparently headed for opposition, become complementary sides of a single coin: Peter's heart, Paul's head; Peter's preaching, Paul's teaching; Peter's emotion, Paul's reason; Peter's Judaism, Paul's Hellenism. Each contrast makes the pair stronger, rather than weaker. This is a testimony to

God's ability to use every person, uniquely gifted as he or she might be, and to increase the power of our ministry through community.

Hope Through Encouragement

The apostles engage in regular and intentional "hope-work" in the early church. Not only do they invite newcomers into the faith, but Luke reports in 14:21–22 that they return to the cities they visited, "strengthening the souls of the disciples, exhorting them to continue in the faith." Encouragement, support, inspiration, and prayer are essential functions of the early church leaders. Hope is a gift and promise to those outside the church; and hope is a primary focus of those within the community of faith as well.

A refreshing feature of Luke's account of the early church is that he doesn't try to sugarcoat it or make it look perfect. Luke reports regular and frequent controversies and conflicts within the church. In the gospel of Luke, most of the controversies are between Jesus and the religious and political authorities. In the Acts of the Apostles, most of the controversies arise within the church (11:1–3; 13:42–45; 15:1–5, 36–51) as it figures out how to live in growing diversity and multiculturalism. In some cases, the solutions work wonderfully, while in others, not so well. As it was in the beginning, is now and ever shall be.

Hope Through a Life with Christ

Two wondrous conversion stories in the Acts of the Apostles are shining examples of hope. The first is found in Acts 8:26–40, the baptism of the Ethiopian eunuch. It is difficult to imagine a character more on the "fringe" than the Ethiopian eunuch. Though he is a steward with great authority, he is still a servant—a member of the slave class. He is a sexual minority. He is a racial minority. He is a social-class minority. He is under the hegemony of a foreign power, and therefore not free to make his own choices about beliefs and personal preferences. He is the most marginalized of the marginalized. And he becomes a Christian: baptized, redeemed, and blessed. Early readers and hearers of this early account would have one of two reactions to such a tale. For those in power and part of the established order, this would be a deeply offensive story. For those on the extreme edges of society, this would be a powerful message of hope.

The second story is the salvation of the Philippian jailer (Acts 16:25–34). One who could only be considered an enemy of the Christian Way is shaken physically, emotionally, and spiritually by an earthquake that opens the doors of the cells and loosens the chains of the Christian prisoners of his jail. Thinking that his prisoners will simply flee and leave him responsible, the jailer prepares to take his own life. Paul stops him and takes the opportunity to share the gospel. The jailer and his entire household are subsequently baptized. It is one thing to offer hope to strangers and those with no power; it is something quite different to offer such grace to your enemies and oppressors, but such is the will of God.

The remainder of the Acts of the Apostles is essentially a travelogue for Paul, with a few highlights. The book includes an intentional parallel to the concluding passages of Luke's gospel, with mounting controversies and a plot to kill Paul that is quite similar to the plot to kill Jesus. Yet Luke is clear: no earthly power comes close to the miraculous power of God manifest through the Holy Spirit. We are a people of the Holy Spirit, and therefore we cannot be defeated!

Paul moves from town to town with a recurrent theme: he preaches and teaches where many are persuaded (for example, Thessalonica, Berea, Athens, Corinth) and then he meets resistance and mockery. Those who get it, get it and those who don't, don't. Paul provides a living example of the parable of the sower from Matthew 13—he does not worry about where the gospel is received and where it grows; he merely moves from place to place spreading the Word of God, allowing God to bless it and multiply it wherever possible. Paul encounters a conflict that results in a riot in Ephesus (19:21–41) when he challenges the money-makers who honor the goddess Diana. Similar to Jesus' cleansing of the temple, Paul moves from the category of "nuisance" to "threat" by challenging those who profit from religious observance. At this point, resistance to and opposition of Paul increase dramatically.

Acts 20:7–12 reports a charming and painfully real incident. Paul finds a friendly and receptive crowd and begins preaching and teaching, and he talks late into the night. A young man, Eutychus, is seated in a high windowsill listening, but as often happens (even with the best preaching), Eutychus begins to drift and nod. The poor boy dozes, loses his balance, and pitches to the stone floor below, dead on impact. Without missing a beat or pausing in his message, Paul brings the lad back to life. The wonderful, implicit message here is that life in Christ becomes the new normal over time. That which seems exceptional to those who do not know Jesus the Christ becomes the expected to those walking in the Way.

Paul's great gift, according to Luke, is empowerment through exhortation (vv. 17–38). He encourages others to do what he has done. He commends people for their best efforts and helps others figure out what needs to be done. He is a wonderful teacher and shepherd, and if he lacks humility it is due to his high standards and personal performance. Paul asks no one else to do what he himself is unwilling to do. Paul led by not only instruction but also example. Many scholars, who acknowledge Jesus Christ as Lord and the one, true Son of God, agree that the early movement would not have survived, and we would not have a church today, without the ministry of the apostle Paul.

Hope That Transcends Time and Place

The final seven chapters of the Acts of the Apostles recount Paul's trials and tribulations in Jerusalem and Rome. Asian Jews are concerned about the teachings of Paul and the ways that he is defiling the Law. In a scene reminiscent of the night before Jesus' crucifixion, a gathered crowd begins to shout, "Away with him!" (21:36). Paul makes appeals to the gathered Jews, and even attempts to evangelize them to the Christian Way by sharing his own story (22:14–16). When the crowd refuses to listen and begins to call out for more serious punishment, Paul claims his Roman citizenship and requests appropriate treatment (vv. 22–29). Some Jews who feel thwarted plot against him and seek ways to put him to death (23:11–22). Paul appears before Governor Felix in a scene eerily similar to Jesus' appearance before Pontius Pilate. Felix attempts, like Pilate, to defer responsibility and leaves Paul's trial in limbo (24:22–26), but when Porcius Festus replaces Felix, Paul requests to be tried in Rome (25:10). Paul creates a defense, and is so persuasive that many of his accusers are almost converted, but once the wheels are in motion to send him to Rome, there is no recourse (26:1–32). Chapter 27 recounts the trip to Rome and the shipwreck in Malta before Paul finally reaches his destination. The Holy Spirit confirms that Paul has been sent to bring salvation to the Gentiles (28:28). The book ends with a report that Paul preached and taught for two years, with the implication that there was more to come.

The significance of Paul's story transcends time and geography. Paul faced opposition at every turn. He took the good news into new and unknown territories, many of them hostile. He faced persecution, beatings, and imprisonment. And he made disciples everywhere he went. At no time did he ever feel alone or that God was not guiding and strengthening him through the Holy Spirit. As we will discover in Paul's letters, he was convinced that he was able to do nothing apart from Christ within him. Paul lived in a blessed and total assurance that God was with him every step of the way. We need to study Paul and contemplate his life and teaching to be reminded that in all places, at all times, Christ is with us. What greater hope could we ever desire?

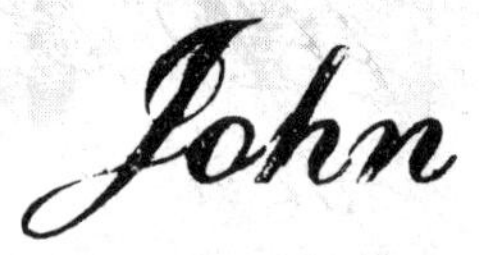

John

The Gospel of Vision

The author of the gospel of John accomplishes a remarkable feat. He creates two very different, somewhat contradictory messages of hope in one book. First, he casts a vision of hope for a remnant community concerned with its own survival. Second and concurrently, he creates a vision of universal and eternal hope.

John's gospel is the last in our New Testament, not only in placement but also chronologically. The Johannine community was a small fringe group, no longer associated with its Jewish forebears and not considered part of the mainstream Christian movement. John's gospel is much more spiritually focused than the Synoptic Gospels (the very similar gospels of Matthew, Mark, and Luke). By the time John's gospel was written, Christian sects were coming under scrutiny and oppression by the Roman Empire. A brief comparison with the other gospels illuminates how very different John's theology and story of Jesus really are. Matthew works hard to connect Christianity to Judaism. Mark labors to distance Christianity from religious and political oppression. Luke champions the cause of the poor and marginalized. John offers a message of hope to an endangered community and casts a vision for a hope that transcends any particular place, time, or people.

Eternal Hope

> In the beginning was the Word, and the Word was with God, and the Word was God. He was in the beginning with God. All things were made through Him, and without Him nothing was made that was made. In Him

> was life, and the life was the light of men. And the light shines in the darkness, and the darkness did not comprehend it.
>
> There was a man sent from God, whose name was John. This man came for a witness, to bear witness of the Light, that all through him might believe. He was not that Light, but was sent to bear witness of that Light. That was the true Light which gives light to every man coming into the world.
>
> He was in the world, and the world was made through Him, and the world did not know Him. He came to His own, and His own did not receive Him. But as many as received Him, to them He gave the right to become children of God, to those who believe in His name: who were born, not of blood, nor of the will of the flesh, nor of the will of man, but of God.
>
> And the Word became flesh and dwelt among us, and we beheld His glory, the glory as of the only begotten of the Father, full of grace and truth.
>
> John bore witness of Him and cried out, saying, "This was He of whom I said, 'He who comes after me is preferred before me, for He was before me.'"
>
> And of His fullness we have all received, and grace for grace. For the law was given through Moses, but grace and truth came through Jesus Christ. No one has seen God at any time. The only begotten Son, who is in the bosom of the Father, He has declared Him. (1:1–18)

Each New Testament author emphasizes the divine nature of Jesus at a different point in his life or death. Paul speaks of Jesus' divine nature assumed after his resurrection. Mark places this at Jesus' baptism. Matthew and Luke speak of Jesus' divinity in his miraculous birth. John sets Jesus' divinity in eternity: "In the beginning . . ."; Jesus was the Word (1:1–5, 14–18). His incarnation is merely his earthly form. Jesus has always been and will always be. (If this isn't a hopeful message, I don't know what is!) John has no need to report a miraculous birth. He moves quickly and directly to Jesus' baptism, the call of the disciples, and the public ministry (1:29–2:12). John's gospel contains many unique stories of Jesus and even recounts familiar stories in new ways.

The other gospels talk about Jesus' fears and struggles, but John displays none of Jesus' human weaknesses. Here, Jesus knows who he is, why he is on earth, and what must be done to fulfill the will of God. He exudes confidence and purpose. He is hope personified. There is absolutely no room for doubt or anxiety. Those who stay faithful to the Way of Jesus Christ have nothing to worry about. This message was especially important for a small community in which things had not gone well; the longer time passed without restoration and redemption, the harder it was to maintain faith.

Hope and Reassurance

John also appreciates dualism more than the other gospel writers. He sees things as "either/or": darkness or light, good or evil, in the community or out, sacred or worldly. In his encounter with Nicodemus (3:1–21), Jesus draws such "either/or" lines. John the Baptist's witness to Christ confirms the same ideas. What comes from God is good; what is of this world is not. Those who believe in Jesus as the Son of God have everlasting life; those who do not are excluded. A common challenge throughout John's gospel is the question, "Are we in or not?" As the story of the Samaritan woman at the well attests (4:1–38), however, Jesus is willing to draw the circle of inclusion very large. The disciples are appalled that Jesus is wasting time talking to a woman (a person of lesser worth in that culture) and a Samaritan as well (considered an enemy not worth noticing). Jesus extends his grace and power to not only the Samaritans but also to a nobleman and his son (vv. 46–54) and all those afflicted and suffering (5:1–16).

The Jesus of John's gospel is a fount of hope and reassurance. He calls God his Father, claims equality with God in both power and authority, and proclaims that God is his witness to the truth of what he says (vv. 17–38). He points to Hebrew scripture, claiming that it testifies to who he is and what he will do (vv. 39–47).

Jesus is in total control, ready to meet every situation, and using miracles and works of power strategically to impress and convince. John's gospel uses the feeding of the five thousand (6:1–14) and walking on water (vv. 15–21) to establish Jesus as a person of power and Spirit.

"I Am" Hope

In John's gospel, Jesus has no problem speaking prophetically, stating God's will and God's mind in declarative terms. The book is known for the seven "I am" statements of Jesus to explain himself and establish a direct connection to the "I am" statement in Exodus when Moses asked God's name (Ex. 3:14). These "I am" statements in John (6:35; 8:12; 10:7, 10:11; 11:25–26; 14:6; 15:5) serve as criteria for inclusion in the community of faith. To agree with the statements is to belong. To reject or disagree with any of them sets one apart from the flock.

A strong element of paranoia and exclusion flows through all of the Johannine literature (John's gospel, the three letters of John, and the book of Revelation). It is important to keep this "either/or" attitude in context and not make it a universal lens through which we interpret what *Jesus* meant. It makes no sense to preference the gospel of John to those of Matthew, Mark, and Luke; each author wrote to a different audience in unique situations, so it is best to keep all four gospels in dialogue. The urgent need for John's community was to establish and preserve a standard for Christianity that wasn't watered down by beliefs that might be more acceptable to Rome. The "I am" statements are prime examples of keeping the faith "pure" in the face of opposition and oppression.

> And Jesus said to them, "I am the bread of life. He who comes to Me shall never hunger, and he who believes in Me shall never thirst. But I said to you that you have seen Me and yet do not believe. All that the Father gives Me will come to Me, and the one who comes to Me I will by no means cast out. For I have come down from heaven, not to do My own will, but the will of Him who sent Me. This is the will of the Father who

> sent Me, that of all He has given Me I should lose nothing, but should raise it up at the last day. And this is the will of Him who sent Me, that everyone who sees the Son and believes in Him may have everlasting life; and I will raise him up at the last day." (6:35–40)

In the first of the "I am" statements (as restated in 6:41), Jesus says, "I am the bread which came down from heaven." This allusion to the manna from heaven that God sent the people during the exodus not only ties Jesus to the ancient tradition but also transcends it. Manna was fleeting and temporary, but Jesus as bread from heaven is permanent and eternal. Those who accept Jesus will never hunger in eternity. For a community that feels betrayed by its spiritual heritage, the majority of whose members live a hand-to-mouth existence on the edge of starvation, this is a powerful claim. Who wouldn't want to put their faith in a source of neverending sustenance and supply?

The second of the "I am" statement claims, "I am the light of the world. He who follows me shall not walk in darkness, but have the light of life" (8:12). The premodern world followed the cycles of nature. Oil was a precious commodity for most people, so the workday was dictated by the sun; people functioned in the light, rested and hid in the darkness. In the dualistic worldview of the Judeo-Christian world, light was associated with life, health, goodness, opportunity, and truth. Darkness indicated death, disease, evil, limitation, and ignorance. Jesus makes a monumental claim here. If he is the light, then one implication is that everything else is darkness. This is the height of "either/or" thinking. It is hopeful only to those who know and believe in Jesus as the Christ, the one, true Son of God. This sentiment taken to extremes has created deep animosity through the ages and, for example, has resulted in horrible acts of violence against Jews, culminating with the Holocaust committed by the Nazis.

Jesus offers the third "I am" statement: "I am the door [gate] of the sheep" (10:7). In context, Jesus employs the metaphor of the shepherd and flock to explain his relationship to those who believe in him. The door, or the gate, into the sheepfold is the threshold from a dangerous and hostile world into a space of safety and comfort. Those who pass through the gate are "inside" where they belong and are cared for by the "good shepherd." The fourth "I am" statement that Jesus makes—"I am the good shepherd. The good shepherd gives his life for his sheep" (v. 11)—is closely related to the third. Offering both a promise of protection and a prophetic statement of his coming crucifixion, this statement is an emphatic assurance that those who believe in Jesus as the Christ will be cared for and kept safe through any and all tribulations. For a community concerned with its very survival, few images could matter more than sheep in the care of a good, courageous shepherd.

Jesus continues the "I am" claims with perhaps the most spectacular statement of all, "I am the resurrection and the life. He who believes in Me, though he may die he shall live. And whoever lives and believes in Me shall never die" (11:25–26). The promise of everlasting life changes everything. If our existence is limited to a few short decades, a life lived in poverty, hopelessness, and indignity is almost too great a burden to bear; but if such a life is a mere moment in the grand span of eternity, it becomes much more tolerable. For Jesus to be the source of salvation in this life and the portal to the life to come makes him worthy of worship and adoration, the very embodiment of hope.

The sixth "I am" statement, taken out of context, has done more damage than good when used to legitimize violence and oppressive behavior. To the members of the Johannine community, Jesus says, "I am the way, the truth, and the life. No one comes to the Father except through Me" (14:6). At the time, many people on the edge of society wondered if it was worth the risk and distress to hold fast to their Christian faith. There were many other alternatives available, including variations on the Christian Way. Jesus warns that no other option will do for John's community. No one in the community will find another faith better than this one, including alternative understandings of Jesus' teaching. This statement was meant to clarify that, for the community of John, there truly was no choice. Fidelity to the beliefs of the community was essential for everyone's survival in this life and for confirmation of life after death.

The last of the "I am" statements occurs in 15:5, "I am the vine, you are the branches. He who abides in Me, and I in him, bears much fruit; for without Me you can do nothing." Only when we stay faithfully connected to Jesus the Christ can we do anything of value. We have no purpose or meaning apart from Jesus. We have no hope separated from the Christ.

Taken together, these seven "I am" statements reinforce that Jesus sees himself as one with God. He makes the same claims that God made to Moses, and he expands them in a variety of ways. Each "I am" statement breeds confidence, courage, comfort, consolation, peace, patience, and most of all, hope. Acknowledging belief in these seven claims serves as a confessional creed. The community stays strong when everyone agrees that Jesus is the bread of life; the light of the world; the door to the sheepfold; the good shepherd; the resurrection and the life; the way, the truth; and the true vine. For the Johannine community, it helped clarify who was a "true" Christian and who was not.

Hope in Community

Idenfitying "true" Christians is vitally important in this gospel. Interspersed with accounts of the adoration and belief of the followers, John offers multiple examples of people who misunderstand and reject Jesus: "many of His disciples" (6:60–66), his family (7:1–5), the crowds (vv. 40–44), the Sanhedrin (vv. 45–52), various Jews (8:33–41), including the Pharisees (9:16). Some Jews in Jerusalem attempt to kill Jesus (10:22–39), and the chief priests and Pharisees (11:45–57) plot his death. John provides a fascinating pendulum swing back and forth between the acceptance of followers and the rejection of others. The Jesus of John's gospel is as divisive as he is reconciling, as exclusive as he is inclusive, and as contemptuous as he is compassionate.

Hope in the Reality of God

John's Passion narrative following the triumphal entry of Jesus into Jerusalem is the longest in the four Gospels. John focuses on the promises and assurances that Jesus makes to his followers, particularly his promise of the Holy Spirit (16:1–15). John selects the words of Jesus that have the greatest potential to keep the community from losing hope and straying from the true faith. Jesus not only predicts his own death in John, he lays out the event itself and the reason it must occur. John wants his audience to know that the ability of the plotters to kill Jesus does not adversely affect Jesus' reality as God incarnate. Some people in the Johannine community claimed that Jesus could not possibly be God because God could not be killed. John crafts his gospel to explain that the resurrection proves that Jesus is indeed God, with the power to conquer death. The same power Jesus possesses in his earthly existence, God grants to those who accept Jesus Christ as bread, light, life, truth, vine, and good shepherd. John's is a finely crafted message of hope, assuring the members of his community that nothing on earth can ever defeat them as long as they stay faithful.

Jesus is intentional in John's gospel to prepare his disciples and followers for his coming death and the tribulations that will follow. He prays for himself (17:1–5), for his disciples (vv. 6–19), and more generally, for all who believe and will believe in the future (vv. 20–26). After providing full instructions, preparations, and offering prayers, Jesus goes forth bravely to meet his fate.

John's gospel shows Jesus in full control throughout his arrest, trials, and beatings. John spends very little time describing the violence done to Jesus, instead focusing on his conversations with Annas (18:12–23), Caiaphas (vv. 24–27), and Pilate (vv. 28–38, 39–19:16). In each of these encounters, the religious and political leaders are bested by the wise and patient Jesus of Nazareth.

By the end of the first century of the Christian era, many Jewish critics and Christian apostates used the crucifixion as their reason for rejecting Jesus as the Messiah. Not only death, but the death of a criminal, made the crucifixion a scandal. The early church understood the death of Jesus as nothing more than the fulfillment of the prophecies of ancient Israel. The absence of a body after the resurrection became another source of contention. In John's gospel, Thomas, the disciple, represents all who question or doubt that Jesus is the one, true Son of God, resurrected from the dead. The resurrected Jesus appears to Mary Magdalene (20:11–18), then to the disciples (minus Thomas, vv. 19–23), then again to the disciples (with Thomas present, vv. 26–29), then to the disciples at the Sea of Tiberias (21:1–23).

This gospel has two endings, each offering hope. The first ending witnesses to the hope of those who believe: "And truly Jesus did many other signs in the presence of His disciples, which are not written in this book; but these are written that you may believe that Jesus is the Christ, the Son of God, and that believing you may have life in His name" (20:30–31). The second ending offers the hope that the story of Jesus, even the Word of God, cannot be contained in words on a page: "And there are also many other things that Jesus did, which if they were written one by one, I suppose that even the world itself could not contain the books that would be written. Amen" (21:25).

The Hope That Prevails

The author of John wrote his gospel to a small, remnant Christian community struggling to survive. At the same time, the words written for a small audience have global implications. Applying the open invitation to believe in Jesus as the Christ, the Son of God, across time and space, Christianity becomes a belief system of hope and promise for all. In combination with the Synoptic Gospels, John's gospel provides an elegant balance between the human Jesus who is so much like one of us with the divine Jesus who is so above us all. Only a Savior who is fully human and fully divine can give us the hope that endures and prevails.

The Letters of Paul

Hope for the World

The church as we know it today was defined less by our gospels than by the teaching of the apostle Paul. Nine of the letters of the New Testament are attributed to Paul. The story Luke offers about Paul in the book of Acts is a little different from the story Paul tells through his own accounts. This is understandable because Luke used secondary sources.

The gospel writers shared very different visions of hope: for the Jews, for the politically oppressed, for the poor and marginalized, and for the community of faith. Paul offers a vision of hope for the world. He takes the universal intimations of John and makes them specific. He attempts to take the grace and love of God in Christ to the ends of the earth, fulfilling the intent of the Great Commission (Matt. 28:18–20). Paul was an apostle in the finest sense of the word: he took the gospel where no one else planned to go.

Each letter of Paul offers instruction for a unique context and congregation. No two letters are the same. Paul's letters are not arranged by chronology or theme, but by length—from the longest to the shortest. This is unfortunate because it denies us an opportunity to see Paul's thinking and theology develop over time. We receive each letter equally, having to wrestle with the contradictions and conflicting messages among them. Some of these dilemmas resolve fairly simply, while others are more challenging.

Were the Pauline letters arranged in the order they were written, we would read first the Thessalonian letters; followed by Galatians, Philemon, and Philippians; then the Corinthian correspondence, Romans, Colossians,

Ephesians, 1 Timothy, Titus, and 2 Timothy. This is important because the letters offer different evidence and rationales for hope to each community, reflecting a growing understanding of the good news and the way to live a life of hope and faith in Christian community.

Romans

Hope in a Complex, Multicultural World

Most scholars agree that Romans contains the most fully developed theology and teaching of the apostle Paul. Rome was a cosmopolitan metropolis where a wide variety of faiths met in the public square. The Christian movement was a newcomer to the large pool of spiritualities. Many small house churches as well as a handful of larger congregations comprised the early Roman Christian representation. Rome was home to Jews who accepted or rejected Hellenism to various degrees, to Jewish converts often called God-fearers, to various Gentile sects, and to a hodgepodge of hybrids.

Paul was writing to those who had accepted Christ, but he also writes to those who might become Christian (1:7, 16–17). Paul launches into an argument against unrighteousness (vv. 18–32) and the righteousness of God's judgment on the unrighteous (2:1–16). This is a clever foundation for the message that is to come. Paul argues that Christianity is not solely a successor to Judaism, but is in fact a perfect alternative for Gentiles as well (vv. 17–29). For centuries, Jews had judged Gentiles as unclean and unworthy, but Paul argues that Jews and Gentiles have failed equally, and all stand in need of what God has to offer (3:9–20).

Hope Through Faith

Paul contends that no one has a claim to superiority. Abraham, for example, became great through faith in God (4:1–4). The same was true of David (vv. 5–8), and the same could be true for us. This kind of greatness cannot be earned and doesn't come through a particular ethnic ritual such as circumcision (vv. 9–12). Abraham was not acceptable to God because of anything he did, but because of his faith, the very same faith that anyone might have (vv. 13–25). "Therefore, having been justified by faith, we have peace with God through our Lord Jesus Christ, through whom also we have access by faith into this grace in which we stand, and rejoice in hope of the glory of God," Paul writes (5:1–2), offering this assurance to all without exception.

The glories of the Christian life are available to all, and this broad equality applies to tribulation as well. To Paul, however, tribulation is not a burden or affliction, but a way to grow strong: "And not only that, but we also glory in tribulations, knowing that tribulation produces perseverance; and perseverance, character; and character, hope. Now hope does not disappoint, because the love of God has been poured out in our hearts by the Holy Spirit who was given to us" (vv. 3–5). Hope does not disappoint. The Holy Spirit instills in us the hope that allows us to trust God and God's promises. Paul indicates that this alone makes our Christian God, Savior, and Spirit superior to other options in the Roman world. Christ himself provides the example we should follow. No one, Jewish or otherwise, has ever been so worthy to emulate as Jesus the Christ. All human life originated in Adam, through whom death came into the world; all life is redeemed and saved through Christ, a free gift given to all from God (vv. 12–21).

It is worth noting that this accepting, inclusive, and tolerant message of hope for a huge Gentile audience is less than well received by Jewish Christians, who struggle with Gentile Christianity for generations before Christianity completely breaks away from Judaism. The apostle Paul is a lightning rod in the early controversies and challenges, but he is convinced from his own experience that true faith in Christ makes a person a new creation. The apostle Paul barely resembles the persecutor Saul. When we come to Christ, we come to life, and our old self is put to death (6:1–14). Paul no longer considers himself a Roman or a Jew, but a Christian. All who accept Christ as Savior die to sin and accept freedom to live in God's grace.

Paul likens sin to slavery, and God's gift to freedom (vv. 15–23), telling the churches in Rome, "the wages of sin is death, but the gift of God is eternal life in Christ Jesus our Lord" (v. 23).

The problem of sin is a central theme for Paul in Romans. The concept of law is important in both Jewish and Roman history and culture. "Breaking the law" is a great concern in both worlds. *Transgression* (to cross the line) and *sin* (to miss the mark) mean a breach of the social contract by which order is maintained. Sinners and lawbreakers are threats to the integrity of the social fabric. Many people become sticklers for right behavior, defining good and evil based on specific acts. Paul tries to offer an alternative to this limited, legalistic perspective. He reminds the churches in Rome that everyone sins, transgresses the law, and makes mistakes. These things make us human and explain why we need a Savior. Using himself as an example, he explains the problem:

> For what I am doing, I do not understand. For what I will to do, that I do not practice; but what I hate, that I do. . . . For the good that I will to do, I do not do; but the evil I will not to do, that I practice. Now if I do what I will not to do, it is no longer I who do it, but sin that dwells in me. (7:15, 19–20)

Sin is a condition that prevents us from becoming who God wants us to be. Christ offers us freedom from sin and opens us to God's will for our lives. "There is therefore now no condemnation to those who are in Christ Jesus, who do not walk according to the flesh, but according to the Spirit" (8:1).

Flesh and Spirit are parallels to law and grace, slavery and freedom. For Paul, there are few ambiguous "gray" areas; either we walk in the flesh or we walk in the Spirit. We are either bound by the snare of sin, or we are freed by the gift of Christ. We have been adopted by God as children and heirs and will fully share the inheritance of Christ (vv. 12–17).

> For I consider that the sufferings of this present time are not worthy to be compared with the glory which shall be revealed in us. For the earnest

expectation of the creation eagerly waits for the revealing of the sons of God. For the creation was subjected to futility, not willingly, but because of Him who subjected it in hope; because the creation itself also will be delivered from the bondage of corruption into the glorious liberty of the children of God. For we know that the whole creation groans and labors with birth pangs together until now. Not only that, but we also who have the firstfruits of the Spirit, even we ourselves groan within ourselves, eagerly waiting for the adoption, the redemption of our body. For we were saved in this hope, but hope that is seen is not hope; for why does one still hope for what he sees? But if we hope for what we do not see, we eagerly wait for it with perseverance.

Likewise the Spirit also helps in our weaknesses. For we do not know what we should pray for as we ought, but the Spirit Himself makes intercession for us with groanings which cannot be uttered. Now He who searches the hearts knows what the mind of the Spirit is, because He makes intercession for the saints according to the will of God.

And we know that all things work together for good to those who love God, to those who are the called according to His purpose. For whom He foreknew, He also predestined to be conformed to the image of His Son, that He might be the firstborn among many brethren. Moreover whom He predestined, these He also called; whom He called, these He also justified; and whom He justified, these He also glorified.

What then shall we say to these things? If God is for us, who can be against us? He who did not spare His own Son, but delivered Him up for us all, how shall He not with Him also freely give us all things? Who shall bring a charge against God's elect? It is God who justifies. Who is he who condemns? It is Christ who died, and furthermore is also risen, who is even at the right hand of God, who also makes intercession for us. Who shall separate us from the love of Christ? Shall tribulation, or distress, or persecution, or famine, or nakedness, or peril, or sword? As it is written:

> "For Your sake we are killed all day long;
> We are accounted as sheep for the slaughter."

Yet in all these things we are more than conquerors through Him who loved us. (vv. 18–37)

No matter how badly things go in our personal lives or how terrible conditions are in the world, the glory of God is greater. The only reason for despair is our inability to see through God's eyes; our knowledge is incomplete, but through faith we learn to see God's purpose in all things. In Paul's theology, we are made powerful through faith. There can be no possible reason to lose hope, for there is no force on earth that can separate us from God—except ourselves.

In chapters 9 and 10, Paul delivers an argument for offering the gospel to the Gentiles, based on the fact that Israel rejected the gospel. In a summary of Hebrew history, Paul recounts the many ways that Israel has rejected God's plan and purpose (9:1–29), including the latest gift, the Christ. What the Jews rejected, God makes available to any and all who will believe (vv. 30–33). In its ignorance, Israel needs the redemption that only Christ can give, but the rejection of the gospel makes this difficult (10:1–21). Paul notes, however, that Israel's rejection is neither total nor permanent (11:1–36), and that there is still hope for all of God's people. Paul believes that God will save Israel; one day all will come to unity in Christ. This will require humility and a fundamental shift in thinking and believing (12:1–2).

God is constantly working in us, whether or not we are aware of it. God activates in us a wide variety of gifts (vv. 3–18) to equip us to do God's work and will. Each of us has gifts to share, but none of us possesses all the gifts. Only together can we fulfill the will and purpose of God. Jew and Gentile are gifted, and stronger together than each is alone. Paul instructs the multifaith, multiheritage, multicultural churches in Rome to commit to what is good and to refrain from anything that might damage unity and harmony (vv. 9–12). His directions are very simple: do what is good, do not do what is not good.

Paul also instructs the churches in Rome not to waste time in senseless struggle with the government. Obeying the rules and regulations of the dominant society will draw the least amount of negative attention, and witness to the world that the Christian Way is not a pathway of destruction and disobedience but is superior in every way (13:1–14:23). In Christ, we have the power to offer a radically countercultural alternative to the way the rest of the world lives. As much as we are able, we should strive to be a stumbling block to no one, and to conduct ourselves in ways that offend none. Christianity is never about getting our own way or imposing our will and beliefs on others. By our thoughts, words, and deeds, we personify God's grace, thereby becoming a beacon of hope in a contentious and restrictive world.

> We then who are strong ought to bear with the scruples of the weak, and not to please ourselves. Let each of us please his neighbor for his good, leading to edification. For even Christ did not please Himself; but as it is written, "The reproaches of those who reproached You fell on Me." For whatever things were written before were written for our learning, that we through the patience and comfort of the Scriptures might have hope. Now may the God of patience and comfort grant you to be like-minded toward one another, according to Christ Jesus, that you may with one mind and one mouth glorify the God and Father of our Lord Jesus Christ.
>
> Therefore receive one another, just as Christ also received us, to the glory of God. Now I say that Jesus Christ has become a servant to the circumcision for the truth of God, to confirm the promises made to the fathers, and that the Gentiles might glorify God for His mercy, as it is written:
>
> "For this reason I will confess to You among the Gentiles,
> And sing to Your name."
>
> And again he says:
>
> "Rejoice, O Gentiles, with His people!"
>
> And again:
>
> "Praise the LORD, all you Gentiles!
> Laud Him, all you peoples!"
>
> And again, Isaiah says:
>
> "There shall be a root of Jesse;
> And He who shall rise to reign over the Gentiles,
> In Him the Gentiles shall hope."
>
> Now may the God of hope fill you with all joy and peace in believing, that you may abound in hope by the power of the Holy Spirit.
>
> Now I myself am confident concerning you, my brethren, that you also are full of goodness, filled with all knowledge, able also to admonish one another. Nevertheless, brethren, I have written more boldly to you on some points, as reminding you, because of the grace given to me by

God, that I might be a minister of Jesus Christ to the Gentiles, ministering the gospel of God, that the offering of the Gentiles might be acceptable, sanctified by the Holy Spirit. Therefore I have reason to glory in Christ Jesus in the things which pertain to God. For I will not dare to speak of any of those things which Christ has not accomplished through me, in word and deed, to make the Gentiles obedient—in mighty signs and wonders, by the power of the Spirit of God, so that from Jerusalem and round about to Illyricum I have fully preached the gospel of Christ. And so I have made it my aim to preach the gospel, not where Christ was named, lest I should build on another man's foundation, but as it is written:

"To whom He was not announced, they shall see;
And those who have not heard shall understand."

For this reason I also have been much hindered from coming to you. But now no longer having a place in these parts, and having a great desire these many years to come to you, whenever I journey to Spain, I shall come to you. For I hope to see you on my journey, and to be helped on my way there by you, if first I may enjoy your company for a while. But now I am going to Jerusalem to minister to the saints. For it pleased those from Macedonia and Achaia to make a certain contribution for the poor among the saints who are in Jerusalem. It pleased them indeed, and they are their debtors. For if the Gentiles have been partakers of their spiritual things, their duty is also to minister to them in material things. Therefore, when I have performed this and have sealed to them this fruit, I shall go by way of you to Spain. But I know that when I come to you, I shall come in the fullness of the blessing of the gospel of Christ.

Now I beg you, brethren, through the Lord Jesus Christ, and through the love of the Spirit, that you strive together with me in prayers to God for me, that I may be delivered from those in Judea who do not believe, and that my service for Jerusalem may be acceptable to the saints, that I may come to you with joy by the will of God, and may be refreshed together with you. Now the God of peace be with you all. Amen. (15:1–33)

From our strength, we should bear the weaknesses of those who have not been equally blessed (vv. 1–6). We who have so much should readily share with those who cannot begin to understand our bounty. Regardless of our physical circumstances, we are rich in the gifts of God (vv. 7–13). Paul offers this spectacular blessing to the believers in Rome: "Now may the God of hope fill you with all joy and peace in believing, that you may abound in hope by the power of the Holy Spirit" (v. 13). Christian communities able to live in such hope have the power to change the world.

The essence of Paul's teaching in Romans is incredibly encouraging. We do not have to try to do good things for God; we have to learn to let God do great things through us by the power of the Holy Spirit; and the Holy Spirit is power indeed. Nothing compares. This power is freely offered to one and all, Jew and Gentile. We don't have to be great men and women of virtue and purity. We need only to believe and commit our lives to Christ. God will lead us to life in the Spirit, and we will be made new beings. Hope abounds.

First and Second *Corinthians*

The majority of modern scholars agree that the two letters to the church at Corinth that we have today are actually a compilation of many letters written over a span of a few years. This theory is based on the evidence contained in the letters themselves. The tone, focus, content, and flow of the two letters are sporadic, and they do not follow a clear, linear path. Paul's emotions swing from positive to negative, and he sometimes seems to ramble from idea to idea before returning to his original point. The bits and pieces of many letters were apparently assembled to preserve the major ideas and key teachings of Paul for the Corinthian church.

The two Corinthian letters are essentially Paul's answer to the question: "What does it really mean to be a church?" It is obvious from both letters that Paul had a long and influential history with this church. Corinth was a crossroads city, a hub between east and west in the ancient world. It represented the height of Greek culture and sophistication. It was a center of philosophy, academia, and the arts. It was as sophisticated a society as any other in its time. We might feel very comfortable in the worldly wise city of Corinth. Paul's messages of challenge and encouragement apply directly to our communities. Such an environment was (and is) a mixed blessing.

First Corinthians

In writing to the church at Corinth, Paul can engage in the most complex and complicated arguments with no fear that he might be talking beyond his audience's capacity to understand. This kind of audience, however, tends to question everything. Debate, schism, and sectarianism were common. Paul writes to address this very situation (1:10–17). Paul declares that the Christian faith isn't primarily about information—it isn't a topic for debate—it is wisdom. We don't believe in Christ because he makes sense or is purely rational. Paul states this simply, "For I determined not to know anything among you except Jesus Christ and Him crucified" (2:2). Paul says he is not interested in being impressive and persuasive through his preaching and teaching, "but in demonstration of the Spirit" (v. 4). He doesn't want people to believe because of the power of human reason but through the power of God (v. 5). Spiritual wisdom rather than human knowledge is the key to truth (vv. 6–16). A community of "intellectuals" may not view this as a message of hope, but Paul has just begun. He knows his audience.

Thinking too hard and making faith in Christ an intellectual exercise is damaging the church in many ways in Corinth. The divisions caused by argument and debate are carnal and worldly (3:1–4). Disagreements over whose argument is most compelling results in people choosing sides and creates adversarial relationships (vv. 5–17). Paul admonishes the church to worry less about who is right and who is wrong, and instead take what is helpful and of value from each. This is a provocative shift from "either/or" to "both/and" thinking. A glimmer of hope appears, a challenge to think in a new way.

In a society that highly values intelligence and rational thought, blind acceptance through faith is viewed as ignorant and foolish. Paul counters that faith is not ignorance, but rather the wisdom of God; it seems foolish simply because we do not fully comprehend it. "Let a man so consider us, as servants of Christ and stewards of the mysteries of God. Moreover it is required in stewards that one be found faithful" (4:1–2). It is not as important to know as it is to believe, to understand as to trust. Paul engages in irony, a rhetorical tactic appealing to his audience, to warn against arrogance and conceit. Their hope lies only in the trust and simplicity, humility and endurance evidenced by Paul:

> We are fools for Christ's sake, but you are wise in Christ! We are weak, but you are strong! You are distinguished, but we are dishonored! To the present hour we both hunger and thirst, and we are poorly clothed, and beaten, and homeless. And we labor, working with our own hands. Being reviled, we bless; being persecuted, we endure; being defamed, we entreat. We have been made as the filth of the world, the offscouring of all things until now.
>
> I do not write these things to shame you, but as my beloved children I warn you. For though you might have ten thousand instructors in Christ, yet you do not have many fathers; for in Christ Jesus I have begotten you through the gospel. Therefore I urge you, imitate me. (vv. 10–16)

Some in Corinth have decided that it doesn't matter how people behave as long as they believe the right things. Sexual immorality, covetousness, and idolatry are practiced by some claiming to be Christian in Corinth; and they defend themselves by compartmentalizing their faith, separating it from their actions (5:1–13). Paul writes that Christian conduct must align with professed beliefs, and that without accountability the integrity of the community will be destroyed (6:1–11).

We must hold one another responsible and not turn to secular courts and institutions to guide us. How we act is a witness to the rest of the world of what it means to be Christian. We are the hope of the world, and we need to pay attention to how our actions and words might be interpreted by or influence others. It was critically important in the first century (as it is today) that Christians do nothing that might dishonor and shame God.

> All things are lawful for me, but all things are not helpful. All things are lawful for me, but I will not be brought under the power of any. Foods for the stomach and the stomach for foods, but God will destroy both it and them. Now the body is not for sexual immorality but for the Lord, and the Lord for the body. And God both raised up the Lord and will also raise us up by His power. . . .
>
> [D]o you not know that your body is the temple of the Holy Spirit who is in you, whom you have from God, and you are not your own? For you were bought at a price; therefore glorify God in your body and in your spirit, which are God's. (vv. 12–20)

Paul's instructions on marriage in chapter 7 may seem odd to us today, but when he wrote to Corinth, Jesus' return was expected at any time. Business-as-usual was displaced by commitment to living life in Christ. Paul was urgent to make sure as many people as possible heard the gospel and had the opportunity to accept life in Christ. There was little time to waste in personal pursuits, including marriage and having families. There was even less time to indulge in carnal activities, so fidelity in marriage served a practical purpose. Husbands and wives could help each other avoid sin. Paul offers some detailed suggestions for how people should handle their relationships and passions in the days anticipating Christ's return. Throughout this chapter, Paul urges focus on the hope of Christ's imminent return rather than on the concerns of this world: "But this I say, brethren, the time is short. . . . For the form of this world is passing away" (vv. 29, 31b). While Paul's specific advice on relationships may not apply in today's world, we would do well to focus our hope and our lives as if Christ were returning in the next moment.

In chapters 8 and 9, Paul attempts to sort out some of the points of contention and issues of debate that the Corinthian Christians wrestle with: eating things offered to idols (8:4–13), supporting ministers and apostles financially (9:1–18), determining who is deserving of ministry (vv. 19–23), and the importance of discipline and self-control (vv. 24–27).

He then addresses a common problem of privilege—thinking more of personal needs and desires than the needs of others. He again pleads with the Corinthian audience to be mindful of the impact their actions have on others. Simply because a person can do something does not mean they should do it, especially when it might affect others adversely (10:23–11:1). Then he offers some basic instructions on behavior and comportment in worship and ritual observance (11:2–16), conduct at the Lord's Supper (vv. 17–26), and personal self-control (vv. 27–34). Paul urges the Corinthians (and us) to shift our focus from personal desires to the good of the community and hope in the kingdom of God.

First Corinthians offers one of the most fully developed expressions of Paul's understanding of the nature of the church; the body of Christ comprised of many gifted members (12:1–31). Greek culture, like our own, was individualistic and competitive. The metaphor of Christian community as one body would be very challenging in Corinth. But Paul links the metaphor with the Greek concept of *synergy* (together we are greater than the sum of our parts): no part can live in isolation, and we can find meaning only in embracing our diversity. The idea of unity from diversity transforms the challenging image of one body to a means of grace in which each individual reaches full potential only in community. This is not one option among many, according to Paul, but an absolute necessity if we ever want to achieve God's will for our lives: "There are diversities of gifts, but the same Spirit. There are differences of ministries, but the same Lord. And there are diversity of activities, but it is the same God who works all in all" (vv. 4–6). Every gift God gives is necessary and important, and only when we combine our gifts with others can we become Christ's body for the world.

Knowing the Corinthian tendency to compete and debate, Paul emphasizes that the gifts are not of greater or lesser importance, and that ultimately there is one universal gift greater than all others:

> Though I speak with the tongues of men and of angels, but have not love, I have become sounding brass or a clanging cymbal. And though I have the gift of prophecy, and understand all mysteries and all knowledge, and though I have all faith, so that I could remove mountains, but have not love, I am nothing. And though I bestow all my goods to feed the poor, and though I give my body to be burned, but have not love, it profits me nothing.
>
> Love suffers long and is kind; love does not envy; love does not parade itself, is not puffed up; does not behave rudely, does not seek its own, is not provoked, thinks no evil; does not rejoice in iniquity, but rejoices in the truth; bears all things, believes all things, hopes all things, endures all things.

> Love never fails. But whether there are prophecies, they will fail; whether there are tongues, they will cease; whether there is knowledge, it will vanish away. For we know in part and we prophesy in part. But when that which is perfect has come, then that which is in part will be done away.
>
> When I was a child, I spoke as a child, I understood as a child, I thought as a child; but when I became a man, I put away childish things. For now we see in a mirror, dimly, but then face to face. Now I know in part, but then I shall know just as I also am known.
>
> And now abide faith, hope, love, these three; but the greatest of these is love. (13:1–13)

In faith, we live with trust in the God of creation who loved us before we knew God. In hope, we live with eager expectation of the coming of the kingdom and the return of Jesus in glory. In love, we live with joy, immersed in the power of the Holy Spirit, as if the kingdom is already here. Unless love is the guiding and governing value of Christian community, nothing else will matter. Without love, our best efforts are inadequate and hollow. Spiritual maturity is measured by our ability to love God, love neighbor, and love our brothers and sisters in Christ.

Paul encourages the community at Corinth to cultivate gifts of prophecy and tongues to enable them to continue the apostolic work of the infant church. Taking God's Word into the world and communicating the good news in other languages guarantees that Christ can be known to the ends of the earth. Speaking in the Spirit may lead to confusion, so interpretation is equally important. God may impart wisdom too great for easy comprehension, especially in foreign cultures (14:1–25). Often, these instructions are interpreted through a spiritualized and mystical lens, but Paul's intention is eminently practical. Rather than a secret, special language, tongues is a way of allowing God to speak through ordinary men and women as a witness to the Spirit's amazing power.

Whenever the community gathers, the focus should be spiritual growth through faith-sharing practices (vv. 26–40). The use of our spiritual gifts serves multiple purposes: to strengthen us within the community, to reveal guidance and inspiration from God, to equip us to be servants of Christ and stewards of God's mysteries, and to allow us to serve others in the world as the incarnate body of Christ. Hope lives, not in some other-worldly and supernatural realm, but in our life as community in this world.

Paul validates his credibility by reminding his hearers that the risen Christ appeared to him in person (15:1–11). He is not teaching hearsay and anecdotal information; his testimony is firsthand witness. He does not conjecture about a mythic resurrection, but testifies to his post-resurrection encounter. He claims for himself a trustworthiness that those who never met Christ do not have. The truth of the Christian faith, for Paul, rests in the truth of the resurrection. Our hope as Christians transcends this life:

> If in this life only we have hope in Christ, we are of all men the most pitiable. But now Christ is risen from the dead, and has become the first fruits of those who have fallen asleep. For since by man came death, my Man also came the resurrection of the dead. For as in Adam all die, even so in Christ all shall be made alive. (vv. 19–22)

Anyone who questions or denies the resurrection is, in effect, denying Christ (vv. 29–34).

First Corinthians 15:35–58 addresses one of the most hotly debated topics of the early church—what form our resurrection will take. Initially, Christ-followers assumed they would return from death just as Jesus did. But with the passage of time, this hope diminished as loved ones passed away and stayed dead. The concept of the Day of the Lord emerged, when God would raise all of the dead in Christ at one time. This general resurrection became tied to the second coming of Jesus. When it became clear that Jesus was not returning quickly, serious questions arose in the beliefs and understanding of many Christians. Paul's response offers hope that we do not believe in vain: "The body is sown in corruption, it is raised in incorruption. It is sown in dishonor, it is raised in glory. It is sown in weakness, it is raised in power. It is sown a natural body, it is raised a spiritual body"

(vv. 42–44). Once again, hope grounded in faith gives us the confidence to persevere. God will surely bless those who hold fast to their faith in spite of disappointments, delays, and distorted interpretations of the end times.

Second Corinthians

Second Corinthians addresses many of the same issues as 1 Corinthians. Misunderstandings, divisions, and debates continue in the Corinthian church, along with individuals who profess new life in Christ while continuing in worldly sin. Paul acknowledges his part in the current controversies and recommends forgiveness and comfort (2:3–11). He suggests that the set-aside community seeks to understand itself as an epistle of Christ, written by the Spirit, hope that may be seen by all the world:

> You are our epistle written in our hearts, known and read by all men; clearly you are an epistle of Christ, ministered by us, written not with ink but by the Spirit of the living God, not on tablets of stone but on tablets of flesh, that is, of the heart.
>
> And we have such trust through Christ toward God. Not that we are sufficient of ourselves to think of anything as being from ourselves, but our sufficiency is from God, who also made us sufficient as ministers of the new covenant, not of the letter but of the Spirit; for the letter kills, but the Spirit gives life.
>
> But if the ministry of death, written and engraved on stones, was glorious, so that the children of Israel could not look steadily at the face of Moses because of the glory of his countenance, which glory was passing away, how will the ministry of the Spirit not be more glorious? . . . For if what is passing away was glorious, what remains is much more glorious.
>
> Therefore, since we have such hope, we use great boldness of speech— . . . Now the Lord is the Spirit; and where the Spirit of the Lord is, there is liberty. But we all, . . . beholding as in a mirror the glory of the Lord, are being transformed into the same image from glory to glory, just as by the Spirit of the Lord. (3:2–18)

Paul honors solidarity and raises the discussion above the level of human disagreement. Just because we may not fully understand God's will or the best way to live our faith, doesn't mean that God cannot bring light from our darkness (4:1–6).

Living in the relentless stress of conflict like that in Corinth elevates tension and fuels conflict. Paul lifts a vision for hope (4:7–5:21). What we desire in our human limitations is of secondary importance to the things God desires for us and from us. We are new creations in Christ, and we have an important purpose to fulfill.

> For we know that if our earthly house, this tent, is destroyed, we have a building from God, a house not made with hands, eternal in the heavens. For in this we groan, earnestly desiring to be clothed with our habitation which is from heaven, if indeed, having been clothed, we shall not be found naked. For we who are in this tent groan, being burdened, not because we want to be unclothed, but further clothed, that mortality may be swallowed up by life. Now He who has prepared us for this very thing is God, who also has given us the Spirit as a guarantee.
>
> So we are always confident, knowing that while we are at home in the body we are absent from the Lord. For we walk by faith, not by sight. . . .
>
> Therefore, if anyone is in Christ, he is a new creation; old things have passed away; behold, all things have become new. Now all things are of God, who has reconciled us to Himself through Jesus Christ, and has given us the ministry of reconciliation, that is, that God was in Christ reconciling the world to Himself, not imputing their trespasses to them, and has committed to us the word of reconciliation.
>
> Now then, we are ambassadors for Christ, as though God were pleading through us: we implore you on Christ's behalf, be reconciled to God. For He made Him who knew no sin to be sin for us, that we might become the righteousness of God in Him. (5:1–7, 17–21)

Paul implores the Corinthians to stay focused and faithful (6:1–10), to be holy and disciplined (6:11–7:1), and to be humble and repentant (7:2–12). He appeals to their generosity to continue supporting ministries that cannot support themselves and to excel in their giving (8:1–9:15). He reminds them that God supplies in abundance that we might share with others. When we live in hopeful anticipation of the coming of the kingdom, we can, indeed, be "cheerful givers" (9:7).

Paul, once again, defends his authority and pleads that the Corinthians be less persuaded by words and arguments than by the character of the speaker (10:1–18). All he says, all he does, and all he intends, flows forth from Christ. Paul confesses sincere concern for the welfare of those in Corinth who are being influenced by teachers with less-clear motives (11:1–15). He hesitates to compete with other apostles (vv. 16–21), but he knows his own motivations. He is troubled by those who seem more interested in stirring up discord than in creating unity.

Paul presents an interesting blend of self-praise and humility in explaining his trustworthiness in chapters 12–13. We sense frustration in his words, disappointment that after so much time and such faithful service he still has to work so hard to justify himself. The fact that he strives so hard is testimony to the depth of his commitment and the purity of his hope.

The Corinthian letters lift up the hope that by the grace and power of the Holy Spirit, all divisions might be healed, true community might emerge, and the church at Corinth might become a witness to the world of the healing power of the Christian faith. May it be so for us as well.

Galatians

The tone of Paul's letter to the church in Galatia is different from any other work in the Bible. Irritation, frustration, contempt, and downright anger seep through the pages to make this a deeply passionate letter. It is sometimes difficult to feel hopeful when being criticized, but there is indeed a subtext of hope in this short message.

The primary problem for the Galatian church is Judaizers—Jewish Christians who believe that Gentile Christians must follow Jewish laws. Paul responds to the Galatians that he did not create the gospel he preaches; it was divinely revealed to him directly through the Holy Spirit, so it should not be altered by human beings (1:6–10). Paul reminds the Galatians that he has put in his time and earned his reputation by consistently preaching one gospel over a wide span of years and geography (1:18–2:10). His ministry was affirmed by the leaders of the Jerusalem church when they extended the right hand of fellowship to Paul and Barnabas.

For Gentile Christians, nothing in Judaism earns God's favor; instead they are justified by faith (3:1–9). The Law brought with it a curse (vv. 10–14), imposed to keep people in line and to keep them from straying from the truth. It set boundaries, by which rewards and punishments might be defined. Faith in Christ completes and fulfills the Law (vv. 15–25), making it unnecessary. The Law defined who belonged to God and who did not. In Christ crucified there is hope for all people because all divisions disappear.

> Is the law then against the promises of God? Certainly not! For if there had been a law given which could have given life, truly righteousness would have been by the law. But the Scripture has confined all under sin, that the promise by faith in Jesus Christ might be given to those who believe. But before faith came, we were kept under guard by the law,

kept for the faith which would afterward be revealed. Therefore the law was our tutor to bring us to Christ, that we might be justified by faith. But after faith has come, we are no longer under a tutor.

For you are all sons of God through faith in Christ Jesus. For as many of you as were baptized into Christ have put on Christ. There is neither Jew nor Greek, there is neither slave nor free, there is neither male nor female; for you are all one in Christ Jesus. And if you are Christ's, then you are Abraham's seed, and heirs according to the promise. (vv. 21–29)

Anger is often an outward response to fear. Paul confesses that he is afraid for the Galatians who are being influenced and persuaded by the Judaizers. You can almost hear him reprimanding them, "I taught you better than that!" He tells them that they will have to choose between the two covenants, one of the flesh and one of the Spirit.

I say then: Walk in the Spirit, and you shall not fulfill the lust of the flesh. For the flesh lusts against the Spirit, and the Spirit against the flesh; and these are contrary to one another, so that you do not do the things that you wish. But if you are led by the Spirit, you are not under the law. (5:16–18)

The old covenant can give nothing that the Galatians have not already received through the new covenant in Christ. Paul further contrasts the two covenants according to *works* of the flesh and *fruits* of the Spirit. Those who live according to the flesh have no hope of the kingdom of God. For those who live in the fullness of the Spirit, however, hope of the kingdom is already fulfilled in the "love, joy, peace, longsuffering, kindness, goodness, faithfulness, gentleness, self-control" (vv. 22–23a) they embody and embrace.

Now the works of the flesh are evident, which are: adultery, fornication, uncleanness, lewdness, idolatry, sorcery, hatred, contentions, jealousies, outbursts of wrath, selfish ambitions, dissensions, heresies, envy, murders, drunkenness, revelries, and the like; of which I tell you beforehand, just as I also told you in time past, that those who practice such things will not inherit the kingdom of God.

> But the fruit of the Spirit is love, joy, peace, longsuffering, kindness, goodness, faithfulness, gentleness, self-control. Against such there is no law. And those who are Christ's have crucified the flesh with its passions and desires. If we live in the Spirit, let us also walk in the Spirit. (vv. 19–25)

Paul's letter to the Galatians is strident and scolding, but just as parents are surprised and disappointed when their children fail to do what they know is right, rebuke is sometimes necessary to provide guidance. In this parallel is the word of hope in Galatians. Parents scold children because they want the very best for them. They understand that some practices and behaviors will help children reach their full potential, while others could hurt them or even ruin their lives. This is the level of threat that Paul perceives in Galatia, and the intensity of his response ("See with what large letters I have written to you with my own hand!" 6:11) reflects Paul's commitment to prevent anyone from destroying the hope of the Christian church.

Ephesians

The letter to the Ephesians shares mystical language similar to that found in Johannine literature, and it reflects a broad, universal church graced by a cosmic Christ. Ephesians represents the most refined theology in the whole Pauline corpus.

Ephesus was the capital of the Roman province of Asia (part of modern Turkey). It was an important trade center and similar to Corinth in terms of its cosmopolitan identity. Contrasted to the church in Galatia, Ephesus had just about everything working right, and it was poised to become a model of what the kingdom of God might look like on the earth (1:13–2:10). Paul writes to commend what is good and reinforce that which might keep the church strong.

The church in Ephesus is living together in a new way. Former divisions have broken down (2:14–18), and the fellowship is being built upon the cornerstone of Christ, a temple, a dwelling place of God's Holy Spirit (vv. 19–22). Paul shares his vision for a church that could unite former Jews and Gentiles, and he encourages the congregation in Ephesus to be that kind of church (3:1–4:6).

The first six verses of chapter 4 provide a personal vision statement for the church in Ephesus:

> I, therefore, the prisoner of the Lord, beseech you to walk worthy of the calling with which you were called, with all lowliness and gentleness, with longsuffering, bearing with one another in love, endeavoring to keep the unity of the Spirit in the bond of peace. There is one body and one Spirit, just as you were called in one hope of your calling; one Lord, one faith, one baptism; one God and Father of all, who is above all, and through all, and in you all. (4:1–6)

The ancient church in Ephesus was living in a reality that eludes most of our churches today.

As in the letters to Rome and Corinth, Paul takes some time to talk about spiritual gifts (vv. 7–16). For Paul and his followers, spiritual gifts define each church as a unique and special community. In Ephesians, Paul goes beyond a focus on the gifts themselves to explain how spiritual gifts have an impact on the church's ministry. God gives gifts

> for the equipping of the saints for the work of ministry, for the edifying of the body of Christ, till we all come to the unity of the faith and of the knowledge of the Son of God, to a perfect man, to the measure of the stature of the fullness of Christ, that we should no longer be children, tossed to and fro and carried about with every wind of doctrine, by the trickery of men, in the cunning craftiness of deceitful plotting, but, speaking the truth in love, may grow up in all things into Him who is the head—Christ—from whom the whole body, joined and knit together by what every joint supplies, according to the effective working by which every part does its share, causes growth of the body for the edifying of itself in love. (vv. 12–16)

This vision includes virtually no focus on the individual; the church is a *communion* in the best sense of the word. We become one in Christ, able to do all that is needed to be God's church. If we are able to live faithfully into this vision, we become not only a true expression of God's hope for the world but also a vibrant model and vital witness of God's hope in the world.

Paul warns the Ephesus community not to "grieve the Holy Spirit" (v. 30) by allowing bitterness, anger, and wrath to remain in the community (v. 31); but to be kind, compassionate, and forgiving with one another, just as God in Christ treats us (v. 32). A summary of Ephesians is a blueprint for an ideal Christian community. Paul offers instructions within the premodern context in how to walk in love and obedience, and avoid uncleanness (5:1–7); walk in the light, righteousness, and truth (vv. 8–14); and walk in wisdom, gratitude, and thanksgiving (vv. 15–21). He also offers practical counsel on marriage and family (5:22–6:4), and slavery

(6:5–9). In whatever circumstance we find ourselves, God's love in Christ is fully available to afford us a life of joy and hope through obedience and true community. This is not a message about "putting up" with what life has to offer; it is about embracing a grace-filled life in the midst of loving, faithful community.

Ephesians is a blessed assurance that God provides us with everything we need in Christ to live as kingdom people in the here and now. We do not have to wait for glory; God is already with us, and through the power of the Holy Spirit, we can rise above every earthly challenge and every division to be one in Christ. All we need to do is choose to let Christ live in us, and to walk in the Spirit, and God will do the rest. Again, hope abounds!

Philippians

It is obvious that Paul holds special affection for the community in Philippi. His opening comments and prayers for the fellowship (1:3–11) indicate that he sees, in this community, the hope of the good news being fulfilled. The church at Philippi offers a wonderful model for our own life of faith and hope.

Paul reassures the congregation that his trials, though severe, have actually been a source of hope for him, allowing him more opportunities to preach the gospel. He rejoices that he still lives and can bring encouragement and joy to the fellowship in Philippi (vv. 12–26). He encourages the church to conduct itself in a way that is above reproach—that will witness to God's power to help them through any situation without complaint (vv. 27–30).

Paul begins the second chapter with a clever challenge to the faith community: "If there is any consolation in Christ, if any comfort of love, if any fellowship of the Spirit, if any affection and mercy, fulfill my joy by being like-minded, having the same love, being of one accord, of one mind" (2:1–2). Paul knows, of course, that consolation, comfort, affection, and mercy exist in the fellowship. His hope-filled prayer is that they will complete his joy and grow into a powerful community of faith, using all of the elements already present.

Chapter 2 contains one of the most powerful early Christian confessions or hymns in scripture:

> Let this mind be in you which was also in Christ Jesus, who, being in the form of God, did not consider it robbery to be equal with God, but made Himself of no reputation, taking the form of a bondservant, and coming in the likeness of men. And being found in appearance as a man,

> He humbled Himself and became obedient to the point of death, even the death of the cross. Therefore God also has highly exalted Him and given Him the name which is above every name, that at the name of Jesus every knee should bow, of those in heaven, and of those on earth, and of those under the earth, and that every tongue should confess that Jesus Christ is Lord, to the glory of God the Father. (vv. 5–11)

Paul lifts up Jesus as a model, who set his own life and power aside to humble himself and accept a punishment and death he did not deserve. If Jesus could do this for us, can we do any less for him? We would not normally consider this a message of hope—allowing ourselves to be vulnerable to others and humble before Christ—but the greatest hope for the community at Philippi, and for us, is to

> work out your own salvation with fear and trembling; for it is God who works in you both to will and to do for His good pleasure.
>
> Do all things without complaining and disputing, that you may become blameless and harmless, children of God without fault in the midst of a crooked and perverse generation, among whom you shine as lights in the world, holding fast the word of life, so that I may rejoice in the day of Christ that I have not run in vain or labored in vain.
>
> Yes, and if I am being poured out as a drink offering on the sacrifice and service of your faith, I am glad and rejoice with you all. For the same reason you also be glad and rejoice with me. (vv. 12–18)

Paul reminds the community to remember that the church exists to understand and do God's will, not to be comfortable and secure. He calls the church to shine as beacons of hope in the world, showing others how to live as true followers of Christ.

Paul calls the church to rejoice and to do all for Christ. Many will attempt to impose rules, rituals, and beliefs that have nothing to do with the gospel of Jesus Christ. Obviously, some Judaizers were claiming a need for circumcision in the Christian community, but Paul refutes their claim. As long as the congregation continues to believe in the resurrected Christ, such outward and visible signs as circumcision are unnecessary and irrelevant (3:1–11). The hope for this community, and for our lives as well, is in Christ crucified, not in the rules, doctrines, beliefs, and rituals that others may try to impose.

Using himself as an example, Paul instructs the Philippian congregation to keep pressing toward the goal of perfection in their faith. We may never attain it in this life, Paul reflects, but as long as we strive toward that end, God will be faithful to strengthen us in our pursuit. We cannot afford to become complacent or content. We must do all in our power to keep our hope alive and attain the goal of glory (3:12–4:1).

Paul commends the generosity of the Phillipians, giving thanks for their support (4:10–20), and he offers a very hopeful request of his brothers and sisters: "Whatever things are true, whatever things are noble, whatever things are just, whatever things are pure, whatever things are lovely, whatever things are of good report, if there is any virtue and if there is anything praiseworthy—meditate on these things" (v. 8). If we, as Christian disciples, will dedicate ourselves to meditating on good and holy things, we won't have time to stray or waste ourselves in hurtful or destructive activities. Press on toward the good, surround ourselves in what is noble, Commit to what is positive; this helps us become the people God needs us to be. Our hope resides in the sure knowledge that Jesus the Christ sets the example for us and continues to guide us through the power of the Holy Spirit.

Colossians

The thinking in the letter to the Colossians aligns well with the rest of Paul's theology. As with many of the letters, Paul begins with general information about right and proper belief, then moves to more specific instructions on conduct. Once more, Paul is deeply concerned by false teaching and its corrupting influence in Colossae.

Paul establishes Christ's supremacy over all other beliefs and the whole created order (1:9–18). The greatness of Christ eliminates the need for any other belief, religion, philosophy, or symbol (2:1–10). Christ is sufficient in himself. Paul writes that this is not a legalism, simply a truth. Others try to impose worldly beliefs and practices on the church, including restrictive lists of rules and regulations (vv. 11–23). Christians don't need a lot of rules and regulation; they have Christ. Christians should stay focused on the "things above," and not be distracted by earthly things (3:1–4). Paul calls the Christians in Colossae to "put to death" all worldly practices—"fornication, uncleanness, passion, evil desire, and covetousness, which is idolatry . . . , anger, wrath, malice, blasphemy, filthy language" and anything else that turns our attention from the things of God" (vv. 5, 8). Instead, Christians should,

> as the elect of God, holy and beloved, put on tender mercies, kindness, humility, meekness, longsuffering; bearing with one another, and forgiving one another, if anyone has a complaint against another; even as Christ forgave you, so you also must do. But above all these things put on love, which is the bond of perfection. And let the peace of God rule in your hearts, to which also you were called in one body; and be thankful. Let the word of Christ dwell in you richly in all wisdom, teaching and admonishing one another in psalms and hymns and spiritual songs, singing with

> grace in your hearts to the Lord. And whatever you do in word or deed, do all in the name of the Lord Jesus, giving thanks to God the Father through Him. (vv. 12–17)

Paul presents an interesting idea here. We have the power to avoid doing the things that make us and others feel hopeless. Many of the destructive behaviors in which we engage are evidence that we have given up hope. If we want to experience hope, we need to live hopefully.

First and Second *Thessalonians*

First and Second Thessalonians have the distinction of being Paul's earliest letters, written to one of the earliest churches he helped found. Thessalonica was an important city to the ancient Roman Empire because of its central location. It became equally important to the apostolic mission of the early Christian movement. First Thessalonians was written to offer some encouragement and guidance to a fledgling congregation where Paul spent far less time than he would have preferred. The congregation's faithfulness is a witness of hope to all developing faith communities, including ours:

> You became followers of us and of the Lord, having received the word in much affliction, with joy of the Holy Spirit, so that you became examples to all in Macedonia and Achaia who believe. For from you the word of the Lord has sounded forth, not only in Macedonia and Achaia, but also in every place. Your faith toward God has gone out, so that we do not need to say anything. For they themselves declare concerning us what manner of entry we had to you, and how you turned to God from idols to serve the living and true God, and to wait for His Son from heaven, whom He raised from the dead, even Jesus who delivers us from the wrath to come. (1 Thess. 1:6–10)

Second Thessalonians is written to address specific concerns regarding the delayed *parousia* (second coming of Christ), "We ask you, not to be soon shaken in mind or troubled, either by spirit or by word or by letter, as if from us, as though the day of Christ had come" (2 Thess. 2:1–2). In both letters, Paul attempts to be hopeful and to encourage congregations dealing with misconceptions and doubts. But another level of hope is also evident in these letters.

Paul sees the spread of Christianity as the hope—the only hope—of a world given over to corruption and evil. He has witnessed Greeks and

Jews, Gentiles and Hellenists choosing to walk in the flesh and accepting the values of the world as their guide. He once shared these values and embraced the ways of the world as his own. But through personal encounter he experienced a radical transformation and has committed his life to helping others experience it as well. The resurrection of Jesus the Christ is his compass, directing his every thought and action following the Damascus Road experience.

Paul writes with urgency and passion, apparent in these two early letters. He is as concerned about his young churches as a parent might be about a child launching into the world on his or her own. Paul's affection for the Thessalonian congregation is pervasive.

First Thessalonians

Paul begins his letter with hopeful and encouraging words, acknowledging that the formation of the church did not happen without affliction, but that it resulted in great joy (1:6) and that its foundation has become an inspiration and model for others (v. 7). The Thessalonians apparently take their responsibility as witnesses of Christ very seriously, and they have sent apostles out to spread the good news (v. 8). When Paul and his associates first came to Thessalonica, they were weary and despondent because of the treatment they received in Philippi (2:1–2). Paul reminds the Thessalonians that the apostles had come in "gentle among you," entrusting themselves to the hospitality of the Thessalonians as they shared the gospel of Jesus the Christ (vv. 7–9). There was no force or coercion, but a simple sharing of truth and encouragement. Obviously, this approach was successful. Apparently, a large number of people accepted Christ and established a church community as active as that in Judea (vv. 13–16). The apostles had a short time in Thessalonica; Paul expresses concern that the church did not have time enough to fully grasp and comprehend the gospel message, but he offers them high praise:

> But we, brethren, having been taken away from you for a short time in presence, not in heart, endeavored more eagerly to see your face with great desire. Therefore we wanted to come to you—even I, Paul, time and again—but Satan hindered us. For what is our hope, or joy, or crown of rejoicing? Is it not even you in the presence of our Lord Jesus Christ at His coming? For you are our glory and joy. (vv. 17–20)

In praising this fledgling faith community, Paul challenges us to become the hope, joy, and crown of rejoicing.

The apostles sent Timothy to check on the young church, and they are encouraged by the report he brought back (3:1–10), again lifting up for the Thessalonians, and for us, the joy and hope that faithful living offers those who guide and pray for the church:

> But now that Timothy has come to us from you, and brought us good news of your faith and love, and that you always have good remembrance of us, greatly desiring to see us, as we also to see you—therefore, brethren, in all our affliction and distress we were comforted concerning you by your faith. For now we live, if you stand fast in the Lord.
>
> For what thanks can we render to God for you, for all the joy with which we rejoice for your sake before our God, night and day praying exceedingly that we may see your face and perfect what is lacking in your faith? (vv. 6–10)

Paul shifts his focus to instruction, advising the congregation to increase its commitment to what is good and to abstain from all forms of sexual immorality and uncleanness (4:1–8). It is unclear if there is a specific reason for this advice or just a general desire for the congregation to remain strong and faithful. When it comes to his advice concerning brotherly love (vv. 9–12), Paul can do little more than encourage them to increase it. Sharing the love of God in Christ seems to be what this young congregation does best.

The generation that lived when Jesus was resurrected believed that Christ would return before they died. As members of this generation die, their passing is characterized as "sleep." When just a few have died, no one is too concerned. But the first letter to Thessalonica is written approximately twenty years after the resurrection of Jesus, and a good portion of one generation has died, with young members of a second generation beginning to join them. This raises concerns that the promise of Christ's return might not be true. Early teaching in the church reasoned that God was delaying Christ's return until the gospel could be spread to all corners of the earth. Those who died in the interim would be raised in full glory at God's command, and each person would be raised as they had been in life. Now, concerns are raised about the condition of the "sleeping" corpses. Detractors from the faith capitalize on people's fears for their loved ones, often undermining the spread of the Christian faith.

Paul writes to address directly these questions and fears. He shares that God knows exactly what must occur, and there is absolutely no reason for concern. All will be raised and caught up together with the Lord:

> But I do not want you to be ignorant, brethren, concerning those who have fallen asleep, lest you sorrow as others who have no hope. For if we believe that Jesus died and rose again, even so God will bring with Him those who sleep in Jesus.
>
> For this we say to you by the word of the Lord, that we who are alive and remain until the coming of the Lord will by no means precede those who are asleep. For the Lord Himself will descend from heaven with a shout, with the voice of an archangel, and with the trumpet of God. And the dead in Christ will rise first. Then we who are alive and remain shall be caught up together with them in the clouds to meet the Lord in the air. And thus we shall always be with the Lord. Therefore comfort one another with these words (vv. 13–18)

There can be no greater message of hope for those who have lost loved ones in Thessalonica or for us. Paul goes on to remind his readers that when the Day of the Lord occurs and Christ returns, it is imperative that believers be on the right side. Those who stay firm in their faith—even in the face of a delayed return—will be blessed (5:1–10).

Paul counsels the congregation members to hold one another accountable to faithful conduct (vv. 12–15); to rejoice, pray without ceasing, and give thanks (vv. 16–18); to do nothing to quench the Spirit (v. 19); and to pay attention to prophecy and test everything (vv. 20–21). Summing up, he tells them to hold fast to what is good and to abstain from what is evil (vv. 21b–22).

There is a simplicity and a joyful spirit here that is not always evident in Paul's writing. It is clear that Paul dotes on this Thessalonian congregation and sees hope for the coming of the kingdom in their faithfulness. Sadly, this light spirit is absent from Paul's second letter to Thessalonica.

Second Thessalonians

The evidence in 2 Thessalonians indicates that the delayed return of the Christ has become a growing point of contention in the congregation. The divisions result in three concerns. First, some claim that the Day of the Lord has already come, and that many in Thessalonica have missed out (2:1–12). Paul writes that this is an absolutely false teaching with no validity or support. Second, a group questions whether the Day of the Lord will come at all. Paul reaffirms that indeed this second coming of Christ is the heart of the gospel and that all will be fine if only the church will stand fast in its hope.

> But we are bound to give thanks to God always for you, brethren beloved by the Lord, because God from the beginning chose you for salvation through sanctification by the Spirit and belief in the truth, to which He called you by our gospel, for the obtaining of the glory of our Lord Jesus Christ. Therefore, brethren, stand fast and hold the traditions which you were taught, whether by word or our epistle.
>
> Now may our Lord Jesus Christ Himself, and our God and Father, who has loved us and given us everlasting consolation and good hope by grace, comfort your hearts and establish you in every good word and work. (vv. 13–17)

The third view is apathy: Why worry about something that hasn't happened so far and probably won't happen for a long time to come (3:6–15)?

Here, Paul warns against idleness and complacency. The delay of the return of Christ does nothing to lift from us our responsibility to do good and spread the gospel.

Summary

The two letters to the church in Thessalonica raise an interesting question: Is hope primarily about the future or is it about the present? The hope as presented in the Gospels helps people live day to day, to find assurance that all will be well in time, and that each new day brings us closer to justice and equity. While the promise is of a better future, the benefit is felt in the here and now. In the Epistles and Revelation, hope is in future events and occurrences, and delays deal a terrible blow to people's confidence in the faith. The early church settled into the complacency of a passive hope, allowing expectation and anticipation to devolve into wishful thinking. Paul's letters to the church at Thessalonica (and to us) offer a corrective to this tendency. They (and we) must hold on to and build our faith, as a lively act of hope for the kingdom of God to come. When Paul speaks of the cross of Christ and his resurrection, he always means a living, rather than passive, hope.

First and Second *Timothy and Titus*

The letters of 1 Timothy, 2 Timothy, and Titus are commonly called the Pastoral Epistles. They are clearly letters of instruction, mentoring church leaders on "how to be church" in the late first and early second centuries. In the chaos of the early stages of the Christian church, as well as suffering under Roman oppression, these letters offer hope through the certainty of structure and guidance from faithful and trustworthy mentors.

First Timothy

First Timothy contains a warning to be on guard against false doctrine and teaching (1:3–11). The prominence of this caution indicates that orthodox doctrine was under siege and in danger. Paul provides a statement of faith and affirmation to clarify right and proper teaching (vv. 12–18). Paul encourages Timothy to pray for all—surrounding leaders in the grace of God:

> Therefore I exhort first of all that supplications, prayers, intercessions, and giving of thanks be made for all men, for kings and all who are in authority, that we may lead a quiet and peaceable life in all godliness and reverence. For this is good and acceptable in the sight of God our Savior, who desires all men to be saved and to come to the knowledge of the truth. For there is one God and one Mediator between God and men, the Man Christ Jesus, who gave Himself a ransom for all, to be testified in due time. (2:1–6)

This author defines a code of conduct for men and women in worship (2:8–15) that is unique in Scripture. Many interpreters believe that this deals with a specific issue in a specific congregation and has no universal application; other epistles offer very different instructions.

First Timothy contains descriptions for offices within the institutional church. Qualifications for bishops (3:1–7) and deacons (vv. 8–13) reflect that the church has adopted a common structure with roles clearly defined. Here is the hope offered by clarity within chaos and disagreement. When leaders are expected to model a life of faithful servant ministry, the entire congregation and all who witness its works are lifted up.

Paul warns that some teachers in the church will expect things that are not true or necessary, such as prohibitions on marriage and abstinence from certain kinds of food (4:1–6). These particular legalisms probably reflect specific incidents in a particular congregation. First Timothy is a wonderful example of helpful guidance for a specific setting being shared and applied universally, but we must remember that not all churches face the same challenges; the solution appropriate in one place might not be helpful in another.

The author writes to Timothy that if he will teach others the lessons contained in the letter, he will be a "good minister of Jesus Christ" (v. 6). He continues to mentor the young minister, supporting him in his authority (even though he is young) and offering him helpful advice in the ways to relate to others in the church.

> Let no one despise your youth, but be an example to the believers in word, in conduct, in love, in spirit, in faith, in purity. Till I come, give attention to reading, to exhortation, to doctrine. Do not neglect the gift that is in you, which was given to you by prophecy with the laying on of the hands of the eldership. Meditate on these things; give yourself entirely to them, that your progress may be evident to all. Take heed to yourself and to the doctrine. Continue in them, for in doing this you will save both yourself and those who hear you. . . .
>
> I charge you before God and the Lord Jesus Christ and the elect angels that you observe these things without prejudice, doing nothing with partiality. Do not lay hands on anyone hastily, nor share in other people's sins; keep yourself pure.
>
> No longer drink only water, but use a little wine for your stomach's sake and your frequent infirmities.

> Some men's sins are clearly evident, preceding them to judgment, but those of some men follow later. Likewise, the good works of some are clearly evident, and those that are otherwise cannot be hidden. (4:12–16; 5:21–25)

Paul concludes the letter by distinguishing between apostasy and good faith. He advises the young leader to avoid envy, strife, reviling, evil suspicions, useless wrangling, and greed (6:3–10). Such wise counsel and mentoring were common in the first few centuries of the church, a valued source of hope for those learning how to lead. The author continues in his guidance by encouraging Timothy to pursue righteousness, godliness, faith, love, patience, and gentleness (v. 11).

Second Timothy

The mentoring continues in 2 Timothy as the author of the letter reminds the young leader to "not be ashamed" (1:8) of the gospel, but to proclaim the good news with courage and conviction (1:3–2:13). The author, Paul, exhorts young Timothy to engage in worthwhile conversation and speech and to avoid idle and worthless chatter (2:14–26). In the early days of the Christian movement, there were only a few central teachings and few questions about them. As time passed, more and more teachings emerged, opening the floor to increased debate. Disagreements arose about contradictory teaching. People were swept into irresolvable debate. The author suggests that Timothy avoid being sucked into such senseless wrangling.

Paul advises Timothy to keep things simple and to preach what he has been taught is true, not to embellish or expand. Stick to the basics and be clear and concise; hope resides in the simplicity of the good news (this is good advice to us as well). Timothy is encouraged to trust the power of the truth:

> But you must continue in the things which you have learned and been assured of, knowing from whom you have learned them, and that from

> childhood you have known the Holy Scriptures, which are able to make you wise for salvation through faith which is in Christ Jesus.
>
> All Scripture is given by inspiration of God, and is profitable for doctrine, for reproof, for correction, for instruction in righteousness, that the man of God may be complete, thoroughly equipped for every good work.
>
> I charge you therefore before God and the Lord Jesus Christ, who will judge the living and the dead at His appearing and His kingdom: Preach the word! Be ready in season and out of season. Convince, rebuke, exhort, with all longsuffering and teaching. For the time will come when they will not endure sound doctrine, but according to their own desires, because they have itching ears, they will heap up for themselves teachers; and they will turn their ears away from the truth, and be turned aside to fables. But you be watchful in all things, endure afflictions, do the work of an evangelist, fulfill your ministry. (3:14–4:5)

Titus

Titus is a close companion to I Timothy, in both style and content. Titus contains the qualifications of an elder (1:5–16), which complement Timothy's list for bishops and deacons. First Timothy focuses on right doctrines for the early church, while the author of Titus pays more attention to proper behaviors and good works: "in all things [show] yourself to be a pattern of good works; in doctrine showing integrity, reverence, incorruptibility, sound speech that cannot be condemned, that one who is an opponent may be ashamed, having nothing evil to say of you" (2:7–8).

Titus is encouraged to preach and teach the saving grace of God and to exhort and rebuke with full authority (vv. 11–15). The message Titus should share is simple: live as though you are grateful for the salvation you have received:

> Remind them to be subject to rulers and authorities, to obey, to be ready for every good work, to speak evil of no one, to be peaceable, gentle, showing all humility to all men. For we ourselves were also once foolish, disobedient, deceived, serving various lusts and pleasures, living in malice and envy, hateful and hating one another. But when the kindness

> and the love of God our Savior toward man appeared, not by works of righteousness which we have done, but according to His mercy He saved us, through the washing of regeneration and renewing of the Holy Spirit, whom He poured out on us abundantly through Jesus Christ our Savior, that having been justified by His grace we should become heirs according to the hope of eternal life. (3:1–7)

Summary

The Pastoral Epistles do not proclaim the mystery of hope; they offer its practical application for church leadership and organization so that the church may become a bastion of hope. As the church developed and grew, many congregations and communities were threatened by disagreements and factions. Those outside the Christian faith experienced the new movement as similar to other groups. The grace and love of God was lost in contention and controversy. The theme of the Pastoral Epistles is that leaders need to work hard to make the church different from other earthly institutions. Where people find despair in the world, they need to be able to find hope in the church.

Philemon

No other book of the New Testament is written as a personal letter to an individual. (The Pastoral Epistles are letters of instruction to church leaders.) In Philemon, Paul writes a personal appeal on behalf of the slave Onesimus. The concept of slavery is foreign to twenty-first-century America, though it is a part of our recent history. In the ancient Middle East, slaves all but lost their personal identity as they sacrificed freedom and autonomy. Hope was one of the first things sacrificed for an entire class of people. Paul connects with Onesimus in prison, and upon their mutual release, Paul endeavors to send Onesimus back to his master. But Paul sends Onesimus to Philemon as a brother in Christ, not as property. He pleads with Philemon:

> For love's sake I rather appeal to you—being such a one as Paul, the aged, and now also a prisoner of Jesus Christ—I appeal to you for my son Onesimus, whom I have begotten while in my chains, who once was unprofitable to you, but now is profitable to you and to me.
>
> I am sending him back. You therefore receive him, that is, my own heart, whom I wished to keep with me, that on your behalf he might minister to me in my chains for the gospel. But without your consent I wanted to do nothing, that your good deed might not be by compulsion, as it were, but voluntary.
>
> For perhaps he departed for a while for this purpose, that you might receive him forever, no longer as a slave but more than a slave—a beloved brother, especially to me but how much more to you, both in the flesh and in the Lord.
>
> If then you count me as a partner, receive him as you would me. (vv. 9–17)

The hopeful significance of this letter is a radical acknowledgment that we become completely new creations when we choose to follow Christ.

We use the language of *change* casually; when we become Christians, everything changes. How deeply do we mean it? Will we not only accept people who are different from us but also embrace them as brothers and sisters, equals in the faith? Will we allow God to eliminate all the distinctions in race, class, gender, intelligence, and social position? Can we treat those we felt superior to on Monday with respect and dignity on Tuesday? Paul issues a provocative challenge to Philemon: set the past behind, ignore what has been, and enter into a brand-new relationship on a level field. For those who have lived in positions of inferiority and subservience, this is more than change; it is transformation and an incredible declaration of hope!

Hebrews

No other writing in the Christian scriptures has such a clear and direct purpose. Hebrews was written to prove that Christianity was the proper and intended successor to Judaism. Many converted Jews wrestled with the decision to become Christians. In the passionate excitement of Christian proselytizing, many took the plunge to become Christians, but then doubts crept in. The unknown author of Hebrews crafted an argument to reinforce the appropriateness of the decision to leave Judaism behind and follow Jesus the Christ.

The author begins his epistle by placing Jesus in the long line of God's many revelations of truth and covenant (1:1–4). Throughout the letter, Jesus is lifted up as the fulfillment of the Hebrew faith, weaving together quotations from Jewish and Christian scriptures to create a single witness. The author draws parallels between Jesus and Moses, emphasizing how Jesus is superior in every way (3:1–6).

Hebrews takes on the spirit and energy of a Christian pep-talk, reminding people of all the wonderful things that are true of Christ. He is the author of our salvation (2:10), God made visible in the flesh (1:3), a merciful and faithful high priest (2:17), and a pathway to a covenant superior to that made with Moses (8:6–13). The Christ is an example, a model, a shepherd, and an advocate. There is no one greater or finer than Christ, and he is present and available to us all. Because Jesus walked this earth as a man, we can relate to him, have confidence that he understands us, and even hope to become like him (4:14–16).

The author of Hebrews warns against complacency and being satisfied with one's progress in spiritual growth and development. He urges us to "go on to perfection" (6:1) and "not to become sluggish" (v. 12) as we pursue Christ. The examples from Judaism for a priesthood were inadequate, because the priests were human. Through Christ, we have a new priesthood (7:1–28). Christ is our high priest, human but more than human, establishing a new covenant (8:1–13). There is no reason to regret leaving the old behind, since in every way it is obsolete and irrelevant.

In chapters 9 and 10, the author explains in detail how the covenant offered through Christ is superior in every way to the old covenants of the Jewish faith. Chapter 11 opens with one of the greatest expressions of "hope" of all time:

> Now faith is the substance of things hoped for, the evidence of things not seen. For by it the elders obtained a good testimony.
>
> By faith we understand that the worlds were framed by the word of God, so that the things which are seen were not made of things which are visible.
>
> By faith Abel offered to God a more excellent sacrifice than Cain, through which he obtained witness that he was righteous, God testifying of his gifts; and through it he being dead still speaks.
>
> By faith Enoch was taken away so that he did not see death, "and was not found, because God had taken him"; for before he was taken he had this testimony, that he pleased God. But without faith it is impossible to please Him, for he who comes to God must believe that He is, and that He is a rewarder of those who diligently seek Him.
>
> By faith Noah, being divinely warned of things not yet seen, moved with godly fear, prepared an ark for the saving of his household, by which he condemned the world and became heir of the righteousness which is according to faith.
>
> By faith Abraham obeyed when he was called to go out to the place which he would receive as an inheritance. And he went out, not knowing where he was going. By faith he dwelt in the land of promise as in a foreign country, dwelling in tents with Isaac and Jacob, the heirs with him of the same promise; for he waited for the city which has foundations, whose builder and maker is God.
>
> By faith Sarah herself also received strength to conceive seed, and she bore a child when she was past the age, because she judged Him faithful who had promised. Therefore from one man, and him as good as

> dead, were born as many as the stars of the sky in multitude—innumerable as the sand which is by the seashore. (vv. 1–12)

Here, *faith* means assurance, *hope* means expectation, and *evidence* means confirmation. More than simple belief, faith is a kind of spiritual knowledge. We hold fast to what we know in our hearts to be true because of the promises of God, which give us expectation of all God will do for us if we live in the confidence of our beliefs.

This does not mean we should be arrogant or superior to those who disagree with us; we have no reason to be defensive or aggressive with those who believe differently. We may live calmly and peacefully in the confidence that God is God and that nothing on earth can sway us from what we know and believe to be true. It gives us a wonderful capacity to agree to disagree and to share our hope with others.

The author traces a history of faith through the great figures of Judaism all the way to Jesus the Christ. From the patriarchs through Moses and the kings and prophets, the author of Hebrews reaffirms the tradition, but explains how Jesus is the culmination of all that came before. Everything throughout history points to Jesus, the "finisher of our faith" (12:2) and "the Mediator of the new covenant" (v. 24). Our hope abides in the knowledge that through Jesus we have "[received] a kingdom which cannot be shaken" (v. 28).

The author of the letter offers some closing advice:

> Let brotherly love continue. Do not forget to entertain strangers, for by so doing some have unwittingly entertained angels. Remember the prisoners as if chained with them—those who are mistreated—since you yourselves are in the body also. . . .
>
> Let your conduct be without covetousness; be content with such things as you have. . . .
>
> But do not forget to do good and to share, for with such sacrifices God is well pleased. (13:1–3, 5, 16)

Such instructions remind us that God is the source of our hope, and that we have many opportunities to be sources of hope for one another.

The closing benediction is both grace-filled and hopeful, a fitting conclusion to such an encouraging letter:

> Now may the God of peace who brought up our Lord Jesus from the dead, that great Shepherd of the sheep, through the blood of the everlasting covenant, make you complete in every good work to do His will, working in you what is well pleasing in His sight, through Jesus Christ, to whom be glory forever and ever. Amen. (vv. 20–21)

James

There are many messages of hope throughout Scripture, but few are more practical and down-to-earth than the hope messages in James's epistle. The audience of this letter seems to be Jews who have converted to the Christian Way (1:1). James writes words of encouragement, instructing readers not to resist or resent trials, but to view such challenges as an opportunity to develop patience and wisdom (vv. 2–8), for that is the hope we have been given through Jesus the Christ. For James, proof of our faith is shown in the way we respond to hardship (vv. 12–20).

James's world includes no social services or safety nets. Communities have to take care of their own. Families and households provide for those within, but this providence does not always extend to widows, orphans, strangers, and the physically and emotionally ill. For those on the fringes of society, only the kindness and charity of strangers makes the hope of survival possible. James understands the needs of his culture and envisions the opportunity of the Christian faith to care for the most vulnerable and needy. We would do well to listen to this call to offer physical care as well as hope to our neighbors. When our modern "safety nets" fail through lack of funding or disaster, James challenges us to live out the hope of our faith in practical terms.

> If a brother or sister is naked and destitute of daily food, and one of you says to them, "Depart in peace, be warmed and filled," but you do not give them the things which are needed for the body, what does it profit? Thus also faith by itself, if it does not have works, is dead.
>
> But someone will say, "You have faith, and I have works." Show me your faith without your works, and I will show you my faith by my works. You believe that there is one God. You do well. Even the demons believe—and tremble! (2:15–19)

The early church wrestled with the relationship of faith and works. Paul was very clear that we could do nothing to earn God's favor, that it is a free gift, undeserved and beyond price. One unintended consequence of this teaching was a tendency on the part of some to decide that their actions meant nothing. As long as a person believed the right things, behaviors didn't matter. James clarifies the conundrum: we do not do works to earn God's favor; because God favors us, we are compelled to do good works. For James, our works are the outward and visible signs of the health and vitality of our relationship with God in Jesus Christ. In James's worldview, good works breed hope, and hope inspires us to perform good works. To live as hope-filled people enables us to inspire hope in others.

This is a powerful and humbling concept. James reminds us that actions have consequences, and Christians need to take responsibility for the things we say and do: "above all, brethren, do not swear, either by heaven or by earth or with any other oath. But let your 'Yes' be 'Yes,' and your 'No,' 'No,' lest you fall into judgment" (5:12). By our conduct, we bear fruit, and by our fruit we will be known. We have the opportunity to be God's hope for others: "Brethren, if anyone among you wanders from the truth, and someone turns him back, let him know that he who turns a sinner from the error of his way will save a soul from death and cover a multitude of sins" (vv. 19–20).

First and Second *Peter*

First and Second Peter are very different letters. Second Peter actually has more in common with the letter from Jude than it does with First Peter. Yet they all share a common focus on holiness and right belief.

First Peter

First Peter is addressed to scattered "pilgrims" (1:1) across Asia Minor. This letter contains a term that actually translates very clearly as "hope," or "living expectation": "Blessed be the God and Father of our Lord Jesus Christ, who according to His abundant mercy has begotten us again to a living hope through the resurrection of Jesus Christ from the dead" (v. 3).

Like James, Peter encourages readers to embrace their trials and understand that through such testing we are strengthened in our faith. He equates our trials to a refiner's fire that purifies gold (vv. 6–9). Peter writes in glowing terms about the privilege and honor we are given to serve God. He celebrates the potential we have to be an example of holiness and righteousness in the world. He famously refers to Christian believers as

> a chosen generation, a royal priesthood, a holy nation, His own special people, that you may proclaim the praises of Him who called you out of darkness into His marvelous light; who once were not a people but are now the people of God, who had not obtained mercy but now have obtained mercy.
>
> Beloved, I beg you as sojourners and pilgrims, abstain from fleshly lusts which war against the soul, having your conduct honorable among the Gentiles, that when they speak against you as evildoers, they may, by your good works which they observe, glorify God in the day of visitation. (2:9–12)

Through these words, Peter validates and honors all who love God. But we are not chosen for special privilege. We are called to be hope for those who do not know God's purifying love. Our honor exists in the ways in which we honor God with our lives of hopeful living.

The central recurrent theme of I Peter is that we are all beneficiaries of the suffering of Jesus Christ for our sake. Since Jesus suffered for us, we should view it as an honor to suffer for Christ (3:18–4:6). A secondary theme is gratitude and appreciation. Since God has done so much for us, we should be ready to do likewise for others. Peter offers the grace-filled reminder that "love will cover a multitude of sins" (4:8). Peter calls for us to serve and care for one another, "As each one has received a gift, minister it to one another, as good stewards of the manifold grace of God" (v. 10). He commands humility and submission (5:5–6), trusting God (v. 7), vigilance and steadfastness (vv. 8–9), and to not despair in suffering (v. 10). For those who lead in the church, Peter offers a message of understanding, comfort, encouragement, and support.

Second Peter

Second Peter is a completely different story. Much more strident and prescriptive, 2 Peter is more of a warning than a letter of encouragement. Echoing the very same sentiments found in Jude, the author of 2 Peter is deeply concerned by false teachers and those who might lead the faithful to destruction (2:1–22). Peter reminds his readers that the message of the eyewitnesses is trustworthy, but false teachers are spreading dangerous heresies. Their hypocrisy is evident "when they speak great swelling words of emptiness" (v. 18), yet behave like "slaves of corruption" (v. 19).

Peter also gives words of comfort and hope in the face of longsuffering and delay in the second coming of Christ. He offers the phrase that frames our understanding of "God's time": "with the Lord one day is as a thousand years, and a thousand years as one day" (3:8). He assures his readers that any delay is simply God's way of allowing more sinners to come to repentance.

Because God's time is not measured as is our time, we must continue to live in hopeful expectation of the Lord's return, enduring with patience and steadfastness. Optimism pervades both letters. Not only should we not lose hope, we should live in a state of constant preparedness.

> Therefore, beloved, looking forward to these things, be diligent to be found by Him in peace, without spot and blameless. (v. 14)

First, Second, Third John, and Jude

The fundamental theme of survival in the face of terrible opposition and oppression that defined the gospel of John continues in the Johannine letters. The common thread running through the Johannine literature is the need to remain faithful in a hostile world, which is trying to destroy our faith. "The world" becomes the antithesis to Christian community, and Christ is the key to overcoming "the world."

First John

In 1 John, the author encourages his audience to remember who they are (1:5–8). He emphasizes how important it is to keep God's commandments (2:3), to walk in light instead of darkness (vv. 7–11), and to renounce the love of the world (vv. 15–17). He warns of the coming of the "Antichrist," and lesser antichrists who threaten to lead true believers astray by perverting the gospel of Jesus Christ and challenging the core beliefs of John's community (vv. 18–23). The author reminds the community to hold fast to what they know to be true and to let the truth abide in them, rejecting anyone who might try to deceive them (vv. 24–27).

John reminds his readers that they are children of God and should live righteously, rejecting everything that is evil (3:1–10). The author proceeds to then offer some of the most memorable and hopeful words in all of Scripture:

> We are of God. He who knows God hears us; he who is not of God does not hear us. By this we know the spirit of truth and the spirit of error.
>
> Beloved, let us love one another, for love is of God; and everyone who loves is born of God and knows God. He who does not love does

> not know God, for God is love. In this the love of God was manifested toward us, that God has sent His only begotten Son into the world, that we might live through Him. In this is love, not that we loved God, but that He loved us and sent His Son to be the propitiation for our sins. Beloved, if God so loved us, we also ought to love one another.
>
> No one has seen God at any time. If we love one another, God abides in us, and His love has been perfected in us. By this we know that we abide in Him, and He in us, because He has given us of His Spirit. And we have seen and testify that the Father has sent the Son as Savior of the world. Whoever confesses that Jesus is the Son of God, God abides in him, and he in God. And we have known and believed the love that God has for us. God is love, and he who abides in love abides in God, and God in him.
>
> Love has been perfected among us in this: that we may have boldness in the day of judgment; because as He is, so are we in this world. There is no fear in love; but perfect love casts out fear, because fear involves torment. But he who fears has not been made perfect in love. We love Him because He first loved us. (4:6–19)

Love is the key. Love gives us the power to overcome the world. Love heals all wounds and protects us from all hurts. Believing in love is equivalent to believing in God because "God is love" (v. 8). Our hope resides in the knowledge that God—perfect love—which "casts out fear" (v. 18) is being perfected in and through us.

The author instructs the community of faith to be watchful and to "test the spirits" (v. 1) in order to guard against false teachings that might undermine the security and strength of the congregation. Truth is very important to the author of I John, and the supreme truth is Jesus. According to John, together we can live in hope because "we know that the Son of God has come and has given us an understanding, that we may know Him who is true; and we are in Him who is true, in His Son Jesus Christ. This is the true God and eternal life" (5:20).

First John is one of the earliest and clearest "Trinitarian" books of the Bible. God the Father, God the Son, and God the Holy Spirit are equal in

John's theology, and they are referenced interchangeably. We are God's children, saved by God's Son, empowered and guided by God's Spirit. The sense of God's presence with the Johannine community is pervasive. As long as the community remains faithful to the teachings of their leaders, all will be well. A shared faith in God through Jesus Christ is the foundation of John's message of hope for the early Christian community and for us. If love is the quality and characteristic that sets the church apart from the world, living in the love of God in Christ through the power of the Holy Spirit (living in hope) could be the very force to bridge our divisions and heal the brokenness between those inside the church and those outside.

Second and Third John

The Johannine community's continued survival was tenuous, and the last two letters from John are cautionary letters to encourage the fellowship to be careful.

The common practice in the late first century and early second century was for communities to welcome itinerant missionary preachers and teachers. The benefit in this process was a constant influx of new thinking, stories, testimonies, and teaching to keep the community from getting too set in its own thinking or limited in its understanding of the scope of the Christian gospel. Engagement with traveling preachers and teachers stimulated deep and regular reflection and growth. False teachers and prophets traveled as frequently as those recognized as worthy and true, however. A constant concern of the early church was not being led astray by false and inaccurate teaching.

Second and Third John warn the fellowship to remember the truth, that is, obedience to the commandments and love of God and neighbor (1:4–6), and to avoid anti-Christian doctrine. The major point of disagreement in John's community relates to the humanity of Jesus. Some teach that

Jesus only appeared to be human, but the leaders of John's community hold fast to the belief that Jesus was both fully human and fully divine. Anyone teaching that Jesus was anything other than or less than human should be rejected. The word of hope here, as in 1 John, is that whoever "abides in the doctrine of Christ has both the Father and the Son" (2 John 9b).

A secondary concern, the focus of 3 John, are those who pretend to be part of the community but are more self-interested and talk badly about others. Anyone who works to bring division to the community should be put out of the church, and no one should imitate such behavior. When we offer God's love to all in the community and to strangers, we honor God. That is the hope of our calling to "walk in the truth" (3 John 3).

Jude

Jude's short letter is often linked to the letters of John because of the common themes. False teachers have crept into the fellowship and corrupted some of the basic teachings. Posing as religious leaders, these men twist and distort common beliefs and practices to their advantages. Under their influence, the church has focused less on obedience to the will of God and more on using the faith for selfish purposes. Jude is angry and outraged by the degradation of the truth. Jude's description of the apostates is a wonderful snapshot of the problem in context:

> These are grumblers, complainers, walking according to their own lusts; and they mouth great swelling words, flattering people to gain advantage. But you, beloved, remember the words which were spoken before by the apostles of our Lord Jesus Christ: how they told you that there would be mockers in the last time who would walk according to their own ungodly lusts. These are sensual persons, who cause divisions, not having the Spirit. (vv. 16–19)

An important function of our spiritual life together in Christian community is to not only remain hopeful but also guard against those who would mislead us and rob us of the hope God wants us to have. We are called: to hope in the promise of Christ's return, to hope for perfection in our life of love, and to hope in the power of the Holy Spirit to protect and guide us into right living and healthy relationships.

Revelation

Apocalyptic literature was a genre of writing in the ancient world that is represented in the Bible in such books as Daniel in the Old Testament and Revelation in the New Testament. Apocalyptic literature uses spiritual and mystical symbolism and imagery to describe things not of this earth. Apocalyptic writing focused on radical change and transformation, often grounded in disaster or earth-shattering events.

In Revelation the author enters into an ethereal realm, moving from body to spirit and back, witnessing things not common to mortal eyes. The book describes a divine vision given by God. It is filled with startling and mystical images. It bridges the heavenly and the earthly, offering instruction to the church on earth as well as focusing on the age to come.

Hope on Earth

The seven churches mentioned are Ephesus, Smyrna, Pergamos, Thyatira, Sardis, Philadelphia, and Laodicea. The seven letters to the seven churches provide a prologue to the prophetic vision and descriptions that follow. The early Christian communities associated with this work of Revelation understood *eschatology* ("end times") as happening in the near future. Revelation was written as an encouragement and guidebook for the early church.

This is a book of urgency. With each passing year the imminent return of the Christ seemed more remote. The first generation after the resurrection assumed Jesus would return in its lifetime. As that generation passed, the message to the next generation was that Jesus would return "soon." With the passing of the second generation, more questions emerged. The apostle Paul taught the first generation about bodily resurrection of the dead. He taught the next generation that at the resurrection, we would be "changed." Later generations taught about a "spiritual" resurrection. Most believers attributed their confusion to their own limited ability to know the mind of God. Others began to ask serious questions and spread virulent doubts. The sense of urgency in the book of Revelation indicates the vital importance of not losing hope in the face of doubts.

Roman opposition toward Christians was on the rise after the fall of the temple in 70 CE. Christianity was a provincial, grassroots movement, and each community developed around an incomplete set of stories, teachings, rituals, and practices. The Christian Way might look radically different in each city, town, village, or region. The early Christian churches included households that closely resembled Jewish synagogues, community gathering spaces guided by a structural hierarchy, and fringe cults engaged in odd and obscure beliefs and practices. A deep desire emerged to develop core orthodoxy to establish the credibility of Christianity as a religion, not a scattered eclectic array of tiny outposts that might be eliminated one by one. Hope for survival of the church depended on developing a unified sense of identity and practice.

In light of the desire to codify and institutionalize the church, Revelation can also be seen as a call to discipleship. The time is now, the need is great, and the key to survival is leadership. The letters to the seven churches in chapters 2 and 3 offer a blend of commendation and criticism to various congregations. These letters are not overly hopeful. It is safe to say that none of the churches is working well (though Philadelphia comes very close), but each describes the mixed success the early church was experiencing.

Christian disciples (following the instructions to the seven churches) must reject evil, be patient, and persevere (2:1–7); bear up under suffering (vv. 8–11); hold fast to the faith (vv. 12–17); perform works of love, service, and fidelity (vv. 18–29); be watchful (3:1–6); stay steadfast and obedient (vv. 7–13); and be passionate and committed (vv. 14–22). The only hope for the church to survive and thrive is for believers to capture the evangelistic zeal of the first disciples.

Revelation is a call to a positive future, not just an encouragement to persevere through suffering, bear unfair oppression, or struggle to survive another dismal day. These early Christians feel that life is little more than an endurance test, with no clear purpose or reward. Many wonder if they have been deluded into believing in something that will never come to pass. John offers a vision of a new heaven and a new earth, and a period of retribution and restoration for those who keep their faith. In short, Revelation is a vision of hope.

Hope in Heaven

John witnesses angelic creatures and heavenly elders gathered in a throne room, and a Lamb taking a scroll with seven seals. The first six seals (6:1–7:8) connote the affliction, hardship, and misery of earthly existence. To be human and alive means to contend with war, conflict, scarcity, hunger, death, persecution, natural disasters, fear, cosmic disturbances, and deprivation. The whole point of faith is to leave all these things behind. John witnesses a multitude gathered around the heavenly throne, crying out together, "Salvation belongs to our God who sits on the throne, and to the Lamb!" (7:10). The message of hope is clear: God in Jesus the Christ offers the means to escape the problems of earthly existence.

The seventh seal is opened, and a short period of silence follows. Seven angels appear with seven trumpets, and as each of the first six trumpets are blown, natural disasters are displayed in extreme measure: hail, lightning, fire, and blood wipe out crops (8:7); seas boil and heave, destroying sea life and ships (vv. 8–9); rivers, creeks, and streams become brackish and poison (vv. 10–11); sun and moon are eclipsed, and day becomes like night (v. 13); volcanoes erupt, ash fills the sky, locusts and scorpions swarm, armored and difficult to kill (9:1–12); and various plagues wipe out huge numbers of people (vv. 13–21). It is important to understand that the Middle Eastern and Mediterranean world experienced such common disasters—plague, famine, drought (resulting in undrinkable water), eclipses, infestation of both locusts and scorpions, volcanic eruptions (and the resulting suffocating ash clouds), earthquakes, and cataclysmic sea disasters—as evidence of a failure of right living, without understanding their natural causes. This was as much a review of the century as it was a prediction of the age to come, and it brought to mind the most terrifying aspects of daily life.

Before the seventh trumpet blows, John sees an image of tragic and violent martyrdom; two witnesses representing the faithful of the Jews and the Christians are killed and mocked. Both, however, are resurrected in three and a half days. The message of hope is clear: death is not the end of the story in the kingdom of heaven! God's power reigns supreme, over even the worst of earth's torments.

The seventh trumpet (11:15–19) ushers in the victory of God over every earthly kingdom and power. Things may become intolerable on earth, but for those who keep hope and remain faithful, God will prevail. In a wonderful contrast, God's victory results in "lightnings, noises, thundering, an earthquake, and great hail" (v. 19). What connotes cataclysm on earth reflects God's power in heaven.

The End of Earthly Hope

Chapter 12 begins a transition in the Revelation narrative, describing the political oppression of Rome in symbolic terms. For citizens throughout the Middle East and Mediterranean world, this section (12:1–14:20) is a potent message of hope.

A dragon (representing Rome, the manifestation of Satan on earth) is ruled by a human child (the Caesars) who conquers the world. The holy forces of heaven—in the form of the Jewish and Christian faiths—are powerless to defeat the beast Rome, and in fact are often mortally injured by the evil empire. While this suggests that the devil holds sway on earth, the vision John receives indicates the ultimate outcome:

> Now salvation, and strength, and the kingdom of our God, and the power of His Christ have come, for the accuser of our brethren, who accused them before our God day and night, has been cast down. And they overcame him by the blood of the Lamb and by the word of their testimony, and they did not love their lives to the death. (12:10–11)

The beast, a manifestation of the dragon, wages war and almost destroys the faithful. From sea and from land the beast does everything in its power to destroy the faith of Abraham and Isaac, as well as the faith of the followers of Jesus the Christ. At the time of John's Revelation, the war is fully underway. Persecutors and oppressors arrive regularly by ship and across land to attack Jewish and Christian communities. The message of hope John wants the communities to hear is contained in the proclamations of three angels:

> "Fear God and give glory to Him, for the hour of His judgment has come; and worship Him who made heaven and earth, the sea and springs of water." . . .
>
> "Babylon is fallen, is fallen, that great city, because she has made all nations drink of the wine of the wrath of her fornication." . . .
>
> "If anyone worships the beast and his image, and receives his mark on his forehead or on his hand, he himself shall also drink of the wine of the wrath of God, which is poured out full strength into the cup of His indignation. He shall be tormented with fire and brimstone in the presence of the holy angels and in the presence of the Lamb. And the smoke of their torment ascends forever and ever; and they have no rest day or night, who worship the beast and his image, and whoever receives the mark of his name." (14:7–11)

To sum up: those who worship God will be rewarded, and those who do not will be punished. Furthermore, those who have persecuted Christians will suffer greatly. This is precisely the message of hope the remnant communities need to hear to bolster them in their faith and to help them hang on.

Modern US culture is built on learning from our history: diplomacy, negotiation, balances of power, and the art of persuasion. None of these features characterized the Roman empire during the first century. Power was the coinage of the empires in the ancient world, and violence was the normative condition of the day. Revelation reflects the worldview of the early church; retribution and restoration cannot be achieved without bloodshed and violence.

In chapters 15–16, John sees that visions indicate the trials and tribulations will continue. Daily life in the world at the end of the first century is dismal, and there is no indication that evil will soon be defeated. Rome is corrupt and powerful, and the early church does everything it can to make Rome look evil and unacceptable. John's vision of seven angels with seven bowls "of the wrath of God" reinforces the corrupt spirit of Rome.

As the angels pour out their bowls, John sees the already horrible circumstances get even worse. The first bowl pours out foul and loathsome sores on those who tolerate and accept Rome (16:2). An outward and visible sign will mark those already corrupted on the inside. The second bowl causes the sea to turn to blood and kill every living thing (v. 3). Everything Rome touches is poisoned. Bowl number three spreads the corruption of the waters to rivers and streams (vv. 4–6). The fourth bowl brings about fire and scorching heat, drought and relentless sunshine (vv. 8–9). The fifth bowl brings on darkness and pain (vv. 10–11). By the sixth bowl, the rivers dry up and the need for water brings remaining nations to war and violence (vv. 12–16). The last bowl ushers in widespread cataclysm as nature is thrown into chaos with storms and earthquakes and hail (vv. 17–21). People curse God in hopeless despair.

As the natural disasters increase and people live in the terror and anxiety of impending chaos, political powers—"Babylon" (Rome)—become even more oppressive and cruel, but even it cannot survive the breakdown of society. Rome—the evil whore—falls. Every human institution and structure of power and control is devastated and destroyed. Chapters 17–18 recount the total collapse of earthly power and the heavenly victory.

The Promise of Hope Fulfilled

As the dust settles, heaven rejoices (19:1–10). Christ arrives in glory, victorious and leading the armies of heaven (vv. 11–16). The forces of evil refuse to give up. Satan is bound for one thousand years, but by the end of this time the future is set.

Earthly life is filled with corruption and evil, heartaches and violence, but these are not our ultimate reality. We may suffer, but suffering is not the final word. If we hold on to hope through the love of God and the power of the Holy Spirit, we grow strong through suffering, and we will be victorious through our faith in Jesus Christ. We may not see it when we look at the world as it is, but through John's vision we see what is really true—we see what God sees, and we live in hope of the final victory.

Death, evil, Satan, Hades, injury, disease, fear, foolishness—all these things will cease to exist in the ultimate reality of God—the kingdom of heaven. Why wait? Since this is what will be, Christians should live as if these things are already true. This is the image of present and future hope John offers struggling Christian communities at the conclusion of his vision report:

> Now I saw a new heaven and a new earth, for the first heaven and the first earth had passed away. Also there was no more sea. Then I, John, saw the holy city, New Jerusalem, coming down out of heaven from God, prepared as a bride adorned for her husband. And I heard a loud voice from heaven saying, "Behold, the tabernacle of God is with men, and He will dwell with them, and they shall be His people. God Himself will be with them and be their God. And God will wipe away every tear from their eyes; there shall be no more death, nor sorrow, nor crying. There shall be no more pain, for the former things have passed away." (21:1–4)

The visions of the New Jerusalem (22:9–27) and the river of life (23:1–6) are the culmination of John's apocalyptic vision. What could be more hopeful than the possibility of a place in which no evil, no pain, no worry, and no fear exist? For many, this is heaven. And this is the promise of hope to all who remain faithful to God in Jesus Christ in the face of persecution, threat, oppression, and despair. John promises that all these things will happen soon, but the delay has caused a wide variety of interpretations, including occasional predictions of the end of the world, throughout church history. Regardless of what interpretation people choose to believe, Revelation offers us all a message of hope and promise.

In today's world we still see the ravages of famine, disease, corruption, and greed. We look at our planet and wonder how we (and it) will survive. As advanced and sophisticated as our science and technology have become, a hurricane or an earthquake can humble us in an instant. We still need God and a Savior who will make all things new. We still need radical and abiding hope that what we see with our eyes is a mere shadow of the truth we know in our hearts.

John closes with his standard instruction: "Blessed are those who do His commandments" (22:14a), who avoid evil and live their lives in love. Then he entreats Christ to do as he promises and come quickly in glory, urging all who read his words to live in hopeful expectation:

> And the Spirit and the bride say, "Come!" And let him who hears say, "Come!" And let him who thirsts come. Whoever desires, let him take the water of life freely. . . .
>
> He who testifies to these things says, "Surely I am coming quickly." Amen. Even so, come, Lord Jesus!
>
> The grace of our Lord Jesus Christ be with you all. Amen. (22:17, 20–21)